Charts

OF THE GOSPELS
AND THE

Life of
Christ

Books in the Zondervan Charts Series

Charts of Christian Theology and Doctrine
Charts of Cults, Sects, and Religious Movements
Charts of the Gospels and the Life of Christ
Chronological and Background Charts of Church History
Chronological and Background Charts of the New Testament
Chronological and Background Charts of the Old Testament
Chronological and Thematic Charts of Philosophies and Philosophers
Taxonomic Charts of Theology and Biblical Studies
Timeline Charts of the Western Church

Charts

OF THE GOSPELS
AND THE

Life of Christ

Robert L. Thomas

ZONDERVAN™

GRAND RAPIDS, MICHIGAN 49530 USA

ZONDERVAN™

Charts of the Gospels and the Life of Christ
Copyright © 2000 by Robert L. Thomas

Requests for information should be addressed to:
Zondervan
Grand Rapids, Michigan 49530

Library of Congress Cataloging-in-Publication Data

Thomas, Robert L., 1928–
    Charts of the Gospels and the life of Christ / Robert L. Thomas
        p. cm — (Zondervan Charts)
    Includes bibliographical references.
    ISBN 0–310–22620–1
    1. Bible. N.T. Gospels—Outlines, syllabi, etc.   2. Jesus Christ—Outlines, syllabi, etc.   I. Title.
    II. Series.
    BS2555.5.T46   2000
    232.9'002'02—dc21   00-039265

Interior design by Sherri L. Hoffman

To J. Dwight Pentecost
who aroused my deep interest in life-of-Christ studies

Contents

Introduction

The *Charts of the Gospels and the Life of Christ* opens many avenues for investigation. The life and ministry of the Lord Jesus Christ on earth was so rich in experiences and his teachings so relevant to everyday life that one could construct an infinite number of varied charts and still not scratch the surface of all the Savior said and did (see John 21:25). The records of that one solitary life furnish a limitless resource for contemplation and challenge.

The tables offered in the following pages provide in varied combinations of factual representations only a beginning to the seemingly endless studies that could sketch the greatest life ever lived. The reader will find four kinds of charted sketches in this presentation: Overview and Distribution Charts, Background Charts, Chronological Charts, and Thematic Charts.

The Overview and Distribution Charts furnish ten perspectives on the Gospels. First of all comes a simplified summary of thirteen periods with their subperiods in Christ's life. The summary labeled "Periods and Period Divisions of Christ's Life" and numbered as Chart #1 includes the period name, time span covered, Scriptures, and a sketch of the period's features. Then in Chart #2 comes a more detailed summary of his life, divided not only into the thirteen periods with their subperiods but also into separate sections that comprise each period or subperiod. This chart includes section titles and Scriptures as well.

Most harmonies of the four Gospels resemble each other fairly closely in their manner of paralleling the four accounts of the life of Christ. The two harmonies chosen to provide the basis for dividing Christ's life into periods, subperiods, and sections are *The NIV Harmony of the Gospels* and *A Harmony of the Gospels (NASB)*, both edited by Robert L. Thomas and Stanley N. Gundry (HarperCollins, 1988 and 1978, respectively). Section numbers from the two harmonies provide a means for cross-referencing the first two charts (as well as most charts in the book) with one of those harmonies for purposes of increased understanding of the Lord's life.

The next eight charts round out the Overview and Distribution portion of the book. A quick glance will yield perspectives on how Gospel material divides itself in describing the life of Christ.

Charts #3–#6 specify sections of Christ's life found in one, two, three, and four Gospels, respectively. Such charts permit a reader to tell how many accounts record each episode in Christ's life and in what Gospels they appear. Chart #3 lists section numbers and titles of those sections appearing in only one Gospel, Chart #4 has those appearing in two Gospels, Chart #5 the ones in three Gospels, and Chart #6 in four Gospels. Charts #7–#10 focus on passages rather than sections. They single out passages of at least one verse in length that are unique to each of the four Gospels. Too often in citing how much of each Gospel is unique, literature on the Gospels calculates percentages of uniqueness based only on section segments. With a focus on individual passages, however, the picture is quite different. For example, the number of passages unique to the Gospel of Mark is much higher than most have realized.

Charts #11–#19 comprise the "Background Charts" division of this work. They portray a variety of information about the Gospels from external sources. "Old Testament Citations in the Gospels" is Chart #11. This set of information lists, of course, the New Testament and Old Testament references, but also describes briefly the contexts of both passages.

"Sects of Judaism in Christ's Time" (Chart #12) lists the principal characteristics of the five major parties that existed in Israel during Christ's life on earth. Chart #13, "The Reigns of the Herods," gives data such as names, dates of reign, titles, territories, and periods of Christ's life for each member of the Herod family who ruled during New Testament times. Chart #14 diagrams "The Herod Family in the New Testament," showing the complex relationships between members of the family, with particular attention given to those members mentioned in the New Testament. "Territorial Rulers during Christ's Life" is Chart #15. It gives dates of rule and territories ruled for both the Herods and Roman procurators (governors). "Roman Rulers of the Land Where Christ Lived" (Chart #16) tells the Roman emperors and procurators of Judea during Christ's life. It includes the lengths of their rule, prominent events during their rule, and where Scripture mentions them.

Chart #17 turns attention to how the early church viewed the Gospels. Entitled "Gospel Origins according to the Early Fathers," it contains select quotations of early church leaders regarding the direct connections between the Gospels and the apostles of Christ. Chart #18 ("The Lineage of the Gospels") builds on Chart #17 in providing a diagram to summarize the church fathers' views of Gospel origins. To wrap up the "Background Charts," Chart #19 has selected quotations from the fathers regarding "Gospel Sequence according to the Early Fathers." That chart indicates how early Christian leaders viewed the sequence in the writing of the four Gospels.

The "Chronological Charts" (Charts #20–#26) are those featuring chronological sequence of periods and events, with specific time designations included. Chart #20 is a brief picture of "Periods of the Life of Christ," noting events, periods, dates, harmony section numbers, and Scriptures. Chart #21 is a similar handling of "The Major Periods of Christ's Ministry," limiting itself to his public ministry and shortly before. Then comes a listing of Christ's discourses and extended teachings on various occasions in Chart #22: "Chronological Chart of Christ's Discourses."

In Charts #23 and #24 (time lines to show Jesus' use of parables) a notable characteristic is conspicuous, namely, how late in his ministry Jesus began using parables. The occasion for his adoption of a new teaching method was the committing of the unpardonable sin by Jewish leaders late during his Galilean ministry. That rejection occasioned his first use of parables, a first use that came on the same day as the rejection. The teaching technique hid new truths from his enemies while revealing them to his followers. From that point on, the nature of his parables differed depending on whether his opponents were in his audience or not. Chart #23 identifies the parables told when his enemies were present, and Chart #24 when they were absent.

Closing out the "Chronological Charts" are "Major Events of Passion Week" and "Chronology of Passion Week." The former of these is a general overview of major events during the week (Chart #25), and the latter a detailed account of what happened each day of that week (Chart #26).

The time designations in the "Chronological Charts" and in all other charts of the book assume with most sources an A.D. 30 date for the crucifixion of Christ. Those readers who prefer an A.D. 33 crucifixion date can simply add three years to the year designations as found in these charts.

The final group of tables, the "Thematic Charts" (Charts #27–#41), deal with a variety of areas. The first four trace themes through each of the four Gospels to show how they emphasize Jesus as King (Matthew, Chart #27), Servant (Mark, Chart #28), Man (Luke, Chart #29), and God (John, Chart #30). Each chart has a summary of and comment about each passage in the thematic survey.

Although many do not realize it, the town of Capernaum was prominent in Jesus' ministry. The next two charts (Charts #31 and #32) relate to that city. The former one scans locations, times, results, and other characteristics of Jesus' miracles in and around the city. The latter does the same with his activities other than miracles in that general territory.

Jesus visited Jerusalem a number of times before Passion Week, a week which he spent in its entirety in that city. Chart #33 outlines Jesus' activities in Jerusalem during his various visits before the week of his crucifixion.

Through the years Bible teachers have focused our attention particularly on certain crises or crisis periods in the life of Christ. Chart #34 pays particular attention to those special times by giving locations, times, occasions, purposes, witnesses, and other relevant data connected with the crises.

Of supreme interest and relevance to Christian discipleship is the way Jesus helped his own disciples along in their spiritual development. Chart #35 on "Seven Lessons of Jesus on Discipleship" is indispensable in any study of his life. On each of the selected occasions he gave a challenge to a specific audience producing important results and/or lessons.

A major area of emphasis in Jesus' teachings and the Gospels was the kingdom of God (heaven). Chart #36 summarizing this important subject suggests vital lessons derived from the scope of these teachings. In each case he spoke of either the present or the future phase of the kingdom and injected remarks about relevant subjects, opportunities, and other factors. Teaching of this sort always expects a specific response.

A number of events in the life of Christ bear resemblances to and are easily confused with each other. A chart enumerating "Similar Events in the Gospels" (Chart #37) will help alleviate that confusion by locating the similar events in their own contexts both scripturally and chronologically. Likewise, most do not realize how often Jesus used the same expressions or illustrations on separate occasions. "Sayings Jesus and Others Repeated on More Than One Occasion" in Chart #38 will impress readers with the fact that our Lord was not afraid to employ the same or similar wordings as used before whenever appropriate to a new occasion. The Gospels may use a similar wording on as many as six separate occasions in some cases.

A depressing but real part of the life of Christ on earth was the opposition he faced. Chart #39 tracing the "Growing Opposition to Jesus" is one of the longer ones in this book. It quotes scriptural instances when his critics sought to halt his mission, giving the outcome of each incident. "Six Phases of Jesus' Trial" in Chart #40 outlines specific details in the stages through which the Son of God received a death sentence. The final chart (Chart # 41) features elements and implications involved in the "Seven Last Words of Christ on the Cross."

Special Features

Most of the charts to follow (all charts except numbers 12–19) list "Harmony Section Numbers." Using these numbers to refer to Chart #2, "A Harmonistic Overview of the Four Gospels," and/or to one of the two harmonies of the Gospels from which the Section Numbers are derived will prove useful. By cross-referencing to one or both of those harmonizations, a chart can take on additional meaning by being located in the biblical context of the life of Christ.

In charts where Periods of Christ's Ministry are listed (all charts except numbers 12–19, 20–26, 31–34, 37–38, 40–41), a heavy horizontal line marks the end of one period and the beginning of another.

Valuable resources about the life of Christ are numerous. I have purposely limited the "Selected Bibliography" at the end of this volume to just a few I deem most appropriate to a chart book of this type. For those who wish to probe aspects of the subject more deeply, I would recommend bibliographical data noted in the additional sources cited.

July 6, 1999—Robert L. Thomas

Abbreviations

for the Books of the Bible

Genesis	Ge	Nahum	Na
Exodus	Ex	Habakkuk	Hab
Leviticus	Lev	Zephaniah	Zep
Numbers	Nu	Haggai	Hag
Deuteronomy	Dt	Zechariah	Zec
Joshua	Jos	Malachi	Mal
Judges	Jdg	Matthew	Mt
Ruth	Ru	Mark	Mk
1 Samuel	1Sa	Luke	Lk
2 Samuel	2Sa	John	Jn
1 Kings	1Ki	Acts	Ac
2 Kings	2Ki	Romans	Ro
1 Chronicles	1Ch	1 Corinthians	1Co
2 Chronicles	2Ch	2 Corinthians	2Co
Ezra	Ez	Galatians	Gal
Nehemiah	Ne	Ephesians	Eph
Esther	Est	Philippians	Php
Job	Job	Colossians	Col
Psalms	Ps	1 Thessalonians	1Th
Proverbs	Pr	2 Thessalonians	2Th
Ecclesiastes	Ecc	1 Timothy	1Ti
Song of Songs	SS	2 Timothy	2Ti
Isaiah	Isa	Titus	Tit
Jeremiah	Jer	Philemon	Phm
Lamentations	La	Hebrews	Heb
Ezekiel	Eze	James	Jas
Daniel	Da	1 Peter	1Pe
Hosea	Hos	2 Peter	2Pe
Joel	Joel	1 John	1Jn
Amos	Am	2 John	2Jn
Obadiah	Ob	3 John	3Jn
Jonah	Jnh	Jude	Jude
Micah	Mic	Revelation	Rev

Overview and Distribution Charts

#1—Periods and Period Divisions of Christ's Life

Period No.	Period Name	Period Divisions	Time Span	Harmony Section No.	Scriptures	Features
1	A Preview of Who Jesus Is	[none]	n/a	NIV§1-3 NASB§1-3	Mt 1:1-17; Lk 1:1-4; 3:23b-38; Jn 1:1-18	Luke's purpose; John's prologue; two genealogies
2	The Early Years of John the Baptist	[none]	6 B.C.-C. A.D. 25	NIV§4-8c NASB§4-10	Lk 1:5-80	John's birth; Jesus' birth foretold; Zechariah's song; John's early development
3	The Early Years of Jesus Christ	[none]	6-5 B.C.- A.D. 26	NIV§9-19 NASB§11-22	Mt 1:18-25; 2:1-23; Lk 2:1-52	Jesus' birth; visit of Magi and flight to Egypt; Jesus' first Passover and growth to adulthood
4	The Public Ministry of John the Baptist	[none]	A.D. 26- 27	NIV§20-23 NASB§23-26	Mt 3:1-12; Mk 1:1-8; Lk 3:1-18	Preaching repentance to Pharisees, Sadducees, crowds, tax collectors, soldiers, predicting Christ's coming
5	The End of John's Ministry and the Beginning of Christ's Ministry (largely in Judea)	[none]	A.D. 26- 27	NIV§24-36 NASB§27-42	Mt 3:13–4:12; Mk 1:9-14a; Lk 3:19-23a; 4:1-14a; Jn 1:19–4:45	Jesus' baptism and temptation; John's identification of Jesus; water to wine; first cleansing of the temple; Nicodemus's interview; Samaritan woman's interview
6	The Ministry of Christ in Galilee	[see below]	fall, A.D. 27- spring, A.D. 29	NIV§37-71b NASB§43-103	Mt 4:17–14:12 [except 8:19-22]; Mk 1:14b-6:30; Lk 4:14b–9:10a	A period of growing fame and growing opposition that prompted a significant change in Jesus' ministry
		Opposition at home and a new headquarters		NIV§37-40 NASB§43-46	Mt 4:13-17; Mk 1:14b- 15; Lk 4:14b-31a; Jn 4:46-54	Rejected by his hometown of Nazareth, Jesus used Capernaum as his base of operations
		Disciples called and ministry throughout Galilee		NIV§41-48 NASB§47-56	Mt 4:18-24; 8:2-4, 14-17; 9:1-17; Mk 1:16–2:22; Lk 4:31b–5:39	Call of five disciples; teaching authenticated by healing; banquet at Matthew's house
		Sabbath controversies and a withdrawal		NIV§49a-52 NASB§57-62	Mt 4:25; 12:1-21; Mk 2:23–3:12; Lk 6:1-11; Jn 5:1-47	Three Sabbath controversies; Jesus' discourse claiming equality with the Father
		Appointment of the Twelve and Sermon on the Mount		NIV§53-54i NASB§63-72	Mt 5:1–7:29; Mk 3:13-19; Lk 6:12-49	Twelve chosen from a larger group; sermon giving prerequisites for entering the Messianic kingdom
		Growing fame emphasis on repentance		NIV§55-59 NASB§73-77	Mt 8:1, 5-13; 11:2-30; Lk 7:1-50	Centurion's faith, widow's son raised, woes to unrepentant, feet anointed by contrite woman
		First public rejection by Jewish leaders		NIV§60-63 NASB§78-81	Mt 12:22-50; Mk 3:20- 35; Lk 8:1-3, 19-21	Blasphemous accusation labeled unpardonable sin

Period No.	Period Name	Period Divisions	Time Span	Harmony Section No.	Scriptures	Features
		Secrets about the kingdom taught in parables		NIV§64a-64k NASB§82-92	Mt 13:1-52; Mk 4:1-34; Lk 8:4-18	Five parables to the crowds and four parables to the disciples
		Continuing opposition		NIV§65-69 NASB§93-97	Mt 8:18, 23-34; 9:18-34; 13:54-58; Mk 4:35–6:6a; Lk 8:22-56	More healing miracles; another blasphemous accusation; final visit to unbelieving Nazareth
		Final Galilean campaign		NIV§70a-71b NASB§98-103	Mt 9:35–11:1; 14:1-12; Mk 6:6b-30; Lk 9:1-10a	The Twelve commissioned and sent out; Antipas's earlier execution of John the Baptist
7	The Ministry of Christ around Galilee	[see below]	spring-summer, A.D. 29	NIV§72a-95 NASB§104-132	Mt 8:19-22; 14:13–18:35; Mk 6:31–9:50; Lk 9:10b-62; Jn 6:1–7:10	A period devoted especially to training the Twelve
		Lesson on the bread of life		NIV§72a-76b NASB§104-110	Mt 14:13-36; Mk 6:31- 56; Lk 9:10b-17; Jn 6:1-71	Feeding the 5,000 and discourse based on the miracle; walking on the water and healings at Gennesaret
		Lesson on the yeast of the Pharisees, Sadducees, and Herodians		NIV§77-81b NASB§111-117	Mt 15:1–16:12; Mk 7:1–8:26; Jn 7:1	Conflict over ceremonial defilement; feeding the 4,000; ministry to a believing Gentile; other healings
		Lesson of Messiahship learned and confirmed		NIV§82-86 NASB§118-123	Mt 16:13–17:13; Mk 8:27–9:13; Lk 9:18-36b	Peter's confession; first prophecy of the church; first prediction of the crucifixion and resurrection; transfiguration
		Lessons on responsibility to others		NIV§87-92 NASB§124-129	Mt 17:14–18:35; Mk 9:14-50; Lk 9:37-50	Second prediction of resurrection; rivalry over greatness; warning against causing believers to stumble; treatment of sinning brother
		Journey to Jerusalem for Feast of Tabernacles		NIV§93-95 NASB§130-132	Mt 8:19-22; Lk 9:51- 62; Jn 7:2-10	Opposition from Jesus' half brothers; complete commitment required
8	The Later Judean Ministry of Christ	[see below]	summer- fall, A.D. 29	NIV§96a-111 NASB§133-160	Lk 10:1–13:21; Jn 7:11–10:39	A series of clashes with Jewish leaders in Jerusalem
		Teachings at the Feast of Tabernacles		NIV§96a-99b NASB§133-138	Jn 7:11–8:59	Frustrated attempt to arrest Jesus; relationship to Abraham and attempted stoning
		Private lessons on loving service and prayer		NIV§102a-105 NASB§139-143	Lk 10:1–11:13	Commissioning of the Seventy-two; good Samaritan; how to pray
		Second debate with the scribes and Pharisees		NIV§106-110 NASB§144-152	Lk 11:14–13:21	A third blasphemous accusation; warnings about the scribes and Pharisees; criticism for healing a woman on the Sabbath
		Teaching at the Feast of Dedication		NIV§100a-101b NIV§111 NASB§153-160	Jn 9:1–10:39	Healing of a blind man; the good shepherd; another attempt to stone Jesus

Period No.	Period Name	Period Divisions	Time Span	Harmony Section No.	Scriptures	Features
9	The Ministry of Christ in and around Perea	[see below]	winter- spring, A.D. 30	NIV§112-127b NASB§161-184	Mt 19:1–20:34; Mk 10:1-52; Lk 13:22–19:28; Jn 10:40–11:54	Emphasis on discipleship; raising of Lazarus; two parables on prayer; third prediction of resurrection; healing of Bartimaeus; salvation to Zacchaeus
		Principles of discipleship		NIV§112-117c NASB§161-169	Lk 13:22–17:10; Jn 10:40-42	Anticipation of coming death and lament over Jerusalem; cost of discipleship; parables to defend associations with sinners and teach the proper use of money; four lessons on discipleship
		Raising of Lazarus and a brief tour through Samaria and Galilee		NIV§118a-120b NASB§170-174	Lk 17:11-37; Jn 11:1- 54	Lazarus's sickness, death, and resurrection; healing of ten lepers; the Son of Man's coming
		Teaching while on the final journey to Jerusalem		NIV§121-127b NASB§175-184	Mt 19:1–20:34; Mk 10:1-52; Lk 18:1–19:28	Two parables on prayer; conflict with Pharisaic teaching on divorce; riches and the kingdom; third prediction of resurrection; parable to teach responsibility while awaiting the kingdom
10	The Formal Presentation of Christ to Israel and the Resulting Conflict	[see below]	Sunday-Tuesday A.M., spring, A.D. 30	NIV§128a-138 NASB§185-201	Mt 21:1–23:39; 26:6-13; Mk 11:1–12:44; 14:3-9; Lk 19:29–21:4; Jn 11:55–12:50	The Triumphal Entry; confrontation by Jewish leaders; Jesus' response
		Triumphal Entry and the fig tree		NIV§128a-131 NASB§185-192	Mt 21:1-22; 26:6-13; Mk 11:1-25; 14:3-9; Lk 19:29-48; Jn 11:55–12:50	Anointing for burial; second cleansing of the temple; request from Greeks; withered fig tree
		Official challenge of Christ's authority		NIV§132a-135 NASB§193-194	Mt 21:23–22:40; Mk 11:27–12:34; Lk 20:1-40	Question by chief priests, scribes, and elders; faithfulness taught by three parables; questions by Pharisees, Herodians, Sadducees, and a Pharisaic scribe
		Christ's response to his enemies' challenges		NIV§136-138 NASB§198-201	Mt 22:41–23:39; Mk 12:35-44; Lk 20:41–21:4	Seven woes against the scribes and Pharisees; lament over Jerusalem; poor widow's gift
11	Prophecies in Preparation for the Death of Christ	[see below]	Tuesday, P.M.- Thursday, P.M., spring, A.D. 30	NIV§139a-152 NASB§202-226	Mt 24:1–26:46; Mk 13:1–14:42; Lk 21:5–22:46; Jn 13:1–18:1	Olivet Discourse; arrangements for betrayal; the Last Supper; Upper Room Discourse
		The Olivet Discourse: prophecies about the temple and the return of Christ		NIV§139a-139g NASB§202-208	Mt 24:1–25:30; Mk 13:1-37; Lk 21:5-36	Beginning of birth pains; abomination of desolation and great tribulation; coming of the Son of Man; signs of nearness
		Arrangements for betrayal		NIV§140, 142 NASB§209-210	Mt 26:1-16; Mk 14:1-11; Lk 21:37–22:6	Sanhedrin's plot to arrest and kill Jesus; Judas's agreement to cooperate

Period No.	Period Name	Period Divisions	Time Span	Harmony Section No.	Scriptures	Features
		The Last Supper		NIV§143-148 NASB§211-217	Mt 26:17-29; Mk 14:12-25; Lk 22:7-38, John 13:1-38	Washing the disciples' feet; identification of the betrayer; first prediction of Peter's denial
		Discourses and prayers from the Upper Room to Gethsemane		NIV§149-152 NASB§218-226	Mt 26:30-46; Mk 14:26-42; Lk 22:39-46; Jn 14:1–18:1	Disciples' questions about Jesus' destination; the vine and the branches; coming of the Spirit; second prediction of Peter's denial; Jesus' three agonizing prayers in Gethsemane
12	The Death of Christ	[see below]	Friday, A.M.-P.M., spring, A.D. 30	NIV§153-168 NASB§227-243	Mt 26:47–27:56; Mk 14:43–15:41; Lk 22:47–23:56; Jn 18:2–19:42	Betrayal; six-stage trial; Peter's denials; Judas's suicide; Jesus' crucifixion; burial
		Betrayal and arrest		NIV§153 NASB§227	Mt 26:47-56; Mk 14:43-52; Lk 22:47-53; Jn 18:2-12	Jesus betrayed, arrested, and forsaken
		Trial		NIV§154-161 NASB§228-235	Mt 26:57–27:26; Mk 14:53–15:15; Lk 22:54–23:25; Jn 18:13–19:16	Three phases before Jewish authorities and three before Roman authorities; Peter's denials, Judas's suicide
		Crucifixion		NIV§162-166 NASB§236-240	Mt 27:27-56; Mk 15:16-41; Lk 23:26-49; Jn 19:17-30	Mockery by Roman soldiers; six hours on the cross, three of which were in darkness; witnesses of Jesus' death
		Burial		NIV§167a-168 NASB§241-243	Mt 27:57-66; Mk 15:42-47; Lk 23:50-56; Jn 19:31-42	Certification of death; tomb watched by women and soldiers
13	The Resurrection and Ascension of Christ	[see below]	Friday, P.M.-Sunday, A.M., spring, A.D. 30	NIV§169-184 NASB§244-259	Mt 28:1-20; Mk 16:1-8; Lk 24:1-53; Jn 20:1–21:25	The empty tomb; post-resurrection appearances
		The empty tomb		NIV§169-172 NASB§244-247	Mt 28:1-8; Mk 16:1-8; Lk 24:1-11; Jn 20:1-10	Stone rolled away; empty tomb witnessed by women, Peter, and John
		The postresurrection appearances		NIV§173-183 NASB§248-258	Mt 28:9-20; Lk 24:13-49; Jn 20:11–21:25; Ac 1:3-8; 1Co 15:5-7	Eleven appearances to different individuals and groups
		The ascension		NIV§184 NASB§259	Lk 24:50-53	Jesus' parting blessing and departure

#2—A Harmonistic Overview of the Four Gospels

Harmony Section Numbers	Section Title	Matthew	Mark	Luke	John	Period of Christ's Ministry
NIV§1 NASB§1	Luke's purpose for writing a Gospel			1:1-4		Preview of Who Jesus Is
NIV§2 NASB§2	John's prologue: from preincarnation to crucifixion				1:1-18	Preview of Who Jesus Is
NIV§3 NASB§3	Jesus' legal lineage through Joseph and natural lineage through Mary	1:1-17		3:23b-38		Preview of Who Jesus Is
NIV§4 NASB§4	John's birth foretold to Zechariah			1:5-25		Early Years of John the Baptist
NIV§5 NASB§5	Jesus' birth foretold to Mary			1:26-38		Early Years of John the Baptist
NIV§6 NASB§6	Mary's visit to Elizabeth			1:39-45		Early Years of John the Baptist
NIV§7 NASB§7	Mary's song of joy			1:46-56		Early Years of John the Baptist
NIV§8a NASB§8	John's birth			1:57-66		Early Years of John the Baptist
NIV§8b NASB§9	Zechariah's prophetic song			1:67-79		Early Years of John the Baptist
NIV§8c NASB§10	John's growth and early life			1:80		Early Years of John the Baptist
NIV§9 NASB§11	Circumstances of Jesus' birth explained to Joseph	1:18-25				Early Years of Jesus Christ
NIV§10 NASB§12	Birth of Jesus			2:1-7		Early Years of Jesus Christ
NIV§11 NASB§13	Witness of the shepherds			2:8-20		Early Years of Jesus Christ
NIV§12 NASB§14	Circumcision of Jesus			2:21		Early Years of Jesus Christ
NIV§13 NASB§15	Jesus presented in the temple			2:22-38		Early Years of Jesus Christ
NIV§16 NASB§16	Return to Nazareth			2:39		Early Years of Jesus Christ
NIV§14 NASB§17	Visit of the Magi	2:1-12				Early Years of Jesus Christ
NIV§15 NASB§18	Flight into Egypt	2:13-18				Early Years of Jesus Christ
NIV§16 NASB§19	New home in Nazareth	2:19-23				Early Years of Jesus Christ
NIV§17 NASB§20	Growth and early life of Jesus			2:40		Early Years of Jesus Christ
NIV§18 NASB§21	Jesus' first Passover in Jerusalem			2:41-50		Early Years of Jesus Christ
NIV§19 NASB§22	Jesus' adolescence and early manhood			2:51-52		Early Years of Jesus Christ

Harmony Section Numbers	Section Title	Matthew	Mark	Luke	John	Period of Christ's Ministry
NIV§20 NASB§23	John's ministry launched		1:1	3:1-2		Public Ministry of John the Baptist
NIV§21 NASB§24	His person, proclamation, and baptism	3:1-6	1:2-6	3:3-6		Public Ministry of John the Baptist
NIV§22 NASB§25	His messages to the Pharisees, Sadducees, multitudes, tax collectors, and soldiers	3:7-10		3:7-14		Public Ministry of John the Baptist
NIV§23 NASB§26	His description of Jesus	3:11-12	1:7-8	3:15-18		Public Ministry of John the Baptist
NIV§24 NASB§27	Jesus' baptism by John	3:13-17	1:9-11	3:21-23a		End of John's Ministry and Beginning of Christ's
NIV§25 NASB§28	Jesus' temptation in the desert	4:1-11	1:12-13	4:1-13		End of John's Ministry and Beginning of Christ's
NIV§26 NASB§29	John's self-identification to the priests and Levites				1:19-28	End of John's Ministry and Beginning of Christ's
NIV§27 NASB§30	John's identification of Jesus as the Son of God				1:29-34	End of John's Ministry and Beginning of Christ's
NIV§28 NASB§31	Jesus' first followers				1:35-51	End of John's Ministry and Beginning of Christ's
NIV§29 NASB§32	First miracle: Water becomes wine				2:1-11	End of John's Ministry and Beginning of Christ's
NIV§30 NASB§33	Visit at Capernaum with his disciples				2:12	End of John's Ministry and Beginning of Christ's
NIV§31 NASB§34	First cleansing of the temple at the Passover				2:13-22	End of John's Ministry and Beginning of Christ's
NIV§32a NASB§35	An early response to Jesus' miracles				2:23-25	End of John's Ministry and Beginning of Christ's
NIV§32b NASB§36	Nicodemus's interview with Jesus				3:1-21	End of John's Ministry and Beginning of Christ's
NIV§33 NASB§37	John superseded by Jesus				3:22-36	End of John's Ministry and Beginning of Christ's
NIV§34 NASB§38	Jesus' departure from Judea	4:12	1:14a	3:19-20; 4:14a	4:1-4	End of John's Ministry and Beginning of Christ's
NIV§35a NASB§39	Discussion with a Samaritan woman				4:5-26	End of John's Ministry and Beginning of Christ's
NIV§35b NASB§40	Challenge of a spiritual harvest				4:27-38	End of John's Ministry and Beginning of Christ's
NIV§35c NASB§41	Evangelization of Sychar				4:39-42	End of John's Ministry and Beginning of Christ's
NIV§36 NASB§42	Arrival in Galilee				4:43-45	End of John's Ministry and Beginning of Christ's

Harmony Section Numbers	Section Title	Matthew	Mark	Luke	John	Period of Christ's Ministry
	Opposition at Home and a New Headquarters					Ministry of Christ in Galilee
NIV§37 NASB§43	Nature of the Galilean ministry	4:17	1:14b-15	4:14b-15		Ministry of Christ in Galilee
NIV§38 NASB§44	Child at Capernaum healed by Jesus while at Cana				4:46-54	Ministry of Christ in Galilee
NIV§39 NASB§45	Ministry and rejection at Nazareth			4:16-31a		Ministry of Christ in Galilee
NIV§40 NASB§46	Move to Capernaum	4:13-16				Ministry of Christ in Galilee
	Disciples Called and Ministry Throughout Galilee					Ministry of Christ in Galilee
NIV§41 NASB§47	First call of the four	4:18-22	1:16-20			Ministry of Christ in Galilee
NIV§42 NASB§48	Teaching in the synagogue of Capernaum authenticated by healing a demoniac		1:21-28	4:31b-37		Ministry of Christ in Galilee
NIV§43 NASB§49	Peter's mother-in-law and others healed	8:14-17	1:29-34	4:38-41		Ministry of Christ in Galilee
NIV§44 NASB§50	Tour of Galilee with Simon and others	4:23-24	1:35-39	4:42-44		Ministry of Christ in Galilee
NIV§41 NASB§51	Second call of the four			5:1-11		Ministry of Christ in Galilee
NIV§45 NASB§52	Cleansing of a leper followed by much publicity	8:2-4	1:40-45	5:12-16		Ministry of Christ in Galilee
NIV§46 NASB§53	Forgiving and healing of a paralytic	9:1-8	2:1-12	5:17-26		Ministry of Christ in Galilee
NIV§47a NASB§54	Call of Matthew	9:9	2:13-14	5:27-28		Ministry of Christ in Galilee
NIV§47b NASB§55	Banquet at Matthew's house	9:10-13	2:15-17	5:29-32		Ministry of Christ in Galilee
NIV§48 NASB§56	Changed conditions with the Messiah present explained by three illustrations	9:14-17	2:18-22	5:33-39		Ministry of Christ in Galilee
	Sabbath Controversies and Withdrawal					Ministry of Christ in Galilee
NIV§49a NASB§57	A lame man healed in Jerusalem on the Sabbath				5:1-9	Ministry of Christ in Galilee
NIV§49b NASB§58	Effort to kill Jesus for breaking the Sabbath and saying he was equal with God				5:10-18	Ministry of Christ in Galilee
NIV§49c NASB§59	Discourse demonstrating the Son's equality with the Father				5:19-47	Ministry of Christ in Galilee

Harmony Section Numbers	Section Title	Matthew	Mark	Luke	John	Period of Christ's Ministry
NIV§50 NASB§60	Controversy over disciples' picking grain on the Sabbath	12:1-8	2:23-28	6:1-5		Ministry of Christ in Galilee
NIV§51 NASB§61	Healing of a man's withered hand on the Sabbath	12:9-14	3:1-6	6:6-11		Ministry of Christ in Galilee
NIV§52 NASB§62	Withdrawal to the Sea of Galilee with a great multitude from many places	12:15-21; 4:25	3:7-12			Ministry of Christ in Galilee
	Appointment of the Twelve and Sermon on the Mount					Ministry of Christ in Galilee
NIV§53 NASB§63	Twelve apostles named		3:13-19	6:12-16		Ministry of Christ in Galilee
NIV§54a NASB§64	Setting of the Sermon	5:1-2		6:17-19		Ministry of Christ in Galilee
NIV§54b NASB§65	Blessings of those who inherit the kingdom and woes to those who do not	5:3-12		6:21-26		Ministry of Christ in Galilee
NIV§54c NASB§66	Responsibility while awaiting the kingdom	5:13-16				Ministry of Christ in Galilee
NIV§54d NASB§67	Law, righteousness, and the kingdom	5:17-20				Ministry of Christ in Galilee
NIV§54e NASB§68	Six contrasts in interpreting the law	5:21-48		6:27-30, 32-36		Ministry of Christ in Galilee
NIV§54f NASB§69	Three hypocritical practices to be avoided	6:1-18				Ministry of Christ in Galilee
NIV§54g NASB§70	Three prohibitions against avarice, harsh judgment, and unwise exposure of sacred things	6:19–7:6		6:37-42		Ministry of Christ in Galilee
NIV§54h NASB§71	Application and conclusion	7:7-27		6:31, 43-49		Ministry of Christ in Galilee
NIV§54i NASB§72	Reaction of the crowds	7:28-29				Ministry of Christ in Galilee
	Growing Fame and Emphasis on Repentance					Ministry of Christ in Galilee
NIV§55 NASB§73	A certain centurion's faith and the healing of his servant	8:1, 5-13		7:1-10		Ministry of Christ in Galilee
NIV§56 NASB§74	A widow's son raised at Nain			7:11-17		Ministry of Christ in Galilee
NIV§57 NASB§75	John the Baptist's relationship to the kingdom	11:2-19		7:18-35		Ministry of Christ in Galilee
NIV§58 NASB§76	Woes upon Chorazin and Bethsaida for failure to repent	11:20-30				Ministry of Christ in Galilee
NIV§59 NASB§77	Jesus' feet anointed by a sinful, but contrite, woman			7:36-50		Ministry of Christ in Galilee

Harmony Section Numbers	Section Title	Matthew	Mark	Luke	John	Period of Christ's Ministry
	First Public Rejection by Jewish Leaders					Ministry of Christ in Galilee
NIV§60 NASB§78	A tour with the Twelve and other followers			8:1-3		Ministry of Christ in Galilee
NIV§61 NASB§79	Blasphemous accusation by the scribes and Pharisees	12:22-37	3:20-30			Ministry of Christ in Galilee
NIV§62 NASB§80	Request for a sign refused	12:38-45				Ministry of Christ in Galilee
NIV§63 NASB§81	Announcement of new spiritual ties	12:46-50	3:31-35	8:19-21		Ministry of Christ in Galilee
	Parabolic Mysteries About the Kingdom					Ministry of Christ in Galilee
NIV§64a NASB§82	The setting of the parables	13:1-3a	4:1-2	8:4		Ministry of Christ in Galilee
NIV§64b NASB§83	The parable of the soils	13:3b-23	4:3-25	8:5-18		Ministry of Christ in Galilee
NIV§64c NASB§84	The parable of the seed's spontaneous growth		4:26-29			Ministry of Christ in Galilee
NIV§64d NASB§85	The parable of the weeds (tares)	13:24-30				Ministry of Christ in Galilee
NIV§64e NASB§86	The parable of the mustard tree	13:31-32	4:30-32			Ministry of Christ in Galilee
NIV§64f NASB§87	The parable of the leavened loaf	13:33-35	4:33-34			Ministry of Christ in Galilee
NIV§64g NASB§88	The parable of the weeds (tares) explained	13:36-43				Ministry of Christ in Galilee
NIV§64h NASB§89	The parable of the hidden treasure	13:44				Ministry of Christ in Galilee
NIV§64i NASB§90	The parable of the valuable pearl	13:45-46				Ministry of Christ in Galilee
NIV§64j NASB§91	The parable of the dragnet	13:47-50				Ministry of Christ in Galilee
NIV§64k NASB§92	The parable of the house owner	13:51-52				Ministry of Christ in Galilee
	Continuing Opposition					Ministry of Christ in Galilee
NIV§65 NASB§93	Crossing the lake and calming the storm	13:53; 8:18, 23-27	4:35-41	8:22-25		Ministry of Christ in Galilee
NIV§66 NASB§94	Healing the Gerasene demoniacs and resultant opposition	8:28-34	5:1-20	8:26-39		Ministry of Christ in Galilee

Harmony Section Numbers	Section Title	Matthew	Mark	Luke	John	Period of Christ's Ministry
NIV§67 NASB§95	Return to Galilee, healing of a woman who touched Jesus' garment, and raising of Jairus's daughter	9:18-26	5:21-43	8:40-56		Ministry of Christ in Galilee
NIV§68 NASB§96	Three miracles of healing and another blasphemous accusation	9:27-34				Ministry of Christ in Galilee
NIV§69 NASB§97	Final visit to unbelieving Nazareth	13:54-58	6:1-6a			Ministry of Christ in Galilee
Final Galilean Campaign						Ministry of Christ in Galilee
NIV§70a NASB§98	Shortage of workers	9:35-38	6:6b			Ministry of Christ in Galilee
NIV§70b NASB§99	Commissioning of the Twelve	10:1-42	6:7-11	9:1-5		Ministry of Christ in Galilee
NIV§70c NASB§100	Workers sent out	11:1	6:12-13	9:6		Ministry of Christ in Galilee
NIV§71a NASB§101	Antipas's mistaken identification of Jesus	14:1-2	6:14-16	9:7-9		Ministry of Christ in Galilee
NIV§71b NASB§102	Earlier imprisonment and beheading of John the Baptist	14:3-12	6:17-29			Ministry of Christ in Galilee
NIV§72a NASB§103	Return of the workers		6:30	9:10a		Ministry of Christ in Galilee
Lesson on the Bread of Life						Ministry of Christ around Galilee
NIV§72b NASB§104	Withdrawal from Galilee	14:13-14	6:31-34	9:10b-11	6:1-3	Ministry of Christ around Galilee
NIV§72c NASB§105	Feeding the five thousand	14:15-21	6:35-44	9:12-17	6:4-13	Ministry of Christ around Galilee
NIV§73 NASB§106	A premature attempt to make Jesus king blocked	14:22-23	6:45-46		6:14-15	Ministry of Christ around Galilee
NIV§74 NASB§107	Walking on the water during a storm at sea	14:24-33	6:47-52		6:16-21	Ministry of Christ around Galilee
NIV§75 NASB§108	Healings at Gennesaret	14:34-36	6:53-56			Ministry of Christ around Galilee
NIV§76a NASB§109	Discourse on the true bread of life				6:22-59	Ministry of Christ around Galilee
NIV§76b NASB§110	Defection among the disciples				6:60-71	Ministry of Christ around Galilee
Lesson on the Yeast (Leaven) of the Pharisees, Sadducees, and Herodians						Ministry of Christ around Galilee
NIV§77 NASB§111	Conflict over the tradition of ceremonial defilement	15:1-20	7:1-23		7:1	Ministry of Christ around Galilee
NIV§78 NASB§112	Ministry to a believing Gentile woman in Tyre and Sidon	15:21-28	7:24-30			Ministry of Christ around Galilee

Harmony Section Numbers	Section Title	Matthew	Mark	Luke	John	Period of Christ's Ministry
NIV§79a NASB§113	Healings in Decapolis	15:29-31	7:31-37			Ministry of Christ around Galilee
NIV§79b NASB§114	Feeding the four thousand in Decapolis	15:32-38	8:1-9			Ministry of Christ around Galilee
NIV§80 NASB§115	Return to Galilee and encounter with the Pharisees and Sadducees	15:39–16:4	8:10-12			Ministry of Christ around Galilee
NIV§81a NASB§116	Warning about the error of the Pharisees, Sadducees, and Herodians	16:5-12	8:13-21			Ministry of Christ around Galilee
NIV§81b NASB§117	Healing a blind man at Bethsaida		8:22-26			Ministry of Christ around Galilee
Lesson of Messiahship Learned and Confirmed						Ministry of Christ around Galilee
NIV§82 NASB§118	Peter's identification of Jesus as the Christ, and first prophecy of the church	16:13-20	8:27-30	9:18-21		Ministry of Christ around Galilee
NIV§83 NASB§119	First direct prediction of the rejection, crucifixion, and resurrection	16:21-26	8:31-37	9:22-25		Ministry of Christ around Galilee
NIV§84 NASB§120	Coming of the Son of Man and judgment	16:27-28	8:38–9:1	9:26-27		Ministry of Christ around Galilee
NIV§85 NASB§121	Transfiguration of Jesus	17:1-8	9:2-8	9:28-36a		Ministry of Christ around Galilee
NIV§86 NASB§122	Command to keep the Transfiguration secret	17:9	9:9-10	9:36b		Ministry of Christ around Galilee
NIV§86 NASB§123	Elijah, John the Baptist, and the Son of Man's coming	17:10-13	9:11-13			Ministry of Christ around Galilee
Lessons on Responsibility to Others						Ministry of Christ around Galilee
NIV§87 NASB§124	Healing of a demoniac boy, and faithlessness rebuked	17:14-20, [21]	9:14-29	9:37-43a		Ministry of Christ around Galilee
NIV§88 NASB§125	Second prediction of the resurrection	17:22-23	9:30-32	9:43b-45		Ministry of Christ around Galilee
NIV§89 NASB§126	Payment of the temple tax	17:24-27				Ministry of Christ around Galilee
NIV§90 NASB§127	Rivalry over greatness dispelled	18:1-5	9:33-37	9:46-48		Ministry of Christ around Galilee
NIV§91 NASB§128	Warning against causing believers to stumble	18:6-14	9:38-59	9:49-50		Ministry of Christ around Galilee
NIV§92 NASB§129	Treatment and forgiveness of a sinning brother	18:15-35				Ministry of Christ around Galilee
Journey to Jerusalem for the Feast of Tabernacles (Booths)						Ministry of Christ around Galilee
NIV§94 NASB§130	Ridicule by the Lord's brothers				7:2-9	Ministry of Christ around Galilee

Harmony Section Numbers	Section Title	Matthew	Mark	Luke	John	Period of Christ's Ministry
NIV§95 NASB§131	Journey through Samaria			9:51-56	7:10	Ministry of Christ around Galilee
NIV§93 NASB§132	Complete commitment required of followers	8:19-22		9:57-62		Ministry of Christ around Galilee
Teachings at the Feast of Tabernacles (Booths)						Later Judean Ministry of Christ
NIV§96a NASB§133	Mixed reaction to Jesus' teaching and miracles				7:11-31	Later Judean Ministry of Christ
NIV§96b NASB§134	Frustrated attempt to arrest Jesus				7:32-52	Later Judean Ministry of Christ
NIV§97 NASB§135	[Jesus' forgiveness of an adulteress]				[7:53–8:11]	Later Judean Ministry of Christ
NIV§98 NASB§136	Conflict over Jesus' claim to be the light of the world				8:12-20	Later Judean Ministry of Christ
NIV§99a NASB§137	Invitation to believe in Jesus				8:21-30	Later Judean Ministry of Christ
NIV§99b NASB§138	Relationship to Abraham, and attempted stoning				8:31-59	Later Judean Ministry of Christ
Private Lessons on Loving Service and Prayer						Later Judean Ministry of Christ
NIV§102a NASB§139	Commissioning of the Seventy			10:1-16		Later Judean Ministry of Christ
NIV§102b NASB§140	Return of the Seventy			10:17-24		Later Judean Ministry of Christ
NIV§103 NASB§141	Story of the good Samaritan			10:25-37		Later Judean Ministry of Christ
NIV§104 NASB§142	Jesus' visit with Mary and Martha			10:38-42		Later Judean Ministry of Christ
NIV§105 NASB§143	Lesson on how to pray and parable of the bold friend			11:1-13		Later Judean Ministry of Christ
Second Debate with the Scribes and Pharisees						Later Judean Ministry of Christ
NIV§106 NASB§144	A third blasphemous accusation and a second debate			11:14-36		Later Judean Ministry of Christ
NIV§107 NASB§145	Woes against the scribes and Pharisees while eating with a Pharisee			11:37-54		Later Judean Ministry of Christ
NIV§108a NASB§146	Warning the disciples about hypocrisy			12:1-12		Later Judean Ministry of Christ
NIV§108b NASB§147	Warning about greed and trust in wealth			12:13-34		Later Judean Ministry of Christ
NIV§108c NASB§148	Warning against being unprepared for the Son of Man's coming			12:35-48		Later Judean Ministry of Christ

Harmony Section Numbers	Section Title	Matthew	Mark	Luke	John	Period of Christ's Ministry
NIV§108d NASB§149	Warning about the coming division			12:49-53		Later Judean Ministry of Christ
NIV§108e NASB§150	Warning against failing to discern the present time			12:54-59		Later Judean Ministry of Christ
NIV§109 NASB§151	Two alternatives: repent or perish			13:1-9		Later Judean Ministry of Christ
NIV§110 NASB§152	Opposition from a synagogue official for healing a woman on the Sabbath			13:10-21		Later Judean Ministry of Christ
Teaching at the Feast of Dedication						Later Judean Ministry of Christ
NIV§100a NASB§153	Healing of a man born blind				9:1-7	Later Judean Ministry of Christ
NIV§100b NASB§154	Reaction of the blind man's neighbors				9:8-12	Later Judean Ministry of Christ
NIV§100c NASB§155	Examination and excommunication of the blind man by the Pharisees				9:13-34	Later Judean Ministry of Christ
NIV§100d NASB§156	Jesus' identification of himself to the blind man				9:35-38	Later Judean Ministry of Christ
NIV§100e NASB§157	Spiritual blindness of the Pharisees				9:39-41	Later Judean Ministry of Christ
NIV§101a NASB§158	Allegory of the good shepherd and the thief				10:1-18	Later Judean Ministry of Christ
NIV§101b NASB§159	Further division among the Jews				10:19-21	Later Judean Ministry of Christ
NIV§111 NASB§160	Another attempt to stone or arrest Jesus for blasphemy				10:22-39	Later Judean Ministry of Christ
Principles of Discipleship						Ministry of Christ in and around Perea
NIV§112 NASB§161	From Jerusalem to Perea				10:40-42	Ministry of Christ in and around Perea
NIV§113a NASB§162	Question about salvation and entering the kingdom			13:22-30		Ministry of Christ in and around Perea
NIV§113b NASB§163	Anticipation of his coming death and lament over Jerusalem			13:31-35		Ministry of Christ in and around Perea
NIV§114 NASB§164	Healing of a man with dropsy while eating with a Pharisaic leader on the Sabbath			14:1-24		Ministry of Christ in and around Perea
NIV§115 NASB§165	Cost of discipleship			14:25-35		Ministry of Christ in and around Perea
NIV§116 NASB§166	Parables in defense of association with sinners			15:1-32		Ministry of Christ in and around Perea
NIV§117a NASB§167	Parable to teach the proper use of money			16:1-13		Ministry of Christ in and around Perea

Harmony Section Numbers	Section Title	Matthew	Mark	Luke	John	Period of Christ's Ministry
NIV§117b NASB§168	Story to teach the danger of wealth			16:14-31		Ministry of Christ in and around Perea
NIV§117c NASB§169	Four lessons on discipleship			17:1-10		Ministry of Christ in and around Perea
Raising of Lazarus and a Brief Tour through Samaria and Galilee						Ministry of Christ in and around Perea
NIV§118a NASB§170	Sickness and death of Lazarus				11:1-16	Ministry of Christ in and around Perea
NIV§118b NASB§171	Lazarus raised from the dead				11:17-44	Ministry of Christ in and around Perea
NIV§119 NASB§172	Decision of the Sanhedrin to put Jesus to death				11:45-54	Ministry of Christ in and around Perea
NIV§120a NASB§173	Healing of ten lepers while passing through Samaria and Galilee			17:11-21		Ministry of Christ in and around Perea
NIV§120b NASB§174	Instructions regarding the Son of Man's coming			17:22-37		Ministry of Christ in and around Perea
Teaching While on Final Journey to Jerusalem						Ministry of Christ in and around Perea
NIV§121 NASB§175	Two parables on prayer: the persistent widow and the Pharisee and the tax collector			18:1-14		Ministry of Christ in and around Perea
NIV§122 NASB§176	Conflict with the Pharisaic teaching on divorce	19:1-12	10:1-12			Ministry of Christ in and around Perea
NIV§123 NASB§177	Example of little children in relation to the kingdom	19:13-15	10:13-16	18:15-17		Ministry of Christ in and around Perea
NIV§124a NASB§178	Riches and the kingdom	19:16-30	10:17-31	18:18-30		Ministry of Christ in and around Perea
NIV§124b NASB§179	Parable of the landowner's sovereignty	20:1-16				Ministry of Christ in and around Perea
NIV§125a NASB§180	Third prediction of the resurrection	20:17-19	10:32-34	18:31-34		Ministry of Christ in and around Perea
NIV§125b NASB§181	Warning against ambitious pride	20:20-28	10:35-45			Ministry of Christ in and around Perea
NIV§126 NASB§182	Healing of Bartimaeus and his companion	20:29-34	10:46-52	18:35-43		Ministry of Christ in and around Perea
NIV§127a NASB§183	Salvation of Zacchaeus			19:1-10		Ministry of Christ in and around Perea
NIV§127b NASB§184	Parable to teach responsibility while the kingdom is delayed			19:11-28		Ministry of Christ in and around Perea
Triumphal Entry and the Fig Tree						Formal Presentation of Christ to Israel
NIV§128a NASB§185	Arrival at Bethany				11:55–12:1	Formal Presentation of Christ to Israel

Harmony Section Numbers	Section Title	Matthew	Mark	Luke	John	Period of Christ's Ministry
NIV§141 NASB§186	Mary's anointing of Jesus for burial	26:6-13	14:3-9		12:2-11	Formal Presentation of Christ to Israel
NIV§128b NASB§187	Triumphal Entry into Jerusalem	21:1-11, 14-17	11:1-11	19:19-44	12:12-19	Formal Presentation of Christ to Israel
NIV§129a NASB§188	Cursing of the fig tree having leaves but no figs	21:18-19a	11:12-14			Formal Presentation of Christ to Israel
NIV§129b NASB§189	Second cleansing of the temple	21:12-13	11:15-18	19:45-48		Formal Presentation of Christ to Israel
NIV§130a NASB§190	Request of some Greeks, and necessity of the Son of Man's being lifted up				12:20-36a	Formal Presentation of Christ to Israel
NIV§130b NASB§191	Departure from the unbelieving crowd and Jesus' response				12:36b-50	Formal Presentation of Christ to Israel
NIV§131 NASB§192	Withered fig tree and the lesson on faith	21:19b-22	11:19-25, [26]			Formal Presentation of Christ to Israel
Official Challenge of Christ's Authority						Formal Presentation of Christ to Israel
NIV§132a NASB§193	A question by the chief priests, scribes, and elders	21:23-27	11:27-33	20:1-8		Formal Presentation of Christ to Israel
NIV§132b NASB§194	Faithful discharge of responsibility taught by three parables	21:28– 22:14	12:1-12	20:9-19		Formal Presentation of Christ to Israel
NIV§133 NASB§195	A question by the Pharisees and Herodians	22:15-22	12:13-17	20:20-26		Formal Presentation of Christ to Israel
NIV§134 NASB§196	A question by the Sadducees	22:23-33	12:18-27	20:27-40		Formal Presentation of Christ to Israel
NIV§135 NASB§197	A question by a Pharisaic scribe	22:34-40	12:28-34			Formal Presentation of Christ to Israel
Christ's Response to His Enemies' Challenges						Formal Presentation of Christ to Israel
NIV§136 NASB§198	Jesus' relationship to David as son and Lord	22:41-46	12:35-37	20:41-44		Formal Presentation of Christ to Israel
NIV§137a NASB§199	Seven woes against the scribes and Pharisees	23:1-36	12:38-40	20:45-47		Formal Presentation of Christ to Israel
NIV§137b NASB§200	Sorrow over Jerusalem	23:37-39				Formal Presentation of Christ to Israel
NIV§138 NASB§201	A poor widow's gift of all she had		12:41-44	21:1-4		Formal Presentation of Christ to Israel
The Olivet Discourse: Prophecies About the Temple and the Return of Christ						Prophecies in Preparation for the Death of Christ
NIV§139a NASB§202	Setting of the discourse	24:1-3	13:1-4	21:5-7		Prophecies in Preparation for the Death of Christ
NIV§139b NASB§203	Beginning of birth pains	24:4-14	13:5-13	21:8-19		Prophecies in Preparation for the Death of Christ

Harmony Section Numbers	Section Title	Matthew	Mark	Luke	John	Period of Christ's Ministry
NIV§139c NASB§204	Abomination of desolation and subsequent distress	24:15-28	13:14-23	21:20-24		Prophecies in Preparation for the Death of Christ
NIV§139d NASB§205	Coming of the Son of Man	24:29-31	13:24-27	21:25-27		Prophecies in Preparation for the Death of Christ
NIV§139e NASB§206	Signs of nearness, but unknown time	24:32-41	13:28-32	21:28-33		Prophecies in Preparation for the Death of Christ
NIV§139f NASB§207	Five parables to teach watchfulness and faithfulness	24:42–25:30	13:33-37	21:34-36		Prophecies in Preparation for the Death of Christ
NIV§139g NASB§208	Judgment at the Son of Man's coming	25:31-46				Prophecies in Preparation for the Death of Christ
Arrangements for Betrayal						Prophecies in Preparation for the Death of Christ
NIV§140 NASB§209	Plot by the Sanhedrin to arrest and kill Jesus	26:1-5	14:1-2	21:37–22:2		Prophecies in Preparation for the Death of Christ
NIV§142 NASB§210	Judas's agreement to betray Jesus	26:14-16	14:10-11	22:3-6		Prophecies in Preparation for the Death of Christ
The Last Supper						Prophecies in Preparation for the Death of Christ
NIV§143 NASB§211	Preparation for the Passover meal	26:17-19	14:12-16	22:7-13		Prophecies in Preparation for the Death of Christ
NIV§144 NASB§212	Beginning of the Passover meal	26:20	14:17	22:14-16		Prophecies in Preparation for the Death of Christ
NIV§145 NASB§213	Washing the disciples' feet				13:1-20	Prophecies in Preparation for the Death of Christ
NIV§146 NASB§214	Identification of the betrayer	26:21-25	14:18-21	22:21-23	13:21-30	Prophecies in Preparation for the Death of Christ
NIV§144 NASB§215	Dissension among the disciples over greatness			22:24-30		Prophecies in Preparation for the Death of Christ
NIV§147 NASB§216	First prediction of Peter's denial			22:31-38	13:31-38	Prophecies in Preparation for the Death of Christ
NIV§148 NASB§217	Conclusion of the meal and the Lord's Supper instituted (1Co 11:23-26)	26:26-29	14:22-25	22:17-20		Prophecies in Preparation for the Death of Christ
Discourses and Prayers from the Upper Room to Gethsemane						Prophecies in Preparation for the Death of Christ
NIV§149 NASB§218	Questions about his destination, the Father, and the Holy Spirit answered				14:1-31	Prophecies in Preparation for the Death of Christ
NIV§150a NASB§219	The vine and the branches				15:1-17	Prophecies in Preparation for the Death of Christ
NIV§150b NASB§220	Opposition from the world				15:18–16:4	Prophecies in Preparation for the Death of Christ
NIV§150c NASB§221	Coming and ministry of the Spirit				16:5-15	Prophecies in Preparation for the Death of Christ

Harmony Section Numbers	Section Title	Matthew	Mark	Luke	John	Period of Christ's Ministry
NIV§150d NASB§222	Prediction of joy over his resurrection				16:16-22	Prophecies in Preparation for the Death of Christ
NIV§150e NASB§223	Promise of answered prayer and peace				16:23-33	Prophecies in Preparation for the Death of Christ
NIV§151 NASB§224	Jesus' prayer for his disciples and all who will believe				17:1-26	Prophecies in Preparation for the Death of Christ
NIV§147, 152 NASB§225	Second prediction of Peter's denial	26:30-35	14:26-31	22:39-40a	18:1	Prophecies in Preparation for the Death of Christ
NIV§152 NASB§226	Jesus' three agonizing prayers in Gethsemane	26:36-46	14:32-42	22:40b-46		Prophecies in Preparation for the Death of Christ
Betrayal and Arrest						Death of Christ
NIV§153 NASB§227	Jesus betrayed, arrested, and forsaken	26:47-56	14:43-52	22:47-53	18:2-12	Death of Christ
The Trial						Death of Christ
NIV§154 NASB§228	First Jewish phase, before Annas				18:13-24	Death of Christ
NIV§155 NASB§229	Second Jewish phase, before Caiaphas and the Sanhedrin	26:57-68	14:53-65	22:54		Death of Christ
NIV§156 NASB§230	Peter's denials	26:69-75	14:66-72	22:55-65	18:25-27	Death of Christ
NIV§157 NASB§231	Third Jewish phase, before the Sanhedrin	27:1	15:1a	22:66-71		Death of Christ
NIV§158 NASB§232	Remorse and suicide of Judas Iscariot (Ac 1:18-19)	27:3-10				Death of Christ
NIV§159 NASB§233	First Roman phase, before Pilate	27:2, 11-14	15:1b-5	23:1-5	18:28-38	Death of Christ
NIV§160 NASB§234	Second Roman phase, before Herod Antipas			23:6-12		Death of Christ
NIV§161 NASB§235	Third Roman phase, before Pilate	27:15-26	15:6-15	23:13-25	18:39–19:16	Death of Christ
The Crucifixion						Death of Christ
NIV§162 NASB§236	Mockery by the Roman soldiers	27:27-30	15:16-19			Death of Christ
NIV§163 NASB§237	Journey to Golgotha	27:31-34	15:20-23	23:26-33a	19:17	Death of Christ
NIV§164 NASB§238	First three hours of crucifixion	27:35-44	15:24-32	23:33b-43	19:18-27	Death of Christ
NIV§165 NASB§239	Last three hours of crucifixion	27:45-50	15:33-37	23:44-45a, 46	19:28-30	Death of Christ

Harmony Section Numbers	Section Title	Matthew	Mark	Luke	John	Period of Christ's Ministry
NIV§166 NASB§240	Witnesses of Jesus' death	27:51-56	15:38-41	23:45b, 47-49		Death of Christ
The Burial						Death of Christ
NIV§167a NASB§241	Certification of death and procurement of the body	27:57-58	15:42-45	23:50-52	19:31-38	Death of Christ
NIV§167b NASB§242	Jesus' body placed in a tomb	27:59-60	15:46	23:53-54	19:39-42	Death of Christ
NIV§168 NASB§243	Tomb watched by the women and guarded by the soldiers	27:61-66	15:47	23:55-56		Death of Christ
The Empty Tomb						Resurrection and Ascension of Christ
NIV§169 NASB§244	The tomb visited by the women	28:1	16:1			Resurrection and Ascension of Christ
NIV§170 NASB§245	The stone rolled away	28:2-4				Resurrection and Ascension of Christ
NIV§171 NASB§246	The tomb found to be empty by the women	28:5-8	16:2-8	24:1-8	20:1	Resurrection and Ascension of Christ
NIV§172 NASB§247	The tomb found to be empty by Peter and John			24:9-11, [12]	20:2-10	Resurrection and Ascension of Christ
Postresurrection Appearances						Resurrection and Ascension of Christ
NIV§173 NASB§248	Appearance to Mary Magdalene		[16:9-11]		20:11-18	Resurrection and Ascension of Christ
NIV§174 NASB§249	Appearance to the other women	28:9-10				Resurrection and Ascension of Christ
NIV§175 NASB§250	Report of the soldiers to the Jewish authorities	28:11-15				Resurrection and Ascension of Christ
NIV§176 NASB§251	Appearance to two disciples traveling to Emmaus		[16:12-13]	24:13-32		Resurrection and Ascension of Christ
NIV§177 NASB§252	Report of the two disciples to the rest (1Co 15:5a)			24:33-35		Resurrection and Ascension of Christ
NIV§178 NASB§253	Appearance to the ten assembled disciples		[16:14]	24:36-43	20:19-25	Resurrection and Ascension of Christ
NIV§179 NASB§254	Appearance to the eleven assembled disciples (1Co 15:5b)				20:26-31	Resurrection and Ascension of Christ
NIV§180 NASB§255	Appearance to the seven disciples while fishing				21:1-25	Resurrection and Ascension of Christ
NIV§181 NASB§256	Appearance to the Eleven in Galilee (1Co 15:6)	28:16-20	[16:15-18]			Resurrection and Ascension of Christ
NIV§182 NASB§257	Appearance to James, his brother (1Co 15:7)					Resurrection and Ascension of Christ

Harmony Section Numbers	Section Title	Matthew	Mark	Luke	John	Period of Christ's Ministry
NIV§183 NASB§258	Appearance to the disciples in Jerusalem (Ac 1:3-8)			24:44-49		Resurrection and Ascension of Christ
The Ascension						Resurrection and Ascension of Christ
NIV§184 NASB§259	Jesus' parting blessing and departure (Ac 1:9-12)		[16:19-20]	24:50-53		Resurrection and Ascension of Christ

#3—Sections Found in Only One Gospel

(A Total of 137 Sections)

(28 sections unique to Matthew, 2 sections to Mark, 54 sections to Luke, and 53 sections to John)

Harmony Section Numbers	Section Title	Gospel	Period of Christ's Ministry
NIV§1 NASB§1	Luke's purpose for writing a Gospel	Lk	Preview of Who Jesus Is
NIV§2 NASB§2	John's prologue: from preincarnation to crucifixion	Jn	Preview of Who Jesus Is
NIV§4 NASB§4	John's birth foretold to Zechariah	Lk	Early Years of John the Baptist
NIV§5 NASB§5	Jesus' birth foretold to Mary	Lk	Early Years of John the Baptist
NIV§6 NASB§6	Mary's visit to Elizabeth	Lk	Early Years of John the Baptist
NIV§7 NASB§7	Mary's song of joy	Lk	Early Years of John the Baptist
NIV§8a NASB§8	John's birth	Lk	Early Years of John the Baptist
NIV§8b NASB§9	Zechariah's prophetic song	Lk	Early Years of John the Baptist
NIV§8c NASB§10	John's growth and early life	Lk	Early Years of John the Baptist
NIV§9 NASB§11	Circumstances of Jesus' birth explained to Joseph	Mt	Early Years of Jesus Christ
NIV§10 NASB§12	Birth of Jesus	Lk	Early Years of Jesus Christ
NIV§11 NASB§13	Witness of the shepherds	Lk	Early Years of Jesus Christ
NIV§12 NASB§14	Circumcision of Jesus	Lk	Early Years of Jesus Christ
NIV§13 NASB§15	Jesus presented in the temple	Lk	Early Years of Jesus Christ
NIV§16 NASB§16	Return to Nazareth	Lk	Early Years of Jesus Christ
NIV§14 NASB§17	Visit of the Magi	Mt	Early Years of Jesus Christ
NIV§15 NASB§18	Flight into Egypt	Mt	Early Years of Jesus Christ
NIV§16 NASB§19	New home in Nazareth	Mt	Early Years of Jesus Christ
NIV§17 NASB§20	Growth and early life of Jesus	Lk	Early Years of Jesus Christ

Harmony Section Numbers	Section Title	Gospel	Period of Christ's Ministry
NIV§18 NASB§21	Jesus' first Passover in Jerusalem	Lk	Early Years of Jesus Christ
NIV§19 NASB§22	Jesus' adolescence and early manhood	Lk	Early Years of Jesus Christ
NIV§26 NASB§29	John's self-identification to the priests and Levites	Jn	End of John's Ministry and Beginning of Christ's
NIV§27 NASB§30	John's identification of Jesus as the Son of God	Jn	End of John's Ministry and Beginning of Christ's
NIV§28 NASB§31	Jesus' first followers	Jn	End of John's Ministry and Beginning of Christ's
NIV§29 NASB§32	First miracle: Water becomes wine	Jn	End of John's Ministry and Beginning of Christ's
NIV§30 NASB§33	Visit at Capernaum with his disciples	Jn	End of John's Ministry and Beginning of Christ's
NIV§31 NASB§34	First cleansing of the temple at the Passover	Jn	End of John's Ministry and Beginning of Christ's
NIV§32a NASB§35	An early response to Jesus' miracles	Jn	End of John's Ministry and Beginning of Christ's
NIV§32b NASB§36	Nicodemus's interview with Jesus	Jn	End of John's Ministry and Beginning of Christ's
NIV§33 NASB§37	John superseded by Jesus	Jn	End of John's Ministry and Beginning of Christ's
NIV§35a NASB§39	Discussion with a Samaritan woman	Jn	End of John's Ministry and Beginning of Christ's
NIV§35b NASB§40	Challenge of a spiritual harvest	Jn	End of John's Ministry and Beginning of Christ's
NIV§35c NASB§41	Evangelization of Sychar	Jn	End of John's Ministry and Beginning of Christ's
NIV§36 NASB§42	Arrival in Galilee	Jn	End of John's Ministry and Beginning of Christ's
NIV§38 NASB§44	Child at Capernaum healed by Jesus while at Cana	Jn	Ministry of Christ in Galilee
NIV§39 NASB§45	Ministry and rejection at Nazareth	Lk	Ministry of Christ in Galilee
NIV§40 NASB§46	Move to Capernaum	Mt	Ministry of Christ in Galilee
NIV§41 NASB§51	Second call of the four	Lk	Ministry of Christ in Galilee
NIV§49a NASB§57	A lame man healed in Jerusalem on the Sabbath	Jn	Ministry of Christ in Galilee
NIV§49b NASB§58	Effort to kill Jesus for breaking the Sabbath and saying he was equal with God	Jn	Ministry of Christ in Galilee

Harmony Section Numbers	Section Title	Gospel	Period of Christ's Ministry
NIV§40c NASB§59	Discourse demonstrating the Son's equality with the Father	Jn	Ministry of Christ in Galilee
NIV§54c NASB§66	Responsibility while awaiting the kingdom	Mt	Ministry of Christ in Galilee
NIV§54d NASB§67	Law, righteousness, and the kingdom	Mt	Ministry of Christ in Galilee
NIV§54f NASB§69	Three hypocritical practices to be avoided	Mt	Ministry of Christ in Galilee
NIV§54i NASB§72	Reaction of the multitudes	Mt	Ministry of Christ in Galilee
NIV§56 NASB§74	A widow's son raised at Nain	Lk	Ministry of Christ in Galilee
NIV§58 NASB§76	Woes upon Chorazin and Bethsaida for failure to repent	Mt	Ministry of Christ in Galilee
NIV§59 NASB§77	Jesus' feet anointed by a sinful, but contrite, woman	Lk	Ministry of Christ in Galilee
NIV§60 NASB§78	A tour with the Twelve and other followers	Lk	Ministry of Christ in Galilee
NIV§62 NASB§80	Request for a sign refused	Mt	Ministry of Christ in Galilee
NIV§64c NASB§84	The parable of the seed's spontaneous growth	Mk	Ministry of Christ in Galilee
NIV§64d NASB§85	The parable of the weeds (tares)	Mt	Ministry of Christ in Galilee
NIV§64g NASB§88	The parable of the weeds (tares) explained	Mt	Ministry of Christ in Galilee
NIV§64h NASB§89	The parable of the hidden treasure	Mt	Ministry of Christ in Galilee
NIV§64i NASB§90	The parable of the valuable pearl	Mt	Ministry of Christ in Galilee
NIV§64j NASB§91	The parable of the dragnet	Mt	Ministry of Christ in Galilee
NIV§64k NASB§92	The parable of the house owner	Mt	Ministry of Christ in Galilee
NIV§68 NASB§96	Three miracles of healing and another blasphemous accusation	Mt	Ministry of Christ in Galilee
NIV§76a NASB§109	Discourse on the true bread of life	Jn	Ministry of Christ around Galilee
NIV§76b NASB§110	Defection among the disciples	Jn	Ministry of Christ around Galilee
NIV§81b NASB§117	Healing a blind man at Bethsaida	Mk	Ministry of Christ around Galilee

Harmony Section Numbers	Section Title	Gospel	Period of Christ's Ministry
NIV§89 NASB§126	Payment of the temple tax	Mt	Ministry of Christ around Galilee
NIV§92 NASB§129	Treatment and forgiveness of a sinning brother	Mt	Ministry of Christ around Galilee
NIV§94 NASB§130	Ridicule by the Lord's brothers	Jn	Ministry of Christ around Galilee
NIV§96a NASB§133	Mixed reaction to Jesus' teaching and miracles	Jn	Later Judean Ministry of Christ
NIV§96b NASB§134	Frustrated attempt to arrest Jesus	Jn	Later Judean Ministry of Christ
NIV§98 NASB§136	Conflict over Jesus' claim to be the light of the world	Jn	Later Judean Ministry of Christ
NIV§99a NASB§137	Invitation to believe in Jesus	Jn	Later Judean Ministry of Christ
NIV§99b NASB§138	Relationship to Abraham, and attempted stoning	Jn	Later Judean Ministry of Christ
NIV§102a NASB§139	Commissioning of the seventy	Lk	Later Judean Ministry of Christ
NIV§102b NASB§140	Return of the seventy	Lk	Later Judean Ministry of Christ
NIV§103 NASB§141	Story of the good Samaritan	Lk	Later Judean Ministry of Christ
NIV§104 NASB§142	Jesus' visit with Mary and Martha	Lk	Later Judean Ministry of Christ
NIV§105 NASB§143	Lesson on how to pray and parable of the bold friend	Lk	Later Judean Ministry of Christ
NIV§106 NASB§144	A third blasphemous accusation and a second debate	Lk	Later Judean Ministry of Christ
NIV§107 NASB§145	Woes against the scribes and Pharisees while eating with a Pharisee	Lk	Later Judean Ministry of Christ
NIV§108a NASB§146	Warning the disciples about hypocrisy	Lk	Later Judean Ministry of Christ
NIV§108b NASB§147	Warning about greed and trust in wealth	Lk	Later Judean Ministry of Christ
NIV§108c NASB§148	Warning against being unprepared for the Son of Man's coming	Lk	Later Judean Ministry of Christ
NIV§108d NASB§149	Warning about the coming division	Lk	Later Judean Ministry of Christ
NIV§108e NASB§150	Warning against failing to discern the present time	Lk	Later Judean Ministry of Christ
NIV§109 NASB§151	Two alternatives: repent or perish	Lk	Later Judean Ministry of Christ

Harmony Section Numbers	Section Title	Gospel	Period of Christ's Ministry
NIV§110 NASB§152	Opposition from a synagogue official for healing a woman on the Sabbath	Lk	Later Judean Ministry of Christ
NIV§100a NASB§153	Healing of a man born blind	Jn	Later Judean Ministry of Christ
NIV§100b NASB§154	Reaction of the blind man's neighbors	Jn	Later Judean Ministry of Christ
NIV§100c NASB§155	Examination and excommunication of the blind man by the Pharisees	Jn	Later Judean Ministry of Christ
NIV§100d NASB§156	Jesus' identification of himself to the blind man	Jn	Later Judean Ministry of Christ
NIV§100e NASB§157	Spiritual blindness of the Pharisees	Jn	Later Judean Ministry of Christ
NIV§101a NASB§158	Allegory of the good shepherd and the thief	Jn	Later Judean Ministry of Christ
NIV§101b NASB§159	Further division among the Jews	Jn	Later Judean Ministry of Christ
NIV§111 NASB§160	Another attempt to stone or arrest Jesus for blasphemy	Jn	Later Judean Ministry of Christ
NIV§112 NASB§161	From Jerusalem to Perea	Jn	Ministry of Christ in and around Perea
NIV§113a NASB§162	Question about salvation and entering the kingdom	Lk	Ministry of Christ in and around Perea
NIV§113b NASB§163	Anticipation of his coming death and lament over Jerusalem	Lk	Ministry of Christ in and around Perea
NIV§114 NASB§164	Healing of a man with dropsy while eating with a Pharisaic leader on the Sabbath	Lk	Ministry of Christ in and around Perea
NIV§115 NASB§165	Cost of discipleship	Lk	Ministry of Christ in and around Perea
NIV§116 NASB§166	Parables in defense of associations with sinners	Lk	Ministry of Christ in and around Perea
NIV§117a NASB§167	Parable to teach the proper use of money	Lk	Ministry of Christ in and around Perea
NIV§117b NASB§168	Story to teach the danger of wealth	Lk	Ministry of Christ in and around Perea
NIV§117c NASB§169	Four lessons on discipleship	Lk	Ministry of Christ in and around Perea
NIV§118a NASB§170	Sickness and death of Lazarus	Jn	Ministry of Christ in and around Perea
NIV§118b NASB§171	Lazarus raised from the dead	Jn	Ministry of Christ in and around Perea
NIV§119 NASB§172	Decision of the Sanhedrin to put Jesus to death	Jn	Ministry of Christ in and around Perea

Harmony Section Numbers	Section Title	Gospel	Period of Christ's Ministry
NIV§120a NASB§173	Healing of ten lepers while passing through Samaria and Galilee	Lk	Ministry of Christ in and around Perea
NIV§120b NASB§174	Instructions regarding the Son of Man's coming	Lk	Ministry of Christ in and around Perea
NIV§121 NASB§175	Two parables on prayer: the persistent widow and the Pharisee and the tax collector	Lk	Ministry of Christ in and around Perea
NIV§124b NASB§179	Parable of the landowner's sovereignty	Mt	Ministry of Christ in and around Perea
NIV§127a NASB§183	Salvation of Zacchaeus	Lk	Ministry of Christ in and around Perea
NIV§127b NASB§184	Parable to teach responsibility while the kingdom is delayed	Lk	Ministry of Christ in and around Perea
NIV§128a NASB§185	Arrival at Bethany	Jn	Formal Presentation of Christ to Israel
NIV§130a NASB§190	Request of some Greeks and necessity of the Son of Man's being lifted up	Jn	Formal Presentation of Christ to Israel
NIV§130b NASB§191	Departure from the unbelieving crowd and Jesus' response	Jn	Formal Presentation of Christ to Israel
NIV§137b NASB§200	Sorrow over Jerusalem	Mt	Formal Presentation of Christ to Israel
NIV§139 NASB§208	Judgment at the Son of Man's coming	Mt	Prophecies in Preparation for the Death of Christ
NIV§145 NASB§213	Washing the disciples' feet	Jn	Prophecies in Preparation for the Death of Christ
NIV§144 NASB§215	Dissension among the disciples over greatness	Lk	Prophecies in Preparation for the Death of Christ
NIV§149 NASB§218	Questions about his destination, the Father, and the Holy Spirit answered	Jn	Prophecies in Preparation for the Death of Christ
NIV§150a NASB§219	The vine and the branches	Jn	Prophecies in Preparation for the Death of Christ
NIV§150b NASB§220	Opposition from the world	Jn	Prophecies in Preparation for the Death of Christ
NIV§150c NASB§221	Coming and ministry of the Spirit	Jn	Prophecies in Preparation for the Death of Christ
NIV§150d NASB§222	Prediction of joy over his resurrection	Jn	Prophecies in Preparation for the Death of Christ
NIV§150e NASB§223	Promise of answered prayer and peace	Jn	Prophecies in Preparation for the Death of Christ
NIV§151 NASB§224	Jesus' prayer for his disciples and all who will believe	Jn	Prophecies in Preparation for the Death of Christ
NIV§154 NASB§228	First Jewish phase, before Annas	Jn	Death of Christ

Harmony Section Numbers	Section Title	Gospel	Period of Christ's Ministry
NIV§158 NASB§232	Remorse and suicide of Judas Iscariot (Ac 1:18-19)	Mt	Death of Christ
NIV§160 NASB§234	Second Roman phase, before Herod Antipas	Lk	Death of Christ
NIV§170 NASB§245	The stone rolled away	Mt	Resurrection and Ascension of Christ
NIV§173 NASB§248	Appearance to Mary Magdalene	Jn	Resurrection and Ascension of Christ
NIV§174 NASB§249	Appearance to the other women	Mt	Resurrection and Ascension of Christ
NIV§175 NASB§250	Report of the soldiers to the Jewish authorities	Mt	Resurrection and Ascension of Christ
NIV§176 NASB§251	Appearance to two disciples traveling to Emmaus	Lk	Resurrection and Ascension of Christ
NIV§177 NASB§252	Report of the two disciples to the rest (1Co 15:5a)	Lk	Resurrection and Ascension of Christ
NIV§179 NASB§254	Appearance to the eleven assembled disciples (1Co 15:5b)	Jn	Resurrection and Ascension of Christ
NIV§180 NASB§255	Appearance to the seven disciples while fishing	Jn	Resurrection and Ascension of Christ
NIV§181 NASB§256	Appearance to the Eleven in Galilee (1Co 15:6)	Mt	Resurrection and Ascension of Christ
NIV§183 NASB§258	Appearance to the disciples in Jerusalem (Ac 1:3-8)	Lk	Resurrection and Ascension of Christ
NIV§184 NASB§259	Jesus' parting blessing and departure (Ac 1:9-12)	Lk	Resurrection and Ascension of Christ

#4—Sections Found in Two Gospels

(A Total of 41 Sections)

(22 sections in Matthew-Mark, 10 sections in Matthew-Luke, 5 sections in Mark-Luke, and 4 sections in Luke-John)

Harmony Section Numbers	Section Title	Gospel	Period of Christ's Ministry
NIV§3 NASB§3	Jesus' legal lineage through Joseph and natural lineage through Mary	Mt, Lk	Preview of Who Jesus Is
NIV§20 NASB§23	His ministry launched	Mk, Lk	Public Ministry of John the Baptist
NIV§22 NASB§25	His messages to the Pharisees, Sadducees, multitudes, tax collectors, and soldiers	Mt, Lk	Public Ministry of John the Baptist
NIV§41 NASB§47	First call of the four	Mt, Mk	Ministry of Christ in Galilee
NIV§42 NASB§48	Teaching in the synagogue of Capernaum authenticated by healing a demoniac	Mk, Lk	Ministry of Christ in Galilee
NIV§52 NASB§62	Withdrawal to the Sea of Galilee with a great multitude from many places	Mt, Mk	Ministry of Christ in Galilee
NIV§53 NASB§63	Twelve apostles named	Mk, Lk	Ministry of Christ in Galilee
NIV§54a NASB§64	Setting of the Sermon	Mt, Lk	Ministry of Christ in Galilee
NIV§54b NASB§65	Blessings of those who inherit the kingdom and woes to those who do not	Mt, Lk	Ministry of Christ in Galilee
NIV§54e NASB§68	Six contrasts in interpreting the law	Mt, Lk	Ministry of Christ in Galilee
NIV§54g NASB§70	Three prohibitions against avarice, harsh judgment, and unwise exposure of sacred things	Mt, Lk	Ministry of Christ in Galilee
NIV§54h NASB§71	Application and conclusion	Mt, Lk	Ministry of Christ in Galilee
NIV§55 NASB§73	A certain centurion's faith and the healing of his servant	Mt, Lk	Ministry of Christ in Galilee
NIV§57 NASB§75	John the Baptist's relationship to the kingdom	Mt, Lk	Ministry of Christ in Galilee
NIV§61 NASB§79	Blasphemous accusation by the scribes and Pharisees	Mt, Mk	Ministry of Christ in Galilee
NIV§64e NASB§86	The parable of the mustard tree	Mt, Mk	Ministry of Christ in Galilee
NIV§64f NASB§87	The parable of the leavened loaf	Mt, Mk	Ministry of Christ in Galilee
NIV§69 NASB§97	Final visit to unbelieving Nazareth	Mt, Mk	Ministry of Christ in Galilee
NIV§70a NASB§98	Shortage of workers	Mt, Mk	Ministry of Christ in Galilee

Harmony Section Numbers	Section Title	Gospel	Period of Christ's Ministry
NIV§71b NASB§102	Earlier imprisonment and beheading of John the Baptist	Mt, Mk	Ministry of Christ in Galilee
NIV§72a NASB§103	Return of the workers	Mk, Lk	Ministry of Christ in Galilee
NIV§75 NASB§108	Healings at Gennesaret	Mt, Mk	Ministry of Christ around Galilee
NIV§78 NASB§112	Ministry to a believing Gentile woman in Tyre and Sidon	Mt, Mk	Ministry of Christ around Galilee
NIV§79a NASB§113	Healings in Decapolis	Mt, Mk	Ministry of Christ around Galilee
NIV§79b NASB§114	Feeding the four thousand in Decapolis	Mt, Mk	Ministry of Christ around Galilee
NIV§80 NASB§115	Return to Galilee and encounter with the Pharisees and Sadducees	Mt, Mk	Ministry of Christ around Galilee
NIV§81a NASB§116	Warning about the error of the Pharisees, Sadducees, and Herodians	Mt, Mk	Ministry of Christ around Galilee
NIV§86 NASB§123	Elijah, John the Baptist, and the Son of Man's coming	Mt, Mk	Ministry of Christ around Galilee
NIV§95 NASB§131	Journey through Samaria	Lk, Jn	Ministry of Christ around Galilee
NIV§93 NASB§132	Complete commitment required of followers	Mt, Lk	Ministry of Christ around Galilee
NIV§122 NASB§176	Conflict with the Pharisaic teaching on divorce	Mt, Mk	Ministry of Christ in and around Perea
NIV§125b NASB§181	Warning against ambitious pride	Mt, Mk	Ministry of Christ in and around Perea
NIV§129a NASB§188	Cursing of the fig tree having leaves but no figs	Mt, Mk	Formal Presentation of Christ to Israel
NIV§131 NASB§192	Withered fig tree and the lesson on faith	Mt, Mk	Formal Presentation of Christ to Israel
NIV§135 NASB§197	A question by a Pharisaic scribe	Mt, Mk	Formal Presentation of Christ to Israel
NIV§138 NASB§201	A poor widow's gift of all she had	Mk, Lk	Formal Presentation of Christ to Israel
NIV§147 NASB§216	First prediction of Peter's denial	Lk, Jn	Prophecies in Preparation for the Death of Christ
NIV§162 NASB§236	Mockery by the Roman soldiers	Mt, Mk	Death of Christ
NIV§169 NASB§244	The tomb visited by the women	Mt, Mk	Resurrection and Ascension of Christ
NIV§172 NASB§247	The tomb found to be empty by Peter and John	Lk, Jn	Resurrection and Ascension of Christ
NIV§178 NASB§253	Appearance to the ten assembled disciples	Lk, Jn	Resurrection and Ascension of Christ

#5—Sections Found in Three Gospels

(A Total of 63 Sections)

(59 sections in Matthew-Mark-Luke and 4 Sections in Matthew-Mark-John)

Harmony Section Numbers	Section Title	Gospel	Period of Christ's Ministry
NIV§21 NASB§24	John the Baptist's person, proclamation, and baptism	Mt, Mk, Lk	Public Ministry of John the Baptist
NIV§23 NASB§26	Description of Christ	Mt, Mk, Lk	Public Ministry of John the Baptist
NIV§24 NASB§27	Jesus' baptism by John	Mt, Mk, Lk	End of John's Ministry and Beginning of Christ's
NIV§25 NASB§28	Jesus' temptation in the desert	Mt, Mk, Lk	End of John's Ministry and Beginning of Christ's
NIV§37 NASB§43	Nature of the Galilean ministry	Mt, Mk, Lk	Ministry of Christ in Galilee
NIV§43 NASB§49	Peter's mother-in-law and others healed	Mt, Mk, Lk	Ministry of Christ in Galilee
NIV§44 NASB§50	Tour of Galilee with Simon and others	Mt, Mk, Lk	Ministry of Christ in Galilee
NIV§45 NASB§52	Cleansing of a leper followed by much publicity	Mt, Mk, Lk	Ministry of Christ in Galilee
NIV§46 NASB§53	Forgiving and healing of a paralytic	Mt, Mk, Lk	Ministry of Christ in Galilee
NIV§47a NASB§54	Call of Matthew	Mt, Mk, Lk	Ministry of Christ in Galilee
NIV§47b NASB§55	Banquet at Matthew's house	Mt, Mk, Lk	Ministry of Christ in Galilee
NIV§48 NASB§56	Changed conditions with the Messiah present explained by three illustrations	Mt, Mk, Lk	Ministry of Christ in Galilee
NIV§50 NASB§60	Controversy over disciples' picking grain on the Sabbath	Mt, Mk, Lk	Ministry of Christ in Galilee
NIV§51 NASB§61	Healing of a man's withered hand on the Sabbath	Mt, Mk, Lk	Ministry of Christ in Galilee
NIV§63 NASB§81	Announcement of new spiritual ties	Mt, Mk, Lk	Ministry of Christ in Galilee
NIV§64a NASB§82	The setting of the parables	Mt, Mk, Lk	Ministry of Christ in Galilee
NIV§64b NASB§83	The parable of the soils	Mt, Mk, Lk	Ministry of Christ in Galilee
NIV§65 NASB§93	Crossing the lake and calming the storm	Mt, Mk, Lk	Ministry of Christ in Galilee
NIV§66 NASB§94	Healing the Gerasene demoniacs and resultant opposition	Mt, Mk, Lk	Ministry of Christ in Galilee

Harmony Section Numbers	Section Title	Gospel	Period of Christ's Ministry
NIV§67 NASB§95	Return to Galilee, healing of a woman who touched Jesus' garment, and raising of Jairus's daughter	Mt, Mk, Lk	Ministry of Christ in Galilee
NIV§70b NASB§99	Commissioning of the Twelve	Mt, Mk, Lk	Ministry of Christ in Galilee
NIV§70c NASB§100	Workers sent out	Mt, Mk, Lk	Ministry of Christ in Galilee
NIV§71a NASB§101	Antipas's mistaken identification of Jesus	Mt, Mk, Lk	Ministry of Christ in Galilee
NIV§73 NASB§106	A premature attempt to make Jesus king blocked	Mt, Mk, Jn	Ministry of Christ around Galilee
NIV§74 NASB§107	Walking on the water during a storm at sea	Mt, Mk, Jn	Ministry of Christ around Galilee
NIV§77 NASB§111	Conflict over the tradition of ceremonial defilement	Mt, Mk, Jn	Ministry of Christ around Galilee
NIV§82 NASB§118	Peter's identification of Jesus as the Christ, and first prophecy of the church	Mt, Mk, Lk	Ministry of Christ around Galilee
NIV§83 NASB§119	First direct prediction of the rejection, crucifixion, and resurrection	Mt, Mk, Lk	Ministry of Christ around Galilee
NIV§84 NASB§120	Coming of the Son of Man and judgment	Mt, Mk, Lk	Ministry of Christ around Galilee
NIV§85 NASB§121	Transfiguration of Jesus	Mt, Mk, Lk	Ministry of Christ around Galilee
NIV§86 NASB§122	Command to keep the transfiguration secret	Mt, Mk, Lk	Ministry of Christ around Galilee
NIV§87 NASB§124	Healing of a demoniac boy, and faithlessness rebuked	Mt, Mk, Lk	Ministry of Christ around Galilee
NIV§88 NASB§125	Second prediction of the resurrection	Mt, Mk, Lk	Ministry of Christ around Galilee
NIV§90 NASB§127	Rivalry over greatness dispelled	Mt, Mk, Lk	Ministry of Christ around Galilee
NIV§91 NASB§128	Warning against causing believers to stumble	Mt, Mk, Lk	Ministry of Christ around Galilee
NIV§123 NASB§177	Example of little children in relation to the kingdom	Mt, Mk, Lk	Ministry of Christ in and around Perea
NIV§124a NASB§178	Riches and the kingdom	Mt, Mk, Lk	Ministry of Christ in and around Perea
NIV§125a NASB§180	Third prediction of the resurrection	Mt, Mk, Lk	Ministry of Christ in and around Perea
NIV§126 NASB§182	Healing of Bartimaeus and his companion	Mt, Mk, Lk	Ministry of Christ in and around Perea
NIV§141 NASB§186	Mary's anointing of Jesus for burial	Mt, Mk, Jn	Formal Presentation of Christ to Israel
NIV§129b NASB§189	Second cleansing of the temple	Mt, Mk, Lk	Formal Presentation of Christ to Israel

Harmony Section Numbers	Section Title	Gospel	Period of Christ's Ministry
NIV§132a NASB§193	A question by the chief priests, scribes, and elders	Mt, Mk, Lk	Formal Presentation of Christ to Israel
NIV§132b NASB§194	Faithful discharge of responsibility taught by three parables	Mt, Mk, Lk	Formal Presentation of Christ to Israel
NIV§133 NASB§195	A question by the Pharisees and Herodians	Mt, Mk, Lk	Formal Presentation of Christ to Israel
NIV§134 NASB§196	A question by the Sadducees	Mt, Mk, Lk	Formal Presentation of Christ to Israel
NIV§136 NASB§198	Jesus' relationship to David as son and Lord	Mt, Mk, Lk	Formal Presentation of Christ to Israel
NIV§137a NASB§199	Seven woes against the scribes and Pharisees	Mt, Mk, Lk	Formal Presentation of Christ to Israel
NIV§139a NASB§202	Setting of the discourse	Mt, Mk, Lk	Prophecies in Preparation for the Death of Christ
NIV§139b NASB§203	Beginning of birth pains	Mt, Mk, Lk	Prophecies in Preparation for the Death of Christ
NIV§139c NASB§204	Abomination of desolation and subsequent distress	Mt, Mk, Lk	Prophecies in Preparation for the Death of Christ
NIV§139d NASB§205	Coming of the Son of Man	Mt, Mk, Lk	Prophecies in Preparation for the Death of Christ
NIV§139e NASB§206	Signs of nearness, but unknown time	Mt, Mk, Lk	Prophecies in Preparation for the Death of Christ
NIV§139f NASB§207	Five parables to teach watchfulness and faithfulness	Mt, Mk, Lk	Prophecies in Preparation for the Death of Christ
NIV§140 NASB§209	Plot by the Sanhedrin to arrest and kill Jesus	Mt, Mk, Lk	Prophecies in Preparation for the Death of Christ
NIV§142 NASB§210	Judas's agreement to betray Jesus	Mt, Mk, Lk	Prophecies in Preparation for the Death of Christ
NIV§143 NASB§211	Preparation for the Passover meal	Mt, Mk, Lk	Prophecies in Preparation for the Death of Christ
NIV§144 NASB§212	Beginning of the Passover meal	Mt, Mk, Lk	Prophecies in Preparation for the Death of Christ
NIV§148 NASB§217	Conclusion of the meal and the Lord's Supper instituted (1Co 11:23-26)	Mt, Mk, Lk	Prophecies in Preparation for the Death of Christ
NIV§152 NASB§226	Jesus' three agonizing prayers in Gethsemane	Mt, Mk, Lk	Prophecies in Preparation for the Death of Christ
NIV§155 NASB§229	Second Jewish phase, before Caiaphas and the Sanhedrin	Mt, Mk, Lk	Death of Christ
NIV§157 NASB§231	Third Jewish phase, before the Sanhedrin	Mt, Mk, Lk	Death of Christ
NIV§166 NASB§240	Witnesses of Jesus' death	Mt, Mk, Lk	Death of Christ
NIV§168 NASB§243	Tomb watched by the women and guarded by the soldiers	Mt, Mk, Lk	Death of Christ

#6—Sections Found in All Four Gospels
(A Total of 16 Sections)

Harmony Section Numbers	Section Title	Period of Christ's Ministry
NIV§34 NASB§38	Jesus' departure from Judea	End of John's Ministry and Beginning of Christ's
NIV§72b NASB§104	Withdrawal from Galilee	Ministry of Christ around Galilee
NIV§72c NASB§105	Feeding the five thousand	Ministry of Christ around Galilee
NIV§128b NASB§187	Triumphal Entry into Jerusalem	Formal Presentation of Christ to Israel
NIV§146 NASB§214	Identification of the betrayer	Prophecies in Preparation for the Death of Christ
NIV§147 NASB§225	Second prediction of Peter's denial	Prophecies in Preparation for the Death of Christ
NIV§153 NASB§227	Jesus betrayed, arrested, and forsaken	Death of Christ
NIV§156 NASB§230	Peter's denials	Death of Christ
NIV§159 NASB§233	First Roman phase, before Pilate	Death of Christ
NIV§161 NASB§235	Third Roman phase, before Pilate	Death of Christ
NIV§163 NASB§237	Journey to Golgotha	Death of Christ
NIV§164 NASB§238	First three hours of crucifixion	Death of Christ
NIV§165 NASB§239	Last three hours of crucifixion	Death of Christ
NIV§167a NASB§241	Certification of death and procurement of the body	Death of Christ
NIV§167b NASB§242	Jesus' body placed in a tomb	Death of Christ
NIV§171 NASB§246	The tomb found to be empty by the women	Resurrection and Ascension of Christ

#7—Passages Unique to Matthew's Gospel

Scripture	Subject	Harmony Section Numbers	Period of Christ's Ministry
1:18-25	Circumstances of Jesus' birth explained to Joseph	NIV§9 NASB§11	Early Years of Jesus Christ
2:1-23	Visit of the Magi; flight into Egypt; new home in Nazareth	NIV§14-16 NASB§17-19	Early Years of Jesus Christ
3:14-15	John's refusal to baptize Jesus and Jesus' insistence	NIV§24 NASB§27	End of John's Ministry and Beginning of Christ's
4:24	News about Jesus spread into Syria and the healing of many with various diseases	NIV§44 NASB§50	Ministry in Galilee
12:6-7	Something greater than the temple is here and citation of Hosea 6:6	NIV§50 NASB§60	Ministry in Galilee
12:17-21	Citation of Isaiah 42:1-4	NIV§52 NASB§62	Ministry in Galilee
5:13-43	Responsibility while awaiting the kingdom; law, righteousness, and the kingdom; six contrasts in interpreting the law	NIV§54c-54e NASB§66-68	Ministry in Galilee
6:1-34, 7:6	Three hypocritical practices to be avoided; a prohibition against unwise exposure of sacred things	NIV§54f-54g NASB§69-70	Ministry in Galilee
7:7-11, 13-17, 28-29	Asking, seeking, knocking; the narrow gate; beware of false prophets; the amazement of the crowd over Jesus' teaching	NIV§54h-54i NASB§71-72	Ministry in Galilee
8:11-12	Sons of the kingdom outside the kingdom while those from the east and west enter it	NIV§55 NASB§73	Ministry in Galilee
11:12-13	The kingdom forcefully advancing and forceful men laying hold of it[1]	NIV§57 NASB§75	Ministry in Galilee
11:20-30	Woes on Chorazin and Bethsaida for failure to repent	NIV§58 NASB§76	Ministry in Galilee
12:22-23, 27-28, 32-37	Jesus' healing of a blind and mute man; Jesus' driving out demons by the Spirit of God and the arrival of the kingdom; responsibility for every word spoken	NIV§61 NASB§79	Ministry in Galilee
12:38-45	Request for a sign refused	NIV§62 NASB§80	Ministry in Galilee
13:12, 16-17, 24-30, 33, 36-52	The receptive receiving more, but the unreceptive losing what he has; the blessedness of those who see and hear; parables of the weeds, yeast, hidden treasure, valuable pearl, net, house owner	NIV§64b-64k NASB§83-92	Ministry in Galilee
9:27-34	Three miracles of healing and another blasphemous accusation	NIV§68 NASB§96	Ministry in Galilee

1. Or, The kingdom suffering violence and violent men taking it by force.

Scripture	Subject	Harmony Section Numbers	Period of Christ's Ministry
9:35-38	Shortage of workers	NIV§70a NASB§98	Ministry in Galilee
10:2-8, 12-13, 15-42	Scattered instructions to the twelve disciples	NIV§70b NASB§99	Ministry in Galilee
14:28-31	Peter attempting to walk on the water	NIV§74 NASB§107	Ministry around Galilee
15:13-14	Strong words against blind Pharisaic leaders	NIV§77 NASB§111	Ministry around Galilee
15:24-25	Jesus' response about being sent only to the lost sheep of the house of Israel and the Canaanite woman's insistence	NIV§78 NASB§112	Ministry around Galilee
16:2-3	Detecting signs of the weather but not signs of the times	NIV§80 NASB§115	Ministry around Galilee
16:17-19	Jesus' commendation of Peter's confession and first prophecy of the church	NIV§82 NASB§118	Ministry around Galilee
17:20	Faith as a mustard seed to move mountains	NIV§87 NASB§124	Ministry around Galilee
18:4	Humility as that of a child determines greatness in the kingdom	NIV§90 NASB§127	Ministry around Galilee
18:12-35	Warning against causing believers to sin and treatment and forgiveness of a sinning brother	NIV§91-92 NASB§128-129	Ministry around Galilee
19:8, 10-12	Hardness of heart and Moses' permission to divorce; difficulty of marriage because of no-divorce principle	NIV§122 NASB§176	Ministry in and around Perea
19:28	The twelve disciples sitting on twelve thrones when the Son of Man sits on the throne of his glory	NIV§124a NASB§178	Ministry in and around Perea
21:4-5, 10-11, 14-16	Citation of Isaiah 62:11; the crowd's response to Jesus' triumphal entry and the objections of the chief priests and scribes	NIV§128b NASB§187	Formal Presentation of Christ to Israel
21:28-32, 43, 45; 22:1-14	Parable of the two sons assigned to the vineyard; the kingdom taken away from Jesus' listeners; the chief priests and Pharisees the object of the parable; the parable of the king and the wedding feast	NIV§132b NASB§194	Formal Presentation of Christ to Israel
22:46	Jesus' opponents unable to answer his question about the Messiah being both David's son and his Lord	NIV§136 NASB§198	Formal Presentation of Christ to Israel
23:2-5, 7-39	Heed the scribes' and Pharisees' instructions but do not follow their deeds; seven woes against the scribes and Pharisees; lament over Jerusalem	NIV§137a-137b NASB§199-200	Formal Presentation of Christ to Israel
24:11-12, 14, 26-28	The arising of false prophets; the gospel of the kingdom preached to the world; the Son of Man's coming will be conspicuous	NIV§139b-139c NASB§203-204	Prophecies in Preparation for the Death of Christ
24:37-41	The arrival of the Son of Man during the normal course of human affairs	NIV§139e NASB§206	Prophecies in Preparation for the Death of Christ

Scripture	Subject	Harmony Section Numbers	Period of Christ's Ministry
24:43–25:46	Parables of the thief, the faithful servant, the ten virgins, and the talents	NIV§139f-139g NASB§207-208	Prophecies in Preparation for the Death of Christ
26:2-3	Gathering of the chief priests and elders two days before the Passover	NIV§140 NASB§209	Prophecies in Preparation for the Death of Christ
26:25	Judas's exchange with Jesus about his coming betrayal	NIV§146 NASB§214	Prophecies in Preparation for the Death of Christ
26:53-54	Jesus' refusal to call on twelve legions of angels	NIV§153 NASB§227	Death of Christ
27:3-10	Remorse and suicide of Judas Iscariot	NIV§158 NASB§232	Death of Christ
27:19, 24-25	The dream of Pilate's wife; Pilate's washing his hands and the crowd's acceptance of the blame for Jesus' crucifixion	NIV§161 NASB§235	Death of Christ
27:52-53	The resurrection of the saints after Jesus' resurrection	NIV§166 NASB§240	Death of Christ
27:62-66	Soldiers sent to guard Jesus' tomb	NIV§168 NASB§243	Death of Christ
28:2-4	The stone rolled away from the tomb	NIV§170 NASB§245	Resurrection and Ascension of Christ
28:9-15	Appearance to more women; report of the soldiers to the Jewish authorities	NIV§174-175 NASB§249-250	Resurrection and Ascension of Christ
28:16-20	Appearance to the Eleven in Galilee and the Great Commission	NIV§181 NASB§256	Resurrection and Ascension of Christ

#8—Passages Unique to Mark's Gospel

Scripture	Subject	Harmony Section Numbers	Period of Christ's Ministry
3:9-11	Jesus' instructions to his disciples to keep a boat ready to protect him from the pressing crowd	NIV§52 NASB§62	Ministry in Galilee
3:15	Jesus gave authority to the Twelve to drive out demons	NIV§53 NASB§63	Ministry in Galilee
3:20-21, 23	The house was so crowded that Jesus and his followers could not eat; his own family thought he had lost his mind; he began speaking to them in parables	NIV§61 NASB§79	Ministry in Galilee
4:24	Jesus told the crowd on the shore to be careful what they listen to	NIV§64b NASB§83	Ministry in Galilee
4:26-29	The parable of the seed's spontaneous growth	NIV§64c NASB§84	Ministry in Galilee
5:4-5	Shackles and chains could not restrain the man with the unclean spirit who was inflicting injury on himself	NIV§66 NASB§94	Ministry in Galilee
5:26	Physicians had been unable to help the woman with the twelve-year hemorrhage	NIV§67 NASB§95	Ministry in Galilee
5:29-30	The woman with the hemorrhage felt her healing immediately; Jesus sensed that power had left him	NIV§67 NASB§95	Ministry in Galilee
6:6	Jesus wondered over the unbelief of the people in his hometown synagogue	NIV§69 NASB§97	Ministry in Galilee
6:13	The Twelve were driving out many demons and anointing many sick with oil and healing them	NIV§70c NASB§100	Ministry in Galilee
6:19-21	Herodias had a grudge against John the Baptist, and Herod feared him and enjoyed listening to him; Herod's birthday banquet included his lords, military commanders, and leading men of Galilee	NIV§71b NASB§102	Ministry in Galilee
6:23-24	Herod offered Herodias's daughter up to half his kingdom; the daughter asked Herodias what to ask for	NIV§71b NASB§102	Ministry in Galilee
6:31	Jesus invited his apostles to come with him to a lonely place to rest	NIV§72b NASB§104	Ministry around Galilee
6:52	Because of hardness of heart the disciples had not understood the miracle of feeding the 5,000 and so were astonished at his walking on the water and stilling the storm	NIV§74 NASB§107	Ministry around Galilee
7:2-4	The Pharisees and scribes followed traditions related to washing hands, cups, pitchers, and copper pots	NIV§77 NASB§111	Ministry around Galilee

Scripture	Subject	Harmony Section Numbers	Period of Christ's Ministry
7:30	The Gentile woman returned to her home and found that the demon had left her child	NIV§78 NASB§112	Ministry around Galilee
7:32-34	Jesus healed a man who was deaf and could hardly talk	NIV§79a NASB§113	Ministry around Galilee
8:22-26	Jesus healed a blind man at Bethsaida	NIV§81b NASB§117	Ministry around Galilee
9:10	Peter, James, and John were discussing among themselves what Jesus meant by "rising from the dead"	NIV§86 NASB§122	Ministry around Galilee
9:14	When Jesus and the three returned from the Mount of Transfiguration, they saw a large crowd around the rest of the disciples and some scribes arguing with them	NIV§87 NASB§124	Ministry around Galilee
9:21-24	Jesus asked the boy's father how long he had been troubled; the father described his situation in some detail and asked for pity; Jesus encouraged him to believe, and the father professed his faith	NIV§87 NASB§124	Ministry around Galilee
9:26-27	After Jesus' command to the demon, the boy went into terrible convulsions and fell over as if dead until Jesus took his hand and raised him	NIV§87 NASB§124	Ministry around Galilee
9:33-34	Jesus asked his disciples what they had been discussing, but they did not tell him because they had been discussing who was the greatest	NIV§90 NASB§127	Ministry around Galilee
9:41	Jesus said whoever gives a cup of water in his name because someone belongs to Christ will not lose his reward	NIV§91 NASB§128	Ministry around Galilee
10:24	Because of his disciples' amazement, Jesus repeated his statement about how hard it is to enter the kingdom	NIV§124a NASB§178	Ministry in and around Perea
11:16	During his second cleansing of the temple, Jesus would not let anyone carry any merchandise through the temple	NIV§129b NASB§189	Formal Presentation of Christ to Israel
11:25	Jesus directed his disciples when praying to forgive so that the Father in heaven may forgive them	NIV§131 NASB§192	Formal Presentation of Christ to Israel
12:32-34	A scribe agreed with Jesus and cited Deuteronomy 4:3 and 6:5; upon hearing this intelligent answer, Jesus told him that he was not far from the kingdom	NIV§135 NASB§197	Formal Presentation of Christ to Israel
14:51-52	A young man following Jesus was seized, but left behind a linen sheet covering his body and escaped	NIV§153 NASB§227	Death of Christ
14:59	Mark for a second time pointed out the inconsistency of the testimony against Jesus at his trial before the high priest	NIV§155 NASB§229	Death of Christ
15:8	The crowd asked Pilate to release a prisoner as had been his custom	NIV§161 NASB§235	Death of Christ

Scripture	Subject	Harmony Section Numbers	Period of Christ's Ministry
15:41	Among the women who witnessed Jesus' death were those who followed and served Jesus in Galilee	NIV§166 NASB§240	Death of Christ
15:44	Pilate summoned a centurion to find out whether Jesus was dead	NIV§167a NASB§241	Death of Christ
16:1	Mary Magdalene, Mary the mother of James, and Salome brought spices to Jesus' grave	NIV§169 NASB§244	Resurrection and Ascension of Christ

#9—Passages Unique to Luke's Gospel

Scripture	Subject	Harmony Section Numbers	Period of Christ's Ministry
1:1-4	Luke's purpose for writing a Gospel	NIV§1 NASB§1	A Preview of Who Jesus Is
1:5-80	John's birth foretold; Jesus' birth foretold to Mary; Mary's visit to Elizabeth and song of joy; John's birth; Zechariah's prophetic song; John's growth and early life	NIV§4-8c NASB§4-10	Early Years of John the Baptist
2:1-39	Birth of Jesus; witness of the shepherds; circumcision of Jesus; Jesus presented in the temple; return to Nazareth	NIV§10-13, 16 NASB§12-16	Early Years of Jesus Christ
2:40-52	Growth and early life of Jesus; Jesus' first Passover in Jerusalem; Jesus' adolescence and early manhood	NIV§17-19 NASB§20-22	Early Years of Jesus Christ
3:1-2	Time of the launching of John the Baptist's ministry	NIV§20 NASB§23	Public Ministry of John the Baptist
3:18	Besides warning the people of the coming of the Messiah, John preached the gospel with many other exhortations	NIV§23 NASB§26	Public Ministry of John the Baptist
3:23	Jesus was about thirty years old when he began his ministry	NIV§24 NASB§27	End of John's Ministry and the Beginning of Christ's
4:15	Jesus began preaching in the synagogues of Galilee and was praised by all	NIV§37 NASB§43	Ministry in Galilee
4:16-31	Ministry and rejection at Nazareth	NIV§39 NASB§45	Ministry in Galilee
5:1-11	Second call of the four	NIV§41 NASB§51	Ministry in Galilee
5:39	No one desires the new wine after drinking the old	NIV§48 NASB§56	Ministry in Galilee
6:18-19	Just before the Sermon on the Plain (Mount), many had come to be healed, and Jesus healed them all	NIV§54a NASB§64	Ministry in Galilee
6:29-30, 34-36	Jesus advocated allowing extra benefits to anyone who hits or robs you; he also suggested lending without expecting anything in return	NIV§54e NASB§68	Ministry in Galilee
6:38-40	Jesus said the giver would receive in return, a blind man cannot guide a blind man, and a pupil is not above his teacher	NIV§54g NASB§70	Ministry in Galilee
7:3-5, 7	Jewish elders represented the centurion in asking Jesus to save his servant, because the centurion did not consider himself worthy	NIV§55 NASB§73	Ministry in Galilee
7:11-17	A widow's son raised at Nain	NIV§56 NASB§74	Ministry in Galilee

Scripture	Subject	Harmony Section Numbers	Period of Christ's Ministry
7:21, 29-30	Jesus healed many people at the time John sent to ask if he was the one to come; tax collectors acknowledged God's justice, but the Pharisees and lawyers did not	NIV§57 NASB§75	Ministry in Galilee
7:36-50	Jesus' feet anointed by a sinful, but contrite woman	NIV§59 NASB§77	Ministry in Galilee
8:1-3	Jesus tours Galilee with the Twelve and other followers	NIV§60 NASB§78	Ministry in Galilee
8:51	Jesus did not allow anyone to enter Jairus's house except Peter, John, James, and the girl's parents	NIV§67 NASB§95	Ministry in Galilee
9:31-32	At the Transfiguration Moses and Elijah were talking to Jesus about his departure; when Peter woke up he saw the three	NIV§85 NASB§121	Ministry around Galilee
9:61-62	To the one who wanted to say good-bye to those at home, Jesus said that no one putting his hand to the plow and looking back is worthy of the kingdom	NIV§93 NASB§132	Ministry around Galilee
10:1–13:21	Commissioning and return of the Seventy; story of the good Samaritan; Jesus' visit with Mary and Martha; lesson on how to pray and parable of the bold friend; a third blasphemous accusation and a second debate; woes against the scribes and Pharisees while eating with a Pharisee; warning the disciples about hypocrisy; warning about greed and trust in wealth; warning against being unprepared for the Son of Man's coming, coming division, and failing to discern the present time; two alternatives of repenting or perishing; opposition from a synagogue official for healing a woman on the Sabbath	NIV§102a-110 NASB§139-152	Later Judean Ministry
13:22–17:10	Question about salvation and entering the kingdom; anticipation of Jesus' coming death and lament over Jerusalem; healing of a man with dropsy on the Sabbath; cost of discipleship; parables in defense of association with sinners; parable to teach the proper use of money; story to teach the danger of wealth; four lessons on discipleship	NIV§113a-117c NASB§162-169	Ministry in and around Perea
17:11–18:14	Healing of ten lepers while passing through Samaria and Galilee; instruction regarding the Son of Man's coming; two parables on prayer	NIV§120a-121 NASB§173-175	Ministry in and around Perea
18:34	When Jesus spoke of his future crucifixion and resurrection, his disciples understood none of it	NIV§125a NASB§180	Ministry in and around Perea
19:1-28	Healing of a blind man; salvation of Zacchaeus	NIV§127a-127b NASB§183-184	Ministry in and around Perea
19:39-44	At Jesus' Triumphal Entry the Pharisees told Jesus to rebuke his disciples; Jesus wept over the city as he approached	NIV§128b NASB§187	Formal Presentation of Christ to Israel

Scripture	Subject	Harmony Section Numbers	Period of Christ's Ministry
20:34, 40	Jesus said that the sons of this age marry and are given in marriage; the Sadducees did not have courage to question Jesus further after this exchange	NIV§134 NASB§196	Formal Presentation of Christ to Israel
21:18-19	Jesus promised his disciples that not a hair on their heads would perish and that they would gain their lives by endurance	NIV§139b NASB§203	Prophecies in Preparation for the Death of Christ
21:20, 22, 24	The surrounding of Jerusalem meant her destruction was near; the days of her surrounding are days of vengeance; many will fall by the sword and Jerusalem will be trampled underfoot	NIV§139c NASB§204	Prophecies in Preparation for the Death of Christ
21:28	People could recognize the nearness of their redemption when they see the signs Jesus described	NIV§139e NASB§206	Prophecies in Preparation for the Death of Christ
Lk 21:37-38	Jesus would teach during the day in the temple but would spend the night on the Mount of Olives	NIV§131 NASB§209	Prophecies in Preparation for the Death of Christ
22:8-9	Jesus sent Peter and John to prepare the Passover	NIV§143 NASB§211	Prophecies in Preparation for the Death of Christ
22:14-16	Beginning of the Passover meal and Jesus' prediction that he would not eat it again until in the kingdom	NIV§144 NASB§212	Prophecies in Preparation for the Death of Christ
22:22	Woe pronounced on the man who betrays the Son of Man	NIV§146 NASB§214	Prophecies in Preparation for the Death of Christ
22:24-30	Dissension among the disciples over greatness	NIV§144 NASB§215	Prophecies in Preparation for the Death of Christ
22:31-32	Simon told of Satan's desire to sift him and of Jesus' prayer that his faith not fail	NIV§147 NASB§216	Prophecies in Preparation for the Death of Christ
22:35-38	Jesus tells his disciples to make adequate preparations for ministry from this point on	NIV§147 NASB§216	Prophecies in Preparation for the Death of Christ
22:43-44	The strengthening of Jesus by an angel and his fervent prayer in Gethsemane	NIV§152 NASB§226	Prophecies in Preparation for the Death of Christ
22:48-49	Jesus asks Judas if he is betraying him with a kiss; Jesus' disciples asked if they should respond with the sword	NIV§153 NASB§227	Death of Christ
22:63-65	The men who were holding Jesus were mocking, beating, blindfolding, and blaspheming against him	NIV§156 NASB§230	Death of Christ
22:67-71	When Jesus told the Sanhedrin he was the Son of God, they accepted that as proving his guilt	NIV§157 NASB§231	Death of Christ
23:6-12	Second phase of Roman trial, before Herod Antipas	NIV§160 NASB§234	Death of Christ
23:13-15, 19	Pilate gathered the chief priests, rulers, and people and told them he and Herod Antipas had found Jesus undeserving of death; Barabbas was guilty of insurrection and murder	NIV§161 NASB§235	Death of Christ
23:27-32	Jesus' words to those who were following him to the place of crucifixion	NIV§163 NASB§237	Death of Christ

Scripture	Subject	Harmony Section Numbers	Period of Christ's Ministry
23:39-43	Words of the two criminals and Jesus' response to the repentant criminal	NIV§164 NASB§238	Death of Christ
23:51	Joseph had not agreed to the plan to crucify Jesus and was waiting for the kingdom	NIV§167a NASB§241	Death of Christ
23:56	The women returned from the tomb, prepared spices, and rested on the Sabbath	NIV§168 NASB§243	Death of Christ
24:15-35	Appearance to the two disciples traveling to Emmaus; report of the two to the rest	NIV§176-177 NASB§251-252	Resurrection and Ascension of Christ
24:41-43	When Jesus asked if these two disciples had anything to eat, they gave him a piece of fish and he ate it	NIV§178 NASB§253	Resurrection and Ascension of Christ
24:44-53	Appearance to the disciples in Jerusalem; parting blessing and departure	NIV§183-184 NASB§258-259	Resurrection and Ascension of Christ

#10—Passages Unique to John's Gospel

Scripture	Subject	Harmony Section Numbers	Period of Christ's Life
1:1-18	John's prologue: from preincarnation to crucifixion	NIV§2 NASB§2	A Preview of Who Jesus Is
1:19–4:4	John's self-identification to the priests and Levites; John's identification of Jesus as the Son of God; Jesus' first followers; first miracle: water becomes wine; visit at Capernaum; first cleansing of the temple at the Passover; an early response to Jesus' miracles; Nicodemus's interview with Jesus; John superseded by Jesus; Jesus' departure from Judea	NIV§26-34 NASB§29-38	End of John's Ministry and the Beginning of Christ's
4:5-45	Discussion with a Samaritan woman; challenge of a spiritual harvest; evangelization of Sychar; arrival in Galilee	NIV§35a-36 NASB§39-42	End of John's Ministry and the Beginning of Christ's
4:46-54	Child at Capernaum healed by Jesus while at Cana	NIV§38 NASB§44	Ministry in Galilee
5:1-47	A lame man healed in Jerusalem on the Sabbath; attempt to kill Jesus for breaking the Sabbath and saying he was equal with God; discourse demonstrating the Son's equality with the Father	NIV§49a-49c NASB§57-59	Ministry in Galilee
6:22-71	Discourse on the true bread of life; defection among the disciples	NIV§76a 76b NASB§109-110	Ministry around Galilee
7:2-9	Ridicule by the Lord's half brothers	NIV§94 NASB§130	Ministry around Galilee
7:11–8:59	Mixed reaction to Jesus' teaching and miracles; frustrated attempt to arrest Jesus; Jesus' forgiveness of an adulteress; conflict over Jesus' claim to be the light of the world; invitation to believe in Jesus; relationship to Abraham and attempted stoning	NIV§96a-99b NASB§133-138	Later Judean Ministry
9:1–10:39	Healing of a man born blind; reaction of the blind man's neighbors; examination and excommunication of the blind man by the Pharisees; Jesus' identification of himself to the blind man; spiritual blindness of the Pharisees; allegory of the good shepherd and the thief; further division among the Jews; another attempt to stone or arrest Jesus for blasphemy	NIV§100a-101b, 111 NASB§153-160	Later Judean Ministry
10:40-42	From Jerusalem to Perea	NIV§112 NASB§161	Ministry in and around Perea
11:1-54	Sickness and death of Lazarus; Lazarus raised from the dead; decision of the Sanhedrin to put Jesus to death	NIV§118a-119 NASB§170-172	Ministry in and around Perea
11:55-12:1	Arrival at Bethany	NIV§128a NASB§185	Formal Presentation of Christ to Israel
12:20-36a	Request of some Greeks and necessity of the Son of Man's being lifted up	NIV§130a NASB§190	Formal Presentation of Christ to Israel

Scripture	Subject	Harmony Section Numbers	Period of Christ's Life
13:1-20	Washing the disciples' feet	NIV§145 NASB§213	Prophecies in Preparation for the Death of Christ
13:23-30	John's question about the betrayer, Satan's entering into Judas, and Judas's departure from the meal	NIV§146 NASB§214	Prophecies in Preparation for the Death of Christ
13:31-35	Jesus tells his disciples of his departure and commands them to love one another	NIV§147 NASB§216	Prophecies in Preparation for the Death of Christ
14:1–17:26	Questions answered about his destination, the Father, and the Holy Spirit; the vine and the branches; opposition from the world; coming and ministry of the Spirit; prediction of joy over Jesus' resurrection; promise of answered prayer and peace; Jesus' prayer for his disciples and all who will believe	NIV§149-151 NASB§218-224	Prophecies in Preparation for the Death of Christ
18:4-9	Jesus' self-identification to the Roman soldiers and officers from the chief priests and Pharisees	NIV§153 NASB§227	Death of Christ
18:13-24	First Jewish phase of Jesus' trial, before Annas	NIV§154 NASB§228	Death of Christ
18:31-32, 35-37	Pilate's offer for the people to try Jesus and their answer that they were not allowed to put anyone to death; Jesus' conversation with Pilate about being King and the origin of his kingdom	NIV§159 NASB§233	Death of Christ
19:1-4, 7-14	Pilate's scourging of Jesus, the crown of thorns and beating, and pronouncement of innocence; the Jews' accusation that Jesus claimed to be the Son of God, Pilate's vacillation about releasing Jesus, and his presentation of Jesus as King of the Jews to be crucified	NIV§161 NASB§235	Death of Christ
19:20-22, 24-27	The inscription in Hebrew, Latin, and Greek and Pilate's insistence on putting "THE KING OF THE JEWS" on a sign; dividing of Jesus' garment by the soldiers; Jesus' committing of his mother to John's care	NIV§164 NASB§238	Death of Christ
19:29	Jesus offered sour wine in a sponge to drink	NIV§165 NASB§239	Death of Christ
19:31-37,	Breaking the legs of the other two victims, but not Jesus' legs	NIV§167a NASB§241	Death of Christ
19:39	Nicodemus brings a mixture of myrrh and aloes to the tomb of Jesus	NIV§167b NASB§242	Death of Christ
20:3-10	Peter and John run to see the empty tomb	NIV§172 NASB§247	Resurrection and Ascension of Christ
20:11-18	Jesus' appearance to Mary Magdalene	NIV§173 NASB§248	Resurrection and Ascension of Christ
20:21-25	Jesus' commissioning of the ten disciples; Thomas's doubt	NIV§178 NASB§253	Resurrection and Ascension of Christ
20:26–21:25	Jesus' appearances to the eleven assembled disciples and to seven disciples while fishing	NIV§179-180 NASB§254-255	Resurrection and Ascension of Christ

Background Charts

#11—Old Testament Citations in the Gospels

NT Scripture	Harmony Sec. Nos.	OT Scripture	OT Context	NT Context	Period of Christ's Ministry
Lk 1:17	NIV§4 NASB§4	Mal 4:6	prophecy of the coming of Elijah	prophecy of the birth of John the Baptist	Early Years of John the Baptist
Lk 1:50	NIV§7 NASB§7	Ps 103:17	a psalm of praise for God's mercies to Israel	Mary's song of joy over the coming birth of her son	Early Years of John the Baptist
Lk 1:53	NIV§7 NASB§7	Ps 107:9	thanksgiving to God for his deliverance of Israel	Mary's song of joy over the coming birth of her son	Early Years of John the Baptist
Lk 1:71	NIV§8b NASB§9	Ps 106:10	thanksgiving to God for his deliverance of Israel from the Egyptians	Zechariah's song of praise to God for his fulfillment of the Davidic covenant through the birth of John the Baptist	Early Years of John the Baptist
Lk 1:76	NIV§8b NASB§9	Mal 3:1	Malachi's prophecy of the messenger coming to prepare the way for the Lord	Zechariah's song of praise to God for his fulfillment of the Abrahamic covenant through the birth of John the Baptist	Early Years of John the Baptist
Lk 1:79	NIV§8b NASB§9	Isa 9:1-2	prophecy of Isaiah about the coming of the Messiah to change darkness to light	Zechariah's song of praise to God for his fulfillment of the new covenant in providing forgiveness of sins	Early Years of John the Baptist
Mt 1:23	NIV§9 NASB§11	Isa 7:14	Isaiah's prophecy to Ahaz of the coming miraculous birth of the Messiah	the angel's assurance to Joseph that Mary's son has been miraculously conceived by the Holy Spirit	Early Years of Jesus Christ
Lk 2:23	NIV§13 NASB§15	Ex 13:2, 12	command of the LORD to Moses to consecrate every first-born male	the occasion of Jesus' circumcision in the temple eight days after his birth	Early Years of Jesus Christ
Lk 2:24	NIV§13 NASB§15	Lev 5:11; 12:8	the LORD's command to Moses about how mothers were to be purified after giving birth to a child	the occasion of Mary's purification in the temple after she gave birth to Jesus	Early Years of Jesus Christ
Lk 2:32	NIV§13 NASB§15	Isa 42:6; 49:6	an excerpt from the first two "servant songs" predicting the future role of the Messiah	Simeon's Spirit-inspired song about the future of the infant Jesus in reaching the Gentiles with the light of God	Early Years of Jesus Christ
Mt 2:6	NIV§14 NASB§17	Mic 5:2	Micah's prophecy of Bethlehem as the birthplace of Israel's coming Messiah	the identification of the Messiah's birthplace for Herod by the chief priests and scribes	Early Years of Jesus Christ
Mt 2:15	NIV§15 NASB§18	Hos 11:1	the LORD recalls his love for Israel in delivering the nation from Egyptian captivity	Matthew connects Jesus' return with his parents from Egypt with Israel's deliverance from Egyptian captivity	Early Years of Jesus Christ

NT Scripture	Harmony Sec. Nos.	OT Scripture	OT Context	NT Context	Period of Christ's Ministry
Mt 2:18	NIV§15 NASB§18	Jer 31:15	the LORD reflects on an Israelite mother in distress over the slaying of her children by the Babylonians	Matthew connects the slaying of infants in Bethlehem after Jesus' birth as Herod tried to kill the newborn King of the Jews	Early Years of Jesus Christ
Mt 3:3; Mk 1:2-3; Lk 3:4-6	NIV§21 NASB§24	Isa 40:3-5	a prophetic exhortation to Israel to prepare for the LORD's glory when the Messiah arrives	a description of the ministry of John the Baptist as he preached a baptism of repentance for the forgiveness of sins	Public Ministry of John the Baptist
Mt 4:4; Lk 4:4	NIV§25 NASB§28	Dt 8:3	the LORD's reminder to Israel that his command created the manna that sustained them in the desert	Jesus' response to Satan's first temptation in the desert that suggested that he turn stones into bread to eat	End of John's Ministry and Beginning of Christ's
Mt 4:6; Lk 4:10-11	NIV§25 NASB§28	Ps 91:11-12	a psalm about God's protection of Israel in her conflicts leading to her promised kingdom	Satan's misleading suggestion that Jesus could presume on God's protection in subjecting himself to danger	End of John's Ministry and Beginning of Christ's
Mt 4:7; Lk 4:12	NIV§25 NASB§28	Dt 6:16	the LORD's prohibition against Israel's testing him as they had done in complaining about no water	Jesus' response to Satan stating that to apply the protection promised in Psalm 91:11-12 in the way Satan suggested would be presumption, not faith in God	End of John's Ministry and Beginning of Christ's
Mt 4:10; Lk 4:8	NIV§25 NASB§28	Dt 6:13	the LORD's caution to Israel against worshiping other gods when they arrive in the promised land	Jesus' response to Satan's third temptation that he worship Satan and receive all the kingdoms of the world and their glory in return	End of John's Ministry and Beginning of Christ's
Jn 1:23	NIV§26 NASB§29	Isa 40:3	a prophetic exhortation to Israel to prepare for the LORD's glory when the Messiah arrives	John the Baptist's description of his role as the forerunner of the Messiah	End of John's Ministry and Beginning of Christ's
Jn 2:17	NIV§31 NASB§34	Ps 69:9	the psalmist's insistence on behavior that matches a claim of devotion to God and therefore his becoming the object of the people's hatred	Jesus became the object of the people's hatred when he cleansed the temple of the merchants and money changers	End of John's Ministry and Beginning of Christ's
Lk 4:18-19	NIV§39 NASB§45	Isa 61:1-2	the Servant of the LORD is the one who will redeem Israel from her captivity in her future kingdom	Jesus applied the future salvation of Israel to his first-advent ministry of serving the spiritually poor, captives, and blind	Ministry of Christ in Galilee
Mt 4:15-16	NIV§40 NASB§46	Isa 9:1-2	the replacement of the gloom of the Assyrian captivity with the light of the Messiah to free Israel	Matthew applies the words referring to the Messiah's second advent to the spiritual light brought at his first advent	Ministry of Christ in Galilee
Mt 8:17	NIV§43 NASB§49	Isa 53:4	prophecy in the fourth "servant song" about the Messiah's bearing of the consequences of the sins of men	Matthew applied the words to Jesus' ministry of healing people's physical ailments	Ministry of Christ in Galilee

NT Scripture	Harmony Sec. Nos.	OT Scripture	OT Context	NT Context	Period of Christ's Ministry
Mt 9:13	NIV§47b NASB§55	Hos 6:6	God wanted genuine devotion from Israel, not superficial sacrificial activity	Jesus compared the superficiality of those who criticized his eating with sinners to Israel's superficial religious activities	Ministry of Christ in Galilee
Mt 12:7	NIV§50 NASB§60	Hos 6:6	God wanted genuine devotion from Israel, not superficial sacrificial activity	Jesus compared the superficiality of those who criticized his disciples' picking and eating grain on the Sabbath to Israel's superficial religious activities	Ministry of Christ in Galilee
Mt 12:18-21	NIV§52 NASB§62	Isa 42:1-4	an excerpt from the first "servant song" depicting his quiet and submissive demeanor	Matthew applies the words to support Jesus' warning to his followers not to publicize his presence	Ministry of Christ in Galilee
Mt 5:21	NIV§54e NASB§68	Ex 20:13; Dt 5:17	the sixth of ten commandments through Moses forbidding murder	Jesus applies the command to a forbidding of inward animosity against another person	Ministry of Christ in Galilee
Mt 5:27	NIV§54e NASB§68	Ex 20:14; Dt 5:18	the seventh of ten commandments through Moses forbidding adultery	Jesus applies the command to lustful thoughts, not just to the overt act of adultery	Ministry of Christ in Galilee
Mt 5:31	NIV§54e NASB§68	Dt 24:1, 3	Moses permitted divorces in Israel because of the hardness of people's hearts (Mt 19:8)	Jesus disallowed divorce and remarriage except in cases of legally binding betrothal relationships[1]	Ministry of Christ in Galilee
Mt 5:33	NIV§54e NASB§68	Lev 19:12; Nu 30:2; Dt 23:21	the LORD's command to Israel not to swear by his name falsely	Jesus used the command to forbid the practice of being untruthful except when bound by certain oaths	Ministry of Christ in Galilee
Mt 5:35	NIV§54e NASB§68	Ps 48:2	the psalmist used the phrase "the city of the Great King" to describe Jerusalem	Jesus used the phrase as an example of what one should not base an oath on to avoid being bound by it	Ministry of Christ in Galilee
Mt 5:38	NIV§54e NASB§68	Ex 21:24; Lev 24:20; Dt 19:21	the principle of retaliation whereby the punishment matched but did not exceed the damage to the victim	Jesus told the Jewish leaders of his day that they had unjustly used the principle for personal rather than legal retaliation	Ministry of Christ in Galilee
Mt 5:43	NIV§54e NASB§68	Lev 19:18	this command was not to hold a grudge against a fellow Israelite, but to love him as one loves oneself	Jesus corrected the Pharisaic interpretation of the command, which dictated hate toward one's enemy	Ministry of Christ in Galilee
Mt 7:23	NIV§54h NASB§71	Ps 6:8	the psalmist rebukes his enemies who have caused his distress	Jesus uses the psalmist's words to rebuke those whose profession of being his followers was only superficial	Ministry of Christ in Galilee
Mt 11:5; Lk 7:22	NIV§57 NASB§75	Isa 35:5-6; 61:1	God's restoration in the future kingdom to include physical restoration for the afflicted	application of the Scriptures to Jesus' ministry at his first coming, which was a foretaste of the future kingdom	Ministry of Christ in Galilee

1. Or, except in cases of unfaithfulness.

NT Scripture	Harmony Sec. Nos.	OT Scripture	OT Context	NT Context	Period of Christ's Ministry
Mt 11:20; Lk 7:27	NIV§57 NASB§75	Mal 3:1	Malachi's prophecy of the messenger coming to prepare the way for the Lord	Jesus' teaching to the crowds about John the Baptist just after he had answered John's question about his Messiahship	Ministry of Christ in Galilee
Mt 11:29	NIV§58 NASB§76	Jer 6:16	the LORD's message to Judah encouraging them to return to the right way they once had walked in	Jesus' invitation to Israelites to follow him to escape the load of external observances imposed by their leaders	Ministry of Christ in Galilee
Mt 12:40	NIV§62 NASB§80	Jnh 1:17	the record of Jonah's remaining inside a big fish for three days and three nights	a comparison of Jesus to the sign of his being in the tomb for three days and three nights	Ministry of Christ in Galilee
Mt 13:14-15; Mk 4:12; Lk 8:10	NIV§64b NASB§83	Isa 6:9-10	an advanced warning from God to Isaiah of the unresponsiveness of Judah to his message and of the hiding of the truth from them	Jesus' use of the words to explain his own use of parables to hide truth from his enemies while revealing new truth about the kingdom to his followers	Ministry of Christ in Galilee
Mt 13:32; Mk 4:32	NIV§64e NASB§86	Eze 17:23; 31:6; Da 4:12	birds of the air picturing inhabitants of the future Messianic kingdom and of Nebuchadnezzar's kingdom	Jesus' way of designating inhabitants of the new form of the kingdom he describes in parables	Ministry of Christ in Galilee
Mt 13:35	NIV§64f NASB§87	Ps 78:2	the psalmist speaking of a story with a spiritual application and the puzzle of Israel's rebellion despite God's grace	Jesus using *parable* in the sense of a particular pedagogical device designed to reveal truth to the receptive and to hide it from the unreceptive	Ministry of Christ in Galilee
Mt 13:43	NIV§64g NASB§88	Da 12:3	Daniel's prediction of the privilege of the wise and those who turn many to righteousness after future resurrection	Jesus' prediction of the privilege of the righteous after the Son of Man's judgment at the end of the age	Ministry of Christ in Galilee
Mt 10:35-36	NIV§70b NASB§99	Mic 7:6	Micah's prophecy of the family divisions resulting from Israel's sin and the consequent inability to find someone to trust	Jesus' description to the Twelve of the unfriendly reception to expect when he sent them out into Galilee preaching the gospel of the kingdom	Ministry of Christ in Galilee
Jn 6:31	NIV§76a NASB§109	Ex 16:4, 15; Ne 9:15; Ps 78:24; 105:40	OT records of the historical fact of God's supply of bread for Israel during their desert wanderings after leaving Egypt	Jesus' listeners recall the historical fact of God's miraculous supply of material food to Israel as they ask Jesus for a sign the day after he fed the 5,000	Ministry of Christ around Galilee
Jn 6:45	NIV§76a NASB§109	Isa 54:13	Isaiah prophesies about how in the Messianic kingdom the Lord himself will teach everyone	Jesus applies the words to everyone who has learned from the Father and is drawn to be a follower of the Son	Ministry of Christ around Galilee
Mt 15:8-9; Mk 7:6-7	NIV§77 NASB§111	Isa 29:13	Isaiah describes the empty ritualism of his day and its inability to bring anyone close to God	Jesus applies the words to describe the empty ritualism of the Judaism of his day, particularly in reference to the tradition of the elders	Ministry of Christ around Galilee

NT Scripture	Harmony Sec. Nos.	OT Scripture	OT Context	NT Context	Period of Christ's Ministry
Mt 15:4; Mk 7:10	NIV§77 NASB§111	Ex 20:12; Dt 5:16	the fifth of ten commandments given through Moses requiring respect for parents and parental authority	Jesus' citation of this commandment as being violated through compliance with the traditions of the elders	Ministry of Christ around Galilee
Mk 8:18	NIV§81a NASB§116	Eze 12:2	the LORD's prophecy through Ezekiel to Ezekiel's fellow exiles who would not accept the prophet's message	Jesus' rebuke of his disciples for not understanding his meaning in referring to the leaven of the Pharisees and Herod	Ministry of Christ around Galilee
Mk 9:48	NIV§91 NASB§128	Isa 66:24	the corpses of those suffering everlasting punishment as a reminder of the terrible consequences of rebellion against God	Jesus' application of the words to describe those who fail to enter the kingdom because of some type of stumbling block	Ministry of Christ around Galilee
Mt 18:16	NIV§92 NASB§129	Dt 19:15	the Mosaic law declaring the insufficiency of one witness to establish guilt of an accused person	Jesus' application of that law to dealing with a brother accused of not responding to reproof for his sin	Ministry of Christ around Galilee
Lk 10:27	NIV§103 NASB§141	Lev 19:18; Dt 6:5	commands to love the one LORD wholeheartedly and to love one's neighbor rather than taking vengeance against him	the lawyer's response to Jesus about how the law says one can inherit eternal life	Later Judean Ministry of Christ
Lk 10:28	NIV§103 NASB§141	Lev 18:5	special blessings promised to the Israelites when they obey God's law	Jesus' response to the lawyer who had correctly cited the love of God and neighbor as conditions for inheriting eternal life	Later Judean Ministry of Christ
Lk 13:19	NIV§110 NASB§152	Eze 17:23; 31:6; Da 4:12	birds of the air picturing inhabitants of the future Messianic kingdom and of Nebuchadnezzar's kingdom	Jesus' way of designating inhabitants of the new form of the kingdom he describes in parables	Later Judean Ministry of Christ
Jn 10:34	NIV§111 NASB§160	Ps 82:6	the psalmist's recognition that kings and judges are appointed by the decree of God, who invests his authority in them	Jesus' question to his critics about why it is wrong to call the Messiah God when the inspired psalm calls human leaders gods	Later Judean Ministry of Christ
Lk 13:27	NIV§113a NASB§162	Ps 6:8	the psalmist rebukes his enemies who have caused his distress	Jesus uses the psalmist's words to rebuke those whose profession of being his followers is only superficial	Ministry of Christ in and around Perea
Lk 13:35	NIV§113b NASB§163	Ps 118:26	part of a song written for Israel after forty years of desert-wandering and used regularly at the Passover	Jesus' prediction that Israel would not genuinely utter these words until his second coming	Ministry of Christ in and around Perea
Mk 10:4	NIV§122 NASB§176	Dt 24:1-4	Moses permitted divorces in Israel because of the hardness of people's hearts (Mt 19:8)	Jesus disallowed divorce and remarriage except in cases of legally binding betrothal relationships[2]	Ministry of Christ in and around Perea

2. Or, except in cases of unfaithfulness.

NT Scripture	Harmony Sec. Nos.	OT Scripture	OT Context	NT Context	Period of Christ's Ministry
Mt 19:4; Mk 10:6	NIV§122 NASB§176	Ge 1:27; 5:2	historical record of God's creation of male and female	the first step in Jesus' reasoning before the Pharisees that the marriage union is indissoluble	Ministry of Christ in and around Perea
Mt 19:5; Mk 10:7	NIV§122 NASB§176	Ge 2:24	the establishment and indissolubility of the marriage union as the first human institution	the second step in Jesus' reasoning before the Pharisees that the marriage union is indissoluble	Ministry of Christ in and around Perea
Mt 19:7	NIV§122 NASB§176	Dt 24:1-4	Moses permitted divorces in Israel because of the hardness of people's hearts (Mt 19:8)	Jesus disallowed divorce and remarriage except in cases of legally binding betrothal relationships[3]	Ministry of Christ in and around Perea
Mt 19:18-19; Mk 10:19	NIV§124a NASB§178	Ex 20:12-16; Dt 5:16-20	the fifth through the ninth of the Ten Commandments as Moses received them from God	Jesus recited these commandments to the rich young ruler in response to his question about how to obtain eternal life	Ministry of Christ in and around Perea
Mt 21:5; Jn 12:15	NIV§128b NASB§187	Zec 9:9	Zechariah's prophecy of the Messiah's entrance on a donkey in contrast to other kings who rode on horses	Jesus fulfilled this prophecy on the occasion of his Triumphal Entry into Jerusalem at the beginning of Passion Week	Formal Presentation of Christ to Israel
Mt 21:9; Mk 11:9; Lk 19:38; Jn 12:13	NIV§128b NASB§187	Ps 118:26	part of a song written for Israel after forty years of desert-wandering and used regularly at the Passover	song of praise by the people of Israel when Jesus entered Jerusalem triumphantly at the beginning of Passion Week	Formal Presentation of Christ to Israel
Mt 21:16	NIV§128b NASB§187	Ps 8:2	the psalmist David contrasts dependent infants with self-sufficient infidels	Jesus uses the words to respond to the objections of the scribes and chief priests over the tributes being given to Jesus	Formal Presentation of Christ to Israel
Mt 21:13; Mk 11:17; Lk 19:46	NIV§129b NASB§189	Isa 56:7; Jer 7:11	in the Messiah's kingdom the Jerusalem temple will be the focal point of worship for all people in the world	Jesus' stern rebuke of the leaders of his day for making the temple a commercial venture in violation of its eventual worldwide role in worship	Formal Presentation of Christ to Israel
Jn 12:38	NIV§130b NASB§191	Isa 53:1	a scarcity of people would recognize the Servant of the LORD when he arrives in spite of the prophecies about him	the prophecy of Isaiah literally fulfilled at Christ's first advent when Israel did not recognize and welcome him	Formal Presentation of Christ to Israel
Jn 12:40	NIV§130b NASB§191	Isa 6:10	an advance warning from God to Isaiah of the unresponsiveness of Judah to his message and of the hiding of the truth from them	Jesus gives God's blinding of Israel as the reason the nation did not recognize and welcome him at his first advent	Formal Presentation of Christ to Israel
Mt 21:33; Mk 12:1	NIV§132b NASB§194	Isa 5:2	God's people compared to a vineyard he planted and cultivated, expecting to receive a good yield from his investment	Jesus uses the words as an introduction to the parable of a landowner who rented his vineyard to farmers who proved to be dishonest	Formal Presentation of Christ to Israel

3. Or, except in cases of unfaithfulness.

NT Scripture	Harmony Sec. Nos.	OT Scripture	OT Context	NT Context	Period of Christ's Ministry
Mt 21:42; Mk 12:10-11; Lk 20:17	NIV§132b NASB§194	Ps 118:22-23	a prophecy of the ultimate triumph of the Messiah after being rejected by the leaders of his people	Jesus' noting of the fulfillment of the rejection part of this prophecy in his extended debate with Jewish leaders on Tuesday of Passion Week	Formal Presentation of Christ to Israel
Mt 22:24; Mk 12:19; Lk 20:28	NIV§134 NASB§196	Dt 25:5	the law of Levirate marriages provided that the brother of a dead man who died childless was to marry the widow in order to provide an heir	the citation of the law by the Sadducees in debating with Jesus over the doctrine of the resurrection of the dead	Formal Presentation of Christ to Israel
Mt 22:32; Mk 12:26; Lk 20:37	NIV§134 NASB§196	Ex 3:6	the LORD's identification of himself to Moses as the God of the patriarchs Abraham, Isaac, and Jacob	Jesus' response to the Sadducees to prove the doctrine of the resurrection of the dead by showing that God is the God of the living, not of the dead	Formal Presentation of Christ to Israel
Mt 22:37; Mk 12:29-30	NIV§135 NASB§197	Dt 6:4-5	command to love the one LORD wholeheartedly	Jesus' response to a lawyer who asked which is the greatest commandment of all	Formal Presentation of Christ to Israel
Mt 22:39; Mk 12:31	NIV§135 NASB§197	Lev 19:18	command to love one's neighbor rather than taking vengeance against him	Jesus' designation of the second greatest commandment in the law	Formal Presentation of Christ to Israel
Mt 22:44; Mk 12:36; Lk 20:42-43	NIV§136 NASB§198	Ps 110:1	a Messianic psalm necessitating that the Messiah be both divine as LORD and human as the son of David (2Sa 7:12)	Jesus' citing of the psalm in his debate with the Pharisees to prove that the Messiah must be both divine and human	Formal Presentation of Christ to Israel
Mt 23:39	NIV§137b NASB§200	Ps 118:26	part of a song written for Israel after forty years of desert wandering and used regularly at the Passover	Jesus' prediction that Israel would not genuinely utter these words until his second coming	Formal Presentation of Christ to Israel
Mt 24:15; Mk 13:14	NIV§139c NASB§204	Da 9:27; 11:31; 12:11	prophecy of the future desecration of the temple by a false christ who will arise as world ruler	Jesus' reference to Daniel's prophecy about the future desecration of the temple during the seventieth prophetic week	Prophecies in Preparation for the Death of Christ
Mt 24:29; Mk 13:24-25	NIV§139d NASB§205	Isa 13:10; 34:4; Eze 32:7; Joel 2:10, 31; 3:15	some of the frequent references to cosmic upheavals associated with the opening phase of the day of the LORD in OT prophecy	Jesus' application of the prophecies of cosmic upheavals to the end of the tribulation that will characterize the fulfillment of Daniel's seventieth prophetic week	Prophecies in Preparation for the Death of Christ
Mt 24:30; Mk 13:26; Lk 21:27	NIV§139d NASB§205	Da 7:13	Daniel's prophecy of the coming of the Son of Man to reign over a worldwide kingdom	Jesus' reinforcement of Daniel's prophecy, the fulfillment of which will come at his second advent	Prophecies in Preparation for the Death of Christ
Mt 24:31	NIV§139d NASB§205	Isa 27:13	Isaiah's prophecy of the restoration of Israel to worship the LORD in Jerusalem	Jesus' prophecy of the role of angels in the regathering of elect Israel at the time of his second advent	Prophecies in Preparation for the Death of Christ

NT Scripture	Harmony Sec. Nos.	OT Scripture	OT Context	NT Context	Period of Christ's Ministry
Jn 13:18	NIV§145 NASB§213	Ps 41:9	a psalm of David about a close companion who betrayed him	Jesus applies the words to Judas at the Last Supper just before Judas departed on his mission of betrayal	Prophecies in Preparation for the Death of Christ
Lk 22:37	NIV§147 NASB§216	Isa 53:12	Isaiah's prophecy of the role of the Servant of the LORD among sinful human beings	Jesus' noting of the fulfillment of Isaiah's prophecy in allowing himself to be captured and crucified as though he were a sinner	Prophecies in Preparation for the Death of Christ
Jn 15:25	NIV§150b NASB§220	Ps 35:19; 69:4	David's laments over being the object of hatred and possible destruction even though he has done no wrong	Jesus' application of David's words to himself as he warns the disciples that they too will be objects of hatred	Prophecies in Preparation for the Death of Christ
Mt 26:31; Mk 14:27	NIV§147 NASB§225	Zec 13:7	Zechariah's prophecy of the striking of the good shepherd and the scattering of his followers	Jesus' application of the prophecy to himself, predicting to his disciples their defection after his arrest	Prophecies in Preparation for the Death of Christ
Mt 26:64; Mk 14:62	NIV§155 NASB§229	Ps 110:1; Da 7:13	a psalm about the position of the Messiah at God's right hand and a prophecy of the coming of the Son of Man to reign over a worldwide kingdom	Jesus' application of the two Messianic prophecies to himself at the second Jewish phase of his trial before Caiaphas and the Sanhedrin	Death of Christ
Mt 27:9-10	NIV§158 NASB§232	Zec 11:12-13; cf. Jer 18:2; 19:2, 11; 32:6-9	prophetic of the mocking response of the Jewish leaders that Jesus was worth no more than a common slave and of the purchase of a potter's field with the money	Matthew's application of these prophecies to Judas's betrayal of Jesus for thirty pieces of silver and to the use of the returned money by the Jewish leaders to purchase the potter's field	Death of Christ
Lk 23:30	NIV§163 NASB§237	Hos 10:8	prophecy that Israel's captivity would be so severe that the people would pray to the mountains to fall on them	Jesus on his way to Golgotha uses the prophecy to predict coming days of desolation for Jerusalem	Death of Christ
Jn 19:24	NIV§164 NASB§238	Ps 22:18	David's lament over being forsaken and having his enemies cast lots for his garments	John's application of the words to the soldiers who cast lots for Jesus' seamless tunic rather than tear it in pieces	Death of Christ
Mt 27:43	NIV§164 NASB§238	Ps 22:8	David's words of personal abandonment and feelings of being abandoned by God	the taunts of those who mocked Jesus as he hung on the cross during the first three hours of his crucifixion	Death of Christ
Mt 27:46; Mk 15:34	NIV§165 NASB§239	Ps 22:1	the psalmist David's desperate cry as though he had been utterly forsaken by God	Jesus' application of David's plea for God's help in the third of his seven last words from the cross	Death of Christ
Lk 23:46	NIV§165 NASB§239	Ps 31:5	in the midst of distressing circumstances David's acknowledgment of trust in God	the seventh of Jesus' seven last words from the cross, expressing trust in God as he breathed his last breath	Death of Christ

NT Scripture	Harmony Sec. Nos.	OT Scripture	OT Context	NT Context	Period of Christ's Ministry
Jn 19:36	NIV§167a NASB§241	Ps 34:20	expression by David of the sufficiency of divine preservation in the midst of human persecution	John's application of the words to the soldiers' decision not to break Jesus' legs because he was already dead	Death of Christ
Jn 19:37	NIV§167a NASB§241	Zec 12:10	Zechariah's prophecy of the future repentance of Israel when they look to Jesus in faith at his second advent	John applies the words to the piercing of Jesus in his crucifixion as a foreshadowing of the fulfillment of Zechariah's prophecy	Death of Christ

#12—Sects of Judaism in Christ's Time

Pharisees	Sadducees	Herodians	Essenes	Zealots
1. Began with the Hasidim in 2nd century B.C.	1. Began during Hasmonean period (166-163 B.C.)	1. Originated when Herod the Great tried to establish his right to rule in Palestine	1. Along with the Pharisees, they traced their origin to the Hasidim	1. Began during reign of Herod the Great c. 6 B.C. and wiped out at Masada in A.D. 73
2. Accepted as inspired and authoritative both the Torah and the oral tradition	2. Accepted only the Torah as authoritative Scripture	2. Supporters of Herod who were men of standing and influence	2. Eventually separated from the Pharisees because of Essene strictness and zeal	2. Opposed paying taxes to Roman emperor, claiming allegiance to God alone
3. Held a mediating view on free will and divine sovereignty	3. Attributed everything to free will rather than divine sovereignty	3. Friendly to the Roman rule and therefore akin to the Sadducees religiously and economically	3. Attributed all things to divine providence	3. Strong loyalty to Jewish traditions
4. Accepted a hierarchical system of angels and demons	4. Did not believe in angels or demons	4. Preferred the leadership of Herod Antipas to that of Roman governors	4. Joined with Maccabeans in a revolt against the Syrians (c. 165-155 B.C.)	4. Opposed to use of Greek language in land of Israel
5. Believed in a future for the dead	5. Denied resurrection and future life	5. Politically opposed to the Pharisees who were anti-Hasmonean, anti-Herodian, and anti-Roman	5. Practiced communal ownership of property	5. Predicted a coming time of salvation
6. Champions of human equality	6. Controlled the high priesthood and the chief priests	6. Joined with Pharisees in opposing Jesus because he introduced a kingdom that neither sect wanted	6. Strong sense of mutual responsibility	6. At times took up the sword to try to expel the Romans by force
7. Separated themselves from ritual uncleanness	7. Very strict in maintaining Levitical purity		7. Offered sacrifices on holy days and during sacred seasons but not in the temple	
8. Emphasized the ethical rather than theological in their teaching	8. Interpreted Mosaic Law more literally than the Pharisees		8. Observed purity laws of the Torah strictly	

Pharisees	Sadducees	Herodians	Essenes	Zealots
9. Opposed Roman rule in Palestine	9. Friendly toward Roman rule in Palestine		9. Practiced daily worship and study of Scripture	
10. Accepted immortality of the soul and rewards and retribution	10. Rejected the existence of a spiritual world		10. Marriage not condemned in principle but not widely practiced	
11. The leading party and rivals of the Sadducees	11. Maintained a majority in the Sanhedrin from A.D. 6 until A.D. 70		11. Bound themselves with oaths of piety and obedience	
12. Survived the fall of Jerusalem in A.D. 70	12. Their party dissolved with the fall of Jerusalem in A.D. 70		12. Showed great hospitality toward one another	

#13—The Reigns of the Herods

Name	Dates of Reign	Title	Territory	NT Period
Herod the Great	37-4 B.C.	King	Judea, Samaria, Galilee, Perea, Idumea, Traconitis	time of Jesus' birth
Herod Philip II	4 B.C.-A.D. 34	Tetrarch	Iturea, Traconitis	Jesus' infancy till after his death and resurrection
Herod Antipas	4 B.C.-A.D. 39	Tetrarch	Galilee and Perea	Jesus' infancy till after his death and resurrection
Herod Archelaus	4 B.C.-A.D. 6	Ethnarch	Judea, Idumea, Samaria	Jesus' infancy till his early childhood
Herod Agrippa I	A.D. 37-44	King	Judea, Samaria, Galilee, Perea, Idumea, northeast Palestine	early years after Pentecost
Herod Agrippa II	A.D. 50-70	Tetrarch	Tiberias, Batanea, Traconitis, Auranitis, Abila	during the spread of Christianity to the Gentiles

#14—The Herod Family in the New Testament

(Note: Names appearing in bold type are those family members who are mentioned in the NT.)

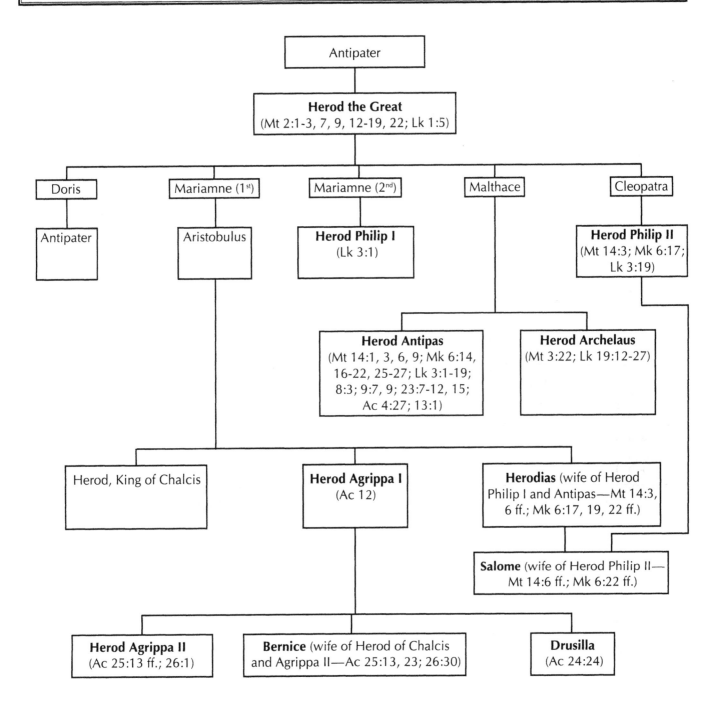

Antipater

Herod the Great
(Mt 2:1-3, 7, 9, 12-19, 22; Lk 1:5)

| Doris | Mariamne (1st) | Mariamne (2nd) | Malthace | Cleopatra |

Antipater

Aristobulus

Herod Philip I
(Lk 3:1)

Herod Philip II
(Mt 14:3; Mk 6:17;
Lk 3:19)

Herod Antipas
(Mt 14:1, 3, 6, 9; Mk 6:14,
16-22, 25-27; Lk 3:1-19;
8:3; 9:7, 9; 23:7-12, 15;
Ac 4:27; 13:1)

Herod Archelaus
(Mt 3:22; Lk 19:12-27)

Herod, King of Chalcis

Herod Agrippa I
(Ac 12)

Herodias (wife of Herod
Philip I and Antipas—Mt 14:3,
6 ff.; Mk 6:17, 19, 22 ff.)

Salome (wife of Herod Philip II—
Mt 14:6 ff.; Mk 6:22 ff.)

Herod Agrippa II
(Ac 25:13 ff.; 26:1)

Bernice (wife of Herod of Chalcis
and Agrippa II—Ac 25:13, 23; 26:30)

Drusilla
(Ac 24:24)

#15—Territorial Rulers during Christ's Life

(Note: Names of members of the Herod family appear in bold type. Others are Roman procurators or governors.)

Dates of Rule	Judea, Samaria, Idumea	Galilee, Perea	Iturea, Trachonitis
37-4 B.C.	**Herod the Great**	**Herod the Great**	**Herod the Great**
4 B.C.-A.D. 6	**Archelaus**	**Antipas**	**Philip II**
A.D. 6-10	Coponius	**Antipas**	**Philip II**
A.D. 10-13	Marcus Ambivius	**Antipas**	**Philip II**
A.D. 13-15	Annius Rufus	**Antipas**	**Philip II**
A.D. 15-26	Valerius Gratus	**Antipas**	**Philip II**
A.D. 26-34	Pontius Pilate	**Antipas**	**Philip II**
A.D. 34-36	Pontius Pilate	**Antipas**	governor of Syria
A.D. 36-37	Marcellus	**Antipas**	governor of Syria
A.D. 37-38	Marcellus	**Antipas**	**Agrippa I**
A.D. 38-39	Maryllus	**Antipas**	**Agrippa I**
A.D. 39-41	Maryllus	**Agrippa I**	**Agrippa I**
A.D. 41-44	**Agrippa I**	**Agrippa I**	**Agrippa I**

#16—Roman Rulers of the Land Where Christ Lived

Name	Position	Length of Rule	Prominent Events	Scriptural Mention
Augustus	Emperor of Rome	30 B.C.-A.D. 14	birth and early years of Christ	Lk 3:1
Tiberius	Emperor of Rome	A.D. 14-37	ministry and death of Christ	Mt 22:17-21; Mk 12:14-17; Lk 3:1; 20:22; 23:1, 2; Jn 19:12-15
Coponius	Procurator of Judea	A.D. 6-10	Christ's childhood years	[not mentioned]
Marcus Ambivius	Procurator of Judea	A.D. 10-13	Christ's middle-teen years	[not mentioned]
Annius Rufus	Procurator of Judea	A.D. 13-15	Christ's early adulthood	[not mentioned]
Valerius Gratus	Procurator of Judea	A.D. 15-26	Christ's adulthood until beginning of his ministry	[not mentioned]
Pontius Pilate	Procurator of Judea	A.D. 26-36	Christ's ministry, trial, and death	Mt 27:2, 13, 17, 22, 24, 58, 62, 65; Mk 15:1-5, 9, 12, 14-15, 43-44; Lk 3:1; 13:1, 23:1, 3-4, 6, 11-13, 20, 24, 52; Jn 18:29, 31, 33, 35, 37-38, 19:1, 4-6, 8, 10, 12-13, 15, 19, 22, 31, 38; Ac 3:13; 4:27; 13:28; 1 Ti 6:13

#17—Gospel Origins according to the Early Fathers
Select Quotations Regarding the Gospels' Direct Connection with the Apostles

Century	Sources of Matthew	Sources of Mark	Sources of Luke	Sources of John	Sources of All
first			"eyewitnesses and servants of the word" - the apostles and other eyewitnesses (Lk 1:2)		
second	**Irenaeus** refers to what Matthew the apostle has written in his Gospel (*Against Heresies* 3.9.3 [*ANF*, 1:423])	**Papias**: "Mark having become the interpreter of Peter, wrote down accurately whatsoever he remembered" (*Fragments of Papias* 6 [*ANF*, 1:154-155])	**Irenaeus**: "Thus did the apostles simply, and without respect of persons, deliver to all what they had themselves learned from the Lord. Thus also does Luke, without respect of persons, deliver to us what he had learned from them as he has himself testified, 'Even as they delivered them to us, who from the beginning were eyewitnesses and ministers of the Word'" (*Against Heresies* 3.15.3 [*ANF*, 1:440])	**Tertullian**: "The same authority of the apostolic churches will afford evidence to the other Gospels also, which we possess equally through their means, and according to their usage—I mean the Gospels of John and Matthew—whilst that which Mark published may be affirmed to be Peter's whose interpreter Mark was. For even Luke's form of the Gospel men usually ascribe to Paul" (Tertullian, *The Five Books Against Marcion* 4.5 [*ANF*, 3:657])	**Justyn Martyr**: "For the apostles, in the memoirs composed by them which are called Gospels, have thus delivered unto us what was enjoined upon them" (*The First Apology of Justin* 6 [*ANF*, 1:185])
second	**Tertullian** called Matthew "the most faithful chronicler of the Gospel, because [he was] the companion of the Lord" (*On the Flesh of Christ* 22 [*ANF*, 3:540])	**Clement of Alexandria**: "Mark, the follower of Peter, while Peter publicly preached the Gospel at Rome before some of Caesar's equities, and adduced many testimonies to Christ, in order that thereby they might be able to commit to memory what was spoken, of what was spoken by Peter, wrote entirely what is called the Gospel according to Mark" (*Fragments* 1, cited by Cassiodorus [*ANF*, 2:573])	**Tertullian**: "Luke, however, was not an apostle, but only an apostolic man; not a master, but a disciple, and so inferior to a master—at least as far subsequent to him as the apostle whom he followed (and that, no doubt was Paul) was subsequent to others . . ." (*The Five Books Against Marcion* 4.2 [*ANF*, 3:347-348])	**Tertullian**: "Of the apostles, therefore, John and Matthew first instill faith into us; whilst of apostolic men, Luke and Mark renew it afterwards" (Tertullian, *The Five Books Against Marcion* 4.2 [*ANF*, 3:651])	**Tertullian**: "The evangelical Testament has apostles for its authors. . . . Since there are apostolic men also, they are not alone, but appear with the apostles and after apostles" (*The Five Books Against Marcion* 4.2 [*ANF*, 3:347])

Century	Sources of Matthew	Sources of Mark	Sources of Luke	Sources of John	Sources of All
second		**Clement of Alexandria**: Peter's hearers "importuned Mark, to whom the Gospel is ascribed, he being the companion of Peter, that he would leave in writing a record of the teaching which had been delivered to them verbally; ... to them we owe the Scripture called the 'Gospel by Mark'" (*Fragments* 3, cited by Cassiodorus [*ANF*, 2:579]; cited by Eusebius, *Ecclesiastical History* 2.15.1)		**Irenaeus**: "John, the disciple of the Lord, ... expresses himself thus: 'In the beginning was the Word, and the Word was with God, and the Word was God; the same was in the beginning with God'" (Irenaeus, *Against Heresies* 1.8.5 [*ANF*, 1:674])	**Tertullian** names John and Matthew as apostles, and as apostolic men Luke and Mark, who possessed "the authority of the masters [i.e., of the apostles]" (*The Five Books Against Marcion* 4.2 [*ANF*, 3:347])
second		**Clement of Alexandria**: "Peter having preached the word publicly at Rome, and by the Spirit proclaimed the Gospel, those who were present, who were numerous, entreated Mark, inasmuch as he had attended him from an early period, and remembered what had been said, to write down what had been spoken" (cited by Eusebius, *Ecclesiastical History* 6.14)		**Irenaeus**: "His own Word is both suitable and sufficient for the formation of all things, even as John, the disciple of the Lord, declares regarding Him: 'All things were made by Him, and without Him was nothing made'" (Irenaeus, *Against Heresies* 2.2.5 [*ANF*, 1:747])	**Irenaeus**: "The opinion of the apostles, therefore, and of those (Mark and Luke) who learned from their words, concerning God, has been made manifest" (*Against Heresies* 3.15.3 [*ANF*, 1:440])
second				**Irenaeus**: "John, the disciple of the Lord, who also had leaned upon His breast, did himself publish a Gospel during his residence at Ephesus in Asia" (Irenaeus, *Against Heresies* 3.1.1 [*ANF*, 1:857])	
second				**Clement of Alexandria**: "John the apostle says: 'No man hath seen God at any time. The only-begotten God, who is in the bosom of the Father, He hath declared Him'" (Clement, *Stromata, or Miscellanies* 12 [*ANF*, 2:959])	

Century	Sources of Matthew	Sources of Mark	Sources of Luke	Sources of John	Sources of All
third	**Hippolytus**, a disciple of Irenaeus - the apostle "Matthew wrote the Gospel in the Hebrew tongue" (*On the Twelve Apostles* 7 [*ANF*, 5:255])	**Origen**: "The second [Gospel] written was that according to Mark, who wrote it according to the instruction of Peter" (*Commentary on Matthew* Book 1 [*ANF*, 10:412])	**Origen**: "And third, was that according to Luke, the Gospel commended by Paul, which he composed for the converts from the Gentiles" (*Commentary on Matthew* Book 1 [*ANF*, 10:412])		
fourth	In describing a statement of Jesus that Matthew allegedly was not present to hear, **Augustine** wrote, "In this way, the Gospels of Luke and Mark, who were companions of the disciples, as well as the Gospel of Matthew, have the same authority as that of [the Gospel of] John" (*Reply to Faustus the Manichaean* 17.3 [*NPNF*, 4:235])		**Chrysostom**: "And why can it have been, that when there were so many disciples, two write only from among the apostles, and two from among their followers? (For one that was a disciple of Paul, and another of Peter, together with Matthew and John, wrote the Gospels.)" (*Homilies of St. John Chrysostom on the Gospel According to St. Matthew* 1.5 [*NPNF*, 10:2])	**Augustine**: Speaking of the apostles, Augustine wrote, "Certain of them also—namely, Matthew and John—gave to the world, in their respective books, a written account of all those matters which it seemed needful to commit to writing concerning Him" (Augustine, *The Harmony of the Gospels* 1.1.1 [*NPNF*, 6:160])	
fourth				**Augustine**: Augustine called the apostle John "the most eminent of the four evangelists" (Augustine, *The Harmony of the Gospels* 2.6.18 [*NPNF*, 6:235])	

#18—The Lineage of the Gospels
A Summary of Patristic Evidence

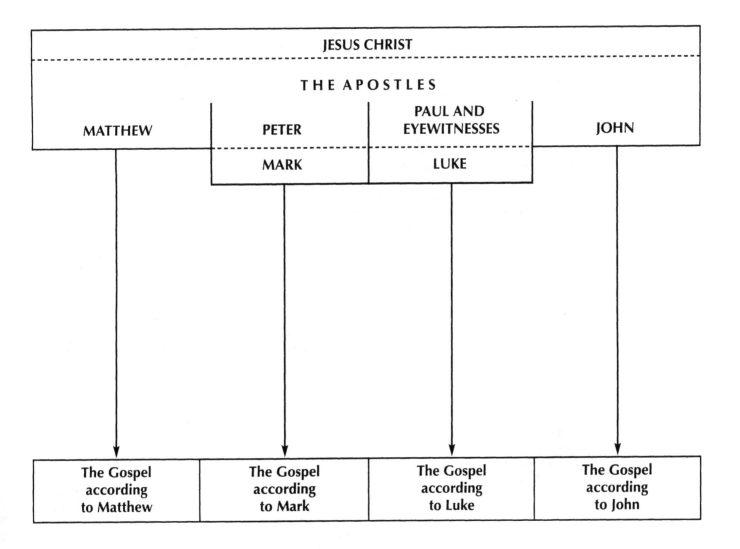

#19—Gospel Sequence according to the Early Fathers

Century	Father	Sequence Quotation or Citation	Sequence Summary	Consensus
2nd	Irenaeus	"Now Matthew published among the Hebrews a written gospel also in their own tongue, while Peter and Paul were preaching in Rome and founding the church. But after their death, Mark also, the disciple and interpreter of Peter, himself handed down to us in writing the things which were preached by Peter and Luke also, who was a follower of Paul, put down in a book the gospel which was preached by him. Then John, the disciple of the Lord who had even rested on his breast, himself also gave forth the gospel, while he was living in Ephesus in Asia." [*Against Heresies* 3.1.1-4]	Matthew, Mark (?), Luke (?), John (sequence of Mark and Luke is in doubt)	Matthew was the first Gospel to be written
2nd	Clement of Alexandria	"And again in the same books Clement has inserted a tradition of the primitive elders with regard to the order of the Gospels, as follows. He said that those Gospels were first written which include the genealogies. . . . But that John, last of all, conscious that the outward facts had been set forth in the Gospels, was urged on by his disciples, and, divinely moved by the Spirit, composed a spiritual Gospel." [cited by Eusebius, *Ecclesiastical History* 6.14.5-7]	Matthew, Luke, Mark, John (clearly places Luke before Mark)	John was the last Gospel to be written
3rd	Origen	"As having learnt by tradition concerning the four Gospels, which alone are unquestionable in the Church of God under heaven, that first was written to Matthew. . . . Secondly, that according to Mark. . . . And thirdly, that according to Luke. . . . After them all, that according to John." [cited by Eusebius, *Ecclesiastical History* 6.25.3-6]	Matthew, Mark (?), Luke (?), John	Differences of opinion exist about the sequence of Mark and Luke
early 4th	Eusebius	"Yet out of them all [i.e., the twelve apostles, the seventy disciples, and countless others] Matthew and John alone have left us memoirs of the Lord's discourses. . . . For Matthew first of all preached to Hebrews; and when he was about to go also to others he committed his Gospel to writing in his native tongue: thus he made his writing compensate those from whom he was departing for the lack of his bodily presence. And when Mark and Luke had already published their Gospels, it is said that John, who all the time had used unwritten preaching, at last came also to write, for the following reason. Those three which we mentioned above having come already into the hands of all, including his own, it is said that he accepted them and attested their truth." [*Ecclesiastical History* 3.24.5-7]	Matthew, Mark (?), Luke (?), John	Probability is that Luke was written second, based on Clement's words
late 4th	Augustine	"Now, these four evangelists . . . are believed to have written in the order which follows: first Matthew, then Mark, thirdly Luke, lastly John." [*The Harmony of the Gospels* 1.2.3]	Matthew, Mark, Luke, John	

Chronological Charts

#20—Periods of the Life of Christ

Year		Event or Period	Harmony Section Numbers	Scripture
6 B.C.		Birth of Christ	NIV§10 NASB§12	Lk 2:1-7
		Death of Herod the Great	NIV§16 NASB§19	Mt 2:19-23
1 B.C.				
A.D. 1				
		Growth and Early Life	NIV§17 NASB§20	Lk 2:40
A.D. 5				
		First Passover in Jerusalem	NIV§18 NASB§21	Lk 2:41-50
A.D.10				
A.D. 15				
		Adolescence and Early Manhood	NIV§19 NASB§22	Lk 2:51-52
A.D. 20				
A.D. 25				
		Baptism of Christ	NIV§24 NASB§27	Mt 3:13-17; Mk 1:9-11; Lk 3:21-23a
		Ministry, Death, and Resurrection	NIV§25-184 NASB§28-259	Mt 4:1–28:30; Mk 1:12–16:8; Lk 4:1–24:53
A.D. 30				

#21—The Major Periods of Christ's Ministry

		Season	Year	Time Span	Period Title	Harmony Section Nos.	Scripture
		winter	A.D. 26			NIV§20-23	Mt 3:1-12; Mk
		spring			Public Ministry of John	NASB§21-26	1:1-8; Lk 3:1-18
		summer					
		fall					Mt 3:13–4:12
		winter	A.D. 27		End of John's Ministry and Beginning of Christ's	NIV§24-36	Mk 1:9-14a
		spring				NASB§27-42	Lk 3:21–4:14a
		summer					Jn 1:19–4:45
		fall					
		winter	A.D. 28				Mt 4:17–14:12
		spring				NIV§37-72a	Mk 1:14b–6:30
		summer			Ministry in Galilee	NASB§43-103	Lk 4:14b–9:10a
		fall					Jn 4:46–5:47
		winter	A.D. 29				
		spring			Ministry around Galilee	NIV§72b-93	Mt 14–18; Mk 6–9; Lk 9; Jn 6–7
		summer				NASB§104-132	
		fall			Later Judean Ministry NIV§96a-111	NASB§133-160	Lk 10–13; Jn 7–10
		winter	A.D. 30		Ministry in and around Perea NIV§112-127b	NASB§161-184	Mt 19–20; Mk 10; Lk 14–19; Jn 11
		spring			Passion Week, Resurrection, and Ascension	NIV§128a-184	Mt 21–28; Mk 14–16; Lk 20–24; Jn 12–21
		summer				NASB§185-259	

#22—Chronological Chart of Christ's Discourses
Extended Teachings of Christ on Various Occasions

Season and Date	Title	Scriptures	Harmony Sec. Nos.	Location	Audience	Occasion	Major Subject(s)
summer, A.D. 27	Nicodemus's interview with Jesus	Jn 3:1-21	NIV§32b NASB§36	Jerusalem	Nicodemus	the signs done by Jesus	the need for the new birth and faith in Jesus
fall, A.D. 27	Discussion with a Samaritan woman	Jn 4:5-26	NIV§35a NASB§39	Sychar in Samaria	a Samaritan woman	Jesus' request for a drink of water and knowledge of the woman's past	the need for living water and worshiping the Father in spirit
fall, A.D. 28	Discourse demonstrating the Son's equality with the Father	Jn 5:19-47	NIV§49c NASB§59	Jerusalem	the Jewish opponents of Jesus	healing of a man who had been sick for thirty-eight years	Jesus' part in judgment and resurrection and witnesses to his authority
fall, A.D. 28	Sermon on the Mount (Plain)	Mt 5:1–7:28; Lk 6:17-49	NIV§54a-54i NASB§64-72	a level place on a mountain in Galilee	the disciples and the crowds	Jesus' growing popularity	righteousness required to enter the promised kingdom
winter, A.D. 29	Parabolic mysteries about the kingdom	Mt 13:1-52; Mk 4:1-34; Lk 8:4-18	NIV§64a-64k NASB§82-92	by the Sea of Galilee	to great crowds and then the disciples	the unpardonable (eternal) sin by Pharisees and scribes	the mysteries of the kingdom to hide truth from Jesus' enemies
winter, A.D. 29	Commissioning of the Twelve	Mt 10:1-42; Mk 6:7-11; Lk 9:1-5	NIV§70b NASB§99	Galilee	the twelve disciples	the need to spread the news about the kingdom in Galilee	nearness of the kingdom
spring, A.D. 29	Discourse on the true bread of life	Jn 6:22-59	NIV§76a NASB§109	Capernaum	the crowd from the feeding of the 5,000	the feeding of the 5,000	Jesus is the bread of life who satisfies
summer, A.D. 29	Warning over causing believers to stumble; forgiveness of a sinning brother	Mt 18:6-35; Mk 9:38-50; Lk 9:49-50	NIV§91-92 NASB§128-129	Capernaum	the disciples	dispute over which disciple was the greatest	the primacy of humility and a forgiving spirit
fall, A.D. 29	Interaction resulting from Jesus' claim to be the light of the world	Jn 8:12-59	NIV§98-99b NASB§136-138	Jerusalem, in the temple	Jesus' friends, enemies, and neutrals	Jesus' claim to be the light of the world	Jesus' claim to present the truth and his preexistence
fall, A.D. 29	Commissioning of the Seventy	Lk 10:1-16	NIV§102a NASB§139	Judea (probably)	seventy disciples	the need to spread the news about the kingdom in Judea	nearness of the kingdom

Season and Date	Title	Scriptures	Harmony Sec. Nos.	Location	Audience	Occasion	Major Subject(s)
fall, A.D. 29	Woes against the scribes and Pharisees while eating with a Pharisee	Lk 17:37-54	NIV§107 NASB§145	Judea (probably)	scribes and Pharisees	Jesus' failure to wash himself ceremonially before the meal	focus of the leaders on outward religion to the neglect of the inner man
fall, A.D. 29	Warnings about various hindrances	Lk 12:1-59	NIV§108a-108e NASB§146-150	Judea (probably)	the disciples and the crowds	assembly of a crowd of many thousands	hypocrisy, greed, preparedness for Jesus' coming, coming division, and discerning the times
fall, A.D. 29	Allegory of the good shepherd	Jn 10:1-18	NIV§101a NASB§158	Jerusalem	Pharisees	expulsion of the healed blind man	the good shepherd and his sheep
winter, A.D. 30	Parables in defense of association with sinners	Lk 15:1-32	NIV§116 NASB§166	Perea (probably)	Pharisees and scribes	Jesus' eating with tax collectors and sinners	the lost sheep, the lost coin, and the lost son
winter, A.D. 30	Story to teach the danger of wealth	Lk 16:14-31	NIV§117b NASB§168	Perea (probably)	Pharisees	Pharisees' love of money	the rich man and the poor man named Lazarus
winter, A.D. 30	Instructions regarding the Son of Man's coming	Lk 17:22-37	NIV§120b NASB§174	Samaria or Galilee	the disciples	Jesus' response to the Pharisees about the presence of the kingdom	imminence of the Son of Man's return
winter, A.D. 30	Two parables on prayer	Lk 18:1-14	NIV§121 NASB§175	journeying toward Jerusalem	the disciples	emphasis on the need for constant prayer	the persistent widow and the Pharisee and the tax collector
winter, A.D. 30	Riches and the kingdom	Mt 19:16-30; Mk 10:17-31; Lk 18:18-30	NIV§124a NASB§178	Perea	a rich man and the disciples	a rich man's question about how to obtain eternal life	the difficulty in a rich person's obtaining treasure in heaven
winter, A.D. 30	Parable of the landowner's sovereignty	Mt 20:1-16	NIV§124b NASB§179	Perea	the disciples	Jesus' comments about rewards to those who follow him sacrificially	a landowner's prerogative of rewarding his laborers according to his own wishes
winter, A.D. 30	Parable to teach responsibility while the kingdom is delayed	Lk 19:11-28	NIV§127b NASB§184	Jericho and the final ascent to Jerusalem	the disciples	the assumption that Jesus would establish his kingdom on earth immediately	the need for diligent service by followers while awaiting Jesus' return
Tuesday of Passion Week, spring, A.D. 30	Faithful discharge of responsibility taught by three parables	Mt 21:28–22:14; Mk 12:1-12; Lk 20:9-19	NIV§132b NASB§194	Jerusalem, in the temple	chief priests, scribes, and elders	an official challenge of Jesus' authority	punishment of leaders who have failed to lead responsibly

Season and Date	Title	Scriptures	Harmony Sec. Nos.	Location	Audience	Occasion	Major Subject(s)
Tuesday of Passion Week, spring, A.D. 30	Seven woes against the scribes and Pharisees	Mt 23:1-36; Mk 12:38-40; Lk 20:45-47	NIV§137a NASB§199	Jerusalem, in the temple	the crowds and the disciples	Jesus' response after his enemies' challenges ended	hypocritical leaders and those who follow them are doomed to hell
Tuesday of Passion Week, spring, A.D. 30	The Olivet Discourse	Mt 24:1–25:46; Mk 13:1-37; Lk 21:5-33	NIV§139a-139g NASB§202-208	from the temple to the Mount of Olives	the disciples	the disciples' question about the temple buildings	signs of Jesus' return and responsible actions while awaiting it
Thursday of Passion Week, spring, A.D. 30	The Upper Room Discourse	Jn 14:1–17:26	NIV§149-151 NASB§218-224	Jerusalem, in the Upper Room	the disciples	Peter's question about where Jesus is going	Jesus' ascension, the coming of the Spirit, and the disciples' enablement while Jesus is away

#23—Time Line to Show Christ's Use of Parables in the Presence of His Enemies

Year	Season	Parables
A.D. 26	winter	
	spring	**Beginning of Jesus' ministry**
	summer	
	fall	
A.D. 27	winter	
	spring	
	summer	
	fall	
A.D. 28	winter	
	spring	
	summer	
	fall	
A.D. 29	winter	◀ 5 parables (Mt 13:3-35[4]; Mk 4:3-34[2]; Lk 8:5-18[1]) (NIV§64b-64f; NASB§83-87)[1]
	spring	
	summer	◀ 1 parable (Mt 15:10-11; Mk 7:14-15) (NIV§77; NASB§111)[2]
	fall	◀ 2 parables (Lk 12:35-48[1]; 13:6-9[1]) (NIV§108c, 109; NASB§148, 151)[3]
A.D. 30	winter	◀ 7 parables (Lk 14:8-24[1]; 15:3-32[3]; 16:19-31[1]; 18:1-14[2]) (NIV§114,116,117b,121;NASB§164,166,168,175)[4]
	spring	◀ 3 parables (Mt 21:28–22:14[3]; Mk 12:1-12[1]; Lk 20:9-19[1]) (NIV§132b; NASB§194)[5] **Crucifixion and Resurrection**
	summer	

1. Parables of the soils, wheat and weeds, mustard seed, yeast, growing seed (in Galilee).
2. Parable of what defiles a person (around Galilee).
3. Parables of wise and wicked servants (in Judea).
4. Parables of the lowest seat at the feast, lost sheep, lost coin, lost son, rich man and Lazarus, persistent widow, Pharisee and tax collector (in and around Perea).
5. Parables of the two sons, wicked tenants, wedding banquet (in Jerusalem, Passion Week).

#24—Time Line to Show Christ's Use of Parables in the Absence of His Enemies

Year	Season	Parables
A.D. 26	winter	
	spring	**Beginning of Jesus' ministry**
	summer	
	fall	
A.D. 27	winter	
	spring	
	summer	
	fall	
A.D. 28	winter	
	spring	
	summer	
	fall	
A.D. 29	winter	4 parables (Mt 13:44-51) (NIV§64h-64k; NASB§89-92)[1]
	spring	
	summer	1 parable (Mt 18:23-35) (NIV§92; NASB§129)[2]
	fall	1 parable (Lk 11:5-13) (NIV§105; NASB§143)[3]
A.D. 30	winter	4 parables (Lk 16:1-13; 17:7-10; 19:11-28; Mt 20:1-16) (NIV§117a,117c,124b,127b;NASB§167,169,179,184)[4]
	spring	5 parables (Mt 24:42–25:30; Mk 13:33-37; Lk 21:34-36) (NIV§139f; NASB§207)[5] **Crucifixion and Resurrection**
	summer	

1. Parables of the hidden treasure, valuable pearl, net, and house owner (in Galilee).
2. Parable of the unmerciful servant (around Galilee).
3. Parable of the bold friend (in Judea).
4. Parables of the wasteful manager, unworthy servants, landowner's sovereignty, and ten minas (in and around Perea).
5. Parables of the watchful servants, thief in the night, wise and wicked servants, ten virgins, and talents (in Jerusalem, Passion Week).

#25—Major Events of Passion Week

Day	Time	Event	Harmony Section Numbers	Scriptures
Sunday	A.M.	Triumphal Entry	NIV§128b NASB§187	Mt 21:1-17; Mk 11:1-11; Lk 19:29-44; Jn 12:12-19
	P.M.			
Monday	A.M.	Cursing of the fig tree	NIV§129a NASB§188	Mt 21:18-19a; Mk 11:12-14
	P.M.	Request of some Greeks	NIV§130a NASB§190	Jn 12:20-36a
Tuesday	A.M.	Withered fig tree	NIV§131 NASB§192	Mt 21:19b-22; Mk 11:19-25
		Official challenge of Jesus' authority	NIV§132a-138 NASB§193-201	Mt 21:23–23:39; Mk 11:27–12:40; Lk 20:1–21:4
	P.M.	Olivet Discourse	NIV§139a-139g NASB§202-208	Mt 24:1–25:46; Mk 13:1-37; Lk 21:5-36
Wednesday	A.M.	Arrangements for betrayal	NIV§140, 142 NASB§209-210	Mt 26:1-5, 14-16; Mk 14:1-2, 10-11; Lk 21:37–22:6
	P.M.			
Thursday	A.M.			
	P.M.	The Last Supper	NIV§143-148 NASB§211-217	Mt 26:17-29; Mk 14:12-25; Lk 22:7-20; Jn 13:1-38
		Upper Room Discourse	NIV§149-151 NASB§218-224	Jn 14:1–17:26
Friday	A.M.	Betrayal and arrest	NIV§153 NASB§227	Mt 26:47-56; Mk 14:43-52; Lk 22:47-53; Jn 18:2-12
		Trial	NIV§154-161 NASB§228-235	Mt 26:57–27:26; Mk 14:53–15:15; Lk 22:54–23:25; Jn 18:13–19:16
	P.M.	Crucifixion	NIV§162-166 NASB§236-240	Mt 27:27-56; Mk 15:16-41; Lk 23:26-49; Jn 19:17-30
		Burial	NIV§167a-168 NASB§241-243	Mt 27:57-66; Mk 15:42-47; Lk 23:50-56; Jn 19:31-42
Saturday	A.M.			
	P.M.			
Sunday	A.M.	Postresurrection appearances	NIV§173-183 NASB§248-258	Mt 28:9-20; [Mk 16:9-20]; Lk 24:13-49; Jn 20:11–21:25
	P.M.			

#26—Chronology of Passion Week

I. The Formal Presentation of Christ to Israel and the Resulting Conflict

	Triumphal Entry and the Fig Tree			
Day	**Subject**	**Scriptures**	**Harmony Section Numbers**	**Other Features**
Saturday	Arrival at Bethany	Jn 11:55–12:1	NIV§128a, NASB§185	Jewish authorities wanted to arrest Jesus
	Mary's anointing of Jesus for burial	Mt 26:6-13; Mk 14:3-9; Jn 12:2-11	NIV§141, NASB§186	Raising of Lazarus attracted a great crowd
Sunday	Triumphal Entry into Jerusalem	Mt 21:1-11, 14-17; Mk 11:1-11; Lk 19:19-44; Jn 12:12-19	NIV§128b, NASB§187	People greeted the King, but were unready spiritually for the kingdom
Monday	Cursing of the fig tree	Mt 21:18-19a; Mk 11:12-14	NIV§129a, NASB§188	Israel's empty ritualism illustrated by fig tree
	Second cleansing of the temple	Mt 21:12-13; Mk 11:15-18; Lk 19:45-48	NIV§129b, NASB§189	Israel's corruption in worship was her problem
	Request of some Greeks	Jn 12:20-36a	NIV§130a, NASB§190	Only after crucifixion could his message go to Gentiles
	Departure from the unbelieving multitude and Jesus' response	Jn 12:36b-50	NIV§130b, NASB§191	Hiding from the crowd because of their unbelief
Tuesday	Withered fig tree and the lesson on faith	Mt 21:19b-22; Mk 11:19-25	NIV§131, NASB§192	Faith to move a mountain
	Official Challenges to Christ's Authority			
Tuesday continued	Questioning of Jesus' authority by the chief priests, teachers of the law, and elders	Mt 21:23-27; Mk 11:27-33; Lk 20:1-8	NIV§132a, NASB§193	Sanhedrin representatives questioned the source of his authority
	Jesus' response with his own question and three parables to teach faithfulness	Mt 21:28–22:14; Mk 12:1-12; Lk 20:9-19	NIV§132b, NASB§194	Two sons and the vineyard, the landowner and his vineyard, the king and the wedding feast
	Questioning by Pharisees and Herodians regarding paying taxes to Caesar	Mt 22:15-22; Mk 12:13-17; Lk 20:20-26	NIV§133, NASB§195	Render to both Caesar and God
	Sadducees' question about conditions after the resurrection	Mt 22:23-33; Mk 12:18-27; Lk 20:27-40	NIV§134, NASB§196	The God of the living, not of the dead

Day	Subject	Scriptures	Harmony Section Numbers	Other Features
Tuesday continued	Question by a Pharisaic legal expert	Mt 22:34-40; Mk 12:28-34	NIV§135, NASB§197	The greatest commandment
Christ's Response to His Enemies' Challenges				
Tuesday continued	Jesus' relationship to David as son and Lord	Mt 22:41-46; Mk 12:35-37; Lk 20:41-44	NIV§136, NASB§198	Messiah is both God and man
	Seven woes against the teachers of the law and Pharisees	Mt 23:1-36; Mk 12:38-40; Lk 20:45-47	NIV§137a, NASB§199	Jewish leaders excluded from the kingdom
	Sorrow over Jerusalem	Mt 23:37-39	NIV§137b, NASB§200	Jerusalem's rejection representative of the whole nation
	A poor widow's gift of all she had	Mk 12:41-44; Lk 21:1-4	NIV§138, NASB§201	An example of true piety

II. Prophecies in Preparation for the Death of Christ

The Olivet Discourse: Prophecies about the Temple and the Return of Christ				
Tuesday continued	Setting of the discourse	Mt 24:1-3; Mk 13:1-4; Lk 21:5-7	NIV§139a, NASB§202	Three questions: about the temple, Jesus' return, and signs to precede them
	Beginning of birth pains	Mt 24:4-14; Mk 13:5-13; Lk 21:8-19	NIV§139b, NASB§203	Beginning of Israel's tribulation
	Abomination of desolation and subsequent distress	Mt 24:15-28; Mk 13:14-23; Lk 21:20-24	NIV§139c, NASB§204	Last half of Daniel's 70th week or the "great tribulation"
	Coming of the Son of Man	Mt 24:29-31; Mk 13:24-27; Lk 21:25-27	NIV§139d, NASB§205	Climax of Israel's hopes
	Signs of nearness, but unknown time	Mt 24:32-41; Mk 13:28-32; Lk 21:28-33	NIV§139e, NASB§206	Foreshadowings of birth pains signal nearness of the time
	Five parables to teach watchfulness and faithfulness	Mt 24:42–25:30; Mk 13:33-37; Lk 21:34-36	NIV§139f, NASB§207	Faithfulness in service must accompany alertness
	Judgment at the Son of Man's coming	Mt 25:31-46	NIV§139g, NASB§208	From David's earthly throne, the King will judge survivors of the "great tribulation"

Day	Subject	Scriptures	Harmony Section Numbers	Other Features
Arrangements for Betrayal				
Wednesday	Plot by the Sanhedrin to arrest and kill Jesus	Mt 26:1-5; Mk 14:1-2; Lk 21:37–22:2	NIV§140, NASB§209	Direct action impossible because of Jesus' popularity
	Judas's agreement to betray Jesus	Mt 26:14-16; Mk 14:10-11; Lk 22:3-6	NIV§142, NASB§210	Selfish motives moved Judas to do the unthinkable
The Last Supper				
Thursday	Preparation for the Passover meal	Mt 26:17-19; Mk 14:12-16; Lk 22:7-13	NIV§143, NASB§211	Daylight preparations for an evening meal
	Beginning of the Passover meal and discussion about greatness	Mt 26:20; Mk 14:17; Lk 22:14-16	NIV§144, NASB§212	Thursday evening after sundown
	Washing the disciples' feet	Jn 13:1-20	NIV§145, NASB§213	Self-sacrificing humility exemplified
	Identification of the betrayer	Mt 26:21-25; Mk 14:18-21; Lk 22:21-23; Jn 13:21-30	NIV§146, NASB§214	Judas identified
	Dissension among the disciples over greatness	Lk 22:24-30	NIV§144, NASB§215	Leadership in the kingdom at stake
	First prediction of Peter's denials	Lk 22:31-38; Jn 13:31-38	NIV§147, NASB§216	In the Upper Room during the Lord's Supper
	Conclusion of the Passover meal and the Lord's Supper instituted	Mt 26:26-29; Mk 14:22-25; Lk 22:17-20; 1Co 11:23-26	NIV§148, NASB§217	The third of four cups at the meal relates to God's promise of Israel's redemption
Discourse and Prayers from the Upper Room to Gethsemane				
Thursday continued	Questions answered about Jesus' destination, the Father, and the Holy Spirit	Jn 14:1-31	NIV§149, NASB§218	Remarks related to the period of Jesus' absence
	The vine and the branches	Jn 15:1-17	NIV§150a, NASB§219	Fruitfulness through abiding in Jesus Christ
	Opposition from the world	Jn 15:18–16:4	NIV§150b, NASB§220	Words of warning because of Jesus' departure
	Coming and ministry of the Holy Spirit	Jn 16:5-15	NIV§150c, NASB§221	Twofold ministry: to the world and to the disciples
	Predicted joy because of Jesus' resurrection	Jn 16:16-22	NIV§150d, NASB§222	Sorrow over departure followed by joy
	Promise of answered prayer and peace	Jn 16:23-33	NIV§150e, NASB§223	Asking the Father in Jesus' name

Day	Subject	Scriptures	Harmony Section Numbers	Other Features
Thursday continued	Jesus' prayer for his disciples and all who believe	Jn 17:1-26	NIV§151, NASB§224	A preview of Jesus' work as our advocate
	Second prediction of Peter's denial	Mt 26:30-35; Mk 14:26-31; Lk 22:39-40a; Jn 18:1	NIV§147, 152, NASB§225	Denials before the cock-crowing at about 3:00 A.M.
	Jesus' three agonizing prayers in Gethsemane	Mt 26:36-46; Mk 14:32-42; Lk 22:40b-46	NIV§152, NASB§226	Prayers not to be separated from the Father

III. The Death of Christ

	Betrayal and Arrest			
Friday	Jesus betrayed, arrested, and forsaken	Mt 26:47-56; Mk 14:43-52; Lk 22:47-53; Jn 18:2-12	NIV§153, NASB§227	Arrested by a large group of Roman soldiers requested by Jewish leaders

	Trial			
Friday continued	First Jewish phase, before Annas	Jn 18:13-24	NIV§154, NASB§228	Annas was an influential former high priest
	Second Jewish phase, before Caiaphas and the Sanhedrin	Mt 26:57-68; Mk 14:53-65; Lk 22:54	NIV§155, NASB§229	At the house of Caiaphas before sunrise
	Three of Peter's denials	Mt 26:69-75; Mk 14:66-72; Lk 22:55-65; Jn 18:25-27	NIV§156, NASB§230	Denials in Caiaphas's courtyard after the Sanhedrin met
	Third Jewish phase, before the Sanhedrin	Mt 27:1; Mk 15:1a; Lk 22:66-71	NIV§157, NASB§231	After sunrise to formalize the verdict reached earlier
	Remorse and suicide of Judas Iscariot	Mt 27:3-10; Ac 1:18-19	NIV§158, NASB§232	Death by hanging and a long fall
	First Roman phase, before Pilate	Mt 27:2, 11-14; Mk 15:1b-5; Lk 23:1-5; Jn 18:28-38	NIV§159, NASB§233	Jesus' kingdom not of earthly origin like Pilate's authority
	Second Roman phase, before Herod Antipas	Lk 23:6-12	NIV§160, NASB§234	The same Herod who beheaded John the Baptist
	Third Roman phase, before Pilate	Mt 27:15-26; Mk 15:6-15; Lk 23:13-25; Jn 18:39—19:16	NIV§161, NASB§235	Barabbas, an insurrectionist, chosen for release

	Crucifixion			
Friday continued	Mockery by the Roman soldiers	Mt 27:27-30; Mk 15:16-19	NIV§162, NASB§236	Brutality after cruel treatment allowed by Pilate
	Journey to Golgotha	Mt 27:31-34; Mk 15:20-23; Lk 23:26-33a; Jn 19:17	NIV§163, NASB§237	Simon of Cyrene forced to help the weakened Jesus with the cross

Day	Subject	Scriptures	Harmony Section Numbers	Other Features
Friday continued	First three hours of crucifixion	Mt 27:35-44; Mk 15:24-32; Lk 23:33b-43; Jn 19:18-27	NIV§164, NASB§238	Prayer for forgiveness and provision for his mother
	Last three hours of crucifixion	Mt 27:45-50; Mk 15:33-37; Lk 23:44-45a, 46; Jn 19:28-30	NIV§165, NASB§239	Cry of dereliction, acknowledgment of thirst, cry of accomplishment, cry of resignation
	Witnesses of Jesus' death	Mt 27:51-56; Mk 15:38-41; Lk 23:45b, 47-49	NIV§166, NASB§240	Centurion and several women

Burial

Day	Subject	Scriptures	Harmony Section Numbers	Other Features
Friday continued	Certification of Jesus' death and procurement of his body	Mt 27:57-58; Mk 15:42-45; Lk 23:50-52; Jn 19:31-38	NIV§167a, NASB§241	Blood and water from Jesus' side indicated his death
	Jesus' body placed in a tomb	Mt 27:59-60; Mk 15:46; Lk 23:53-54; Jn 19:39-42	NIV§167b, NASB§242	Joseph of Arimathea and Nicodemus arranged the burial
	Tomb watched by the women and guarded by the soldiers	Mt 27:61-66; Mk 15:47; Lk 23:55-56	NIV§168, NASB§243	Jesus' enemies remembered his promise to rise again

IV. The Resurrection and Ascension of Christ

The Empty Tomb

Day	Subject	Scriptures	Harmony Section Numbers	Other Features
Sunday	The tomb visited by the women	Mt 28:1; Mk 16:1	NIV§169, NASB§244	Mary Magdalene, Mary the mother of James, Salome
	The stone rolled away	Mt 28:2-4	NIV§170, NASB§245	Allowed witnesses to see empty tomb
	The tomb found empty by the women	Mt 28:5-8; Mk 16:2-8; Lk 24:1-8; Jn 20:1	NIV§171, NASB§246	At about the time of sunrise
	The tomb found empty by Peter and John	Lk 24:9-11, [12]; Jn 20:2-10	NIV§172, NASB§247	Orderly arrangement of grave clothes proved resurrection

Postresurrection Appearances

Day	Subject	Scriptures	Harmony Section Numbers	Other Features
Sunday continued	Appearance to Mary Magdalene	[Mk 16:9-11]; Jn 20:11-18	NIV§173, NASB§248	Jesus predicts his ascension
	Appearance to the other women	Mt 28:9-10	NIV§174, NASB§249	Instruction to meet in Galilee
	Report of the soldiers to the Jewish authorities	Mt 28:11-15	NIV§175, NASB§250	Sanhedrin's absurd explanation

Day	Subject	Scriptures	Harmony Section Numbers	Other Features
Sunday continued	Appearance to the two disciples traveling to Emmaus	[Mk 16:12-13]; Lk 24:13-32	NIV§176, NASB§251	Did not believe the women's report about empty tomb
	Report of the two disciples to the rest, including an appearance to Peter	Lk 24:33-35; 1Co 15:5a	NIV§177; NASB§252	The two reported an appearance to Peter
	Appearance to the ten assembled disciples	[Mk 16:14]; Lk 24:36-43; Jn 20:19-25	NIV§178; NASB§253	Characteristics of Jesus' resurrection body revealed
Sunday, one week later	Appearance to the eleven assembled disciples	Jn 20:26-31; 1 Cor 15:5b	NIV§179; NASB§254	Thomas's doubt removed
Some time later	Appearance to seven disciples while fishing in Galilee	Jn 21:1-25	NIV§180, NASB§255	Peter told to feed and care for Jesus' sheep
Still later	Appearance to the Eleven in Galilee, then to the 500	Mt 28:16-20; [Mk 16:15-18]; 1Co 15:6	NIV§181, NASB§256	Great Commission to large number of followers
Again still later	Appearance to James, Jesus' brother	1Co 15:7	NIV§182; NASB§257	James became a believer
Forty days after Jesus' resurrection	Appearance to the disciples in Jerusalem	Lk 24:44-59; Ac 1:3-8	NIV§183, NASB§258	Preparation for the coming of the Spirit
The Ascension				
Still forty days later	Jesus' parting blessing and departure	[Mk 16:19-20]; Lk 24:50-53; Ac 1:9-12	NIV§184, NASB§259	Ascended from the Mount of Olives

Thematic Charts

#27—Matthew's Emphasis on Jesus as King

(Key Verse: See Matthew 21:5 below.)

* Scriptures marked by an asterisk have no parallels in the other three Gospels.

Summary	Scripture	Harmony Sec. Nos.	Comment	Period of Christ's Ministry
Jesus a descendant of David the king	Mt 1:1, 6, 17*	NIV§3 NASB§3	Genealogy of Jesus' legal lineage through Joseph	A Preview of Who Jesus Is
Jesus' legal father Joseph a descendant of David	Mt 1:20*	NIV§9 NASB§11	Jesus' birth explained to Joseph	Early Years of Jesus Christ
Jesus called "King of the Jews"	Mt 2:2, 11*	NIV§14 NASB§17	The Magi referred to Jesus this way and brought gifts befitting a King	Early Years of Jesus Christ
The kingdom is near because the King is near	Mt 3:2-3*	NIV§21 NASB§24	John the Baptist knew his role of preparing the way for the King	Public Ministry of John the Baptist
John recognized the presence of one greater than himself	Mt 3:11	NIV§23 NASB§26	Baptizing with the Spirit and with fire was the role of the Messiah King	Public Ministry of John the Baptist
John recognized his own unworthiness to baptize Jesus	Mt 3:14, 16-17	NIV§24 NASB§27	The recognition of Jesus as God's Son verified Jesus' kingly role	End of John's Ministry and Beginning of Christ's
Jesus proved his moral fitness to be King by resisting the devil's temptations	Mt 4:8-9	NIV§25 NASB§28	Satan offered Jesus a way to avert sufferings in becoming King	End of John's Ministry and Beginning of Christ's
Jesus preached the nearness of the kingdom because of the nearness of the King	Mt 4:17	NIV§37 NASB§43	Such a message permeated Jesus' Galilean ministry	Ministry in Galilee
Matthew cited the fulfillment of Isa 9:1-2, a Messianic context	Mt 4:14-16*	NIV§40 NASB§46	Isaiah 9 goes on to speak of the one who would rule from the throne of David (Isa 9:7)	Ministry in Galilee
Matthew cited the fulfillment of the Messianic passage Isa 53:4	Mt 8:17*	NIV§43 NASB§49	The suffering servant of Isaiah 53 was destined to rule as King (Isa 52:15)	Ministry in Galilee
Jesus preached the gospel of the kingdom	Mt 4:23*	NIV§44 NASB§50	Jesus carried the message about the kingdom all over Galilee	Ministry in Galilee
Jesus had the authority to forgive sins	Mt 9:6	NIV§46 NASB§53	Only the King can forgive sins	Ministry in Galilee
Jesus was an exception to the law just as David was	Mt 12:3-4	NIV§50 NASB§60	What was lawful for David the king was lawful for David's descendant	Ministry in Galilee
Jesus fulfilled Isa 42:1-4, which predicted the coming servant of the LORD	Mt 12:16-21*	NIV§52 NASB§62	Matthew cited a well-known prophecy of the coming Messiah-King	Ministry in Galilee
Jesus taught authoritatively about possessors of the kingdom	Mt 5:3, 10	NIV§54b NASB§65	Jesus prescribed ethical qualities for those who would be benefited in the kingdom	Ministry in Galilee

Summary	Scripture	Harmony Sec. Nos.	Comment	Period of Christ's Ministry
Jesus set ethical standards for entering the kingdom	Mt 5:20*	NIV§54d NASB§67	External righteousness of the scribes and Pharisees was insufficient to enter	Ministry in Galilee
Jesus prescribed prayer for the kingdom	Mt 6:10	NIV§54f NASB§69	As King, Jesus was in position to tell those awaiting the kingdom how to pray	Ministry in Galilee
Jesus gave the kingdom priority over material goods	Mt 6:33*	NIV§54g NASB§70	The King can guarantee the supplying of all needs for those with right priorities	Ministry in Galilee
Jesus had the authority to exclude from the kingdom	Mt 7:21*	NIV§54h NASB§71	Mere profession cannot replace doing God's will	Ministry in Galilee
The King prescribes faith as a prerequisite for entering the kingdom	Mt 8:10-12*	NIV§55 NASB§73	Through faith Gentiles will enter; without it Israelites will be excluded	Ministry in Galilee
The King recognizes the greatness of the one least in the kingdom	Mt 11:11-12	NIV§57 NASB§75	John was great, but those in the kingdom are greater	Ministry in Galilee
The King announces the presence of the kingdom	Mt 12:28	NIV§61 NASB§79	Jesus' exorcism of demons evidenced the arrival of the kingdom	Ministry in Galilee
The King announces a new phase of the kingdom through parables	Mt 13:1-52	NIV§64a-64k NASB§82-92	Jesus used parables to reveal to the receptive and to hide from the unreceptive	Ministry in Galilee
Two blind men recognized Jesus as the son of David the king	Mt 9:27*	NIV§68 NASB§96	In recognizing Jesus' authority, the men asked for healing	Ministry in Galilee
Jesus continued proclaiming the gospel of the kingdom in Galilee	Mt 9:35*	NIV§70a NASB§98	As their King, Jesus had compassion on the people	Ministry in Galilee
Jesus sent the Twelve to proclaim the kingdom's nearness	Mt 10:7*	NIV§70b NASB§99	Jesus granted them kingly authority to perform the miraculous (Mt 10:8)	Ministry in Galilee
Matthew records the disciples' recognition of Jesus as the Son of God	Mt 14:33*	NIV§74 NASB§107	Jesus' miracles of walking on the water and calming the storm were his credentials	Ministry around Galilee
The Canaanite woman called Jesus the "Son of David"	Mt 15:22*	NIV§78 NASB§112	Only Matthew records the woman's use of this title	Ministry around Galilee
Peter calls Jesus "the Christ, the Son of the living God"	Mt 16:16*	NIV§82 NASB§118	Only such a person as this could be the Messiah-King	Ministry around Galilee
Jesus speaks of the Son of Man coming in his kingdom	Mt 16:28*	NIV§84 NASB§120	Only Matthew calls it *his* (Jesus') kingdom	Ministry around Galilee
Jesus was transfigured as a preview of his coming kingdom	Mt 17:2	NIV§85 NASB§121	This followed immediately after Jesus' words about coming in his kingdom	Ministry around Galilee
Jesus classed himself among the sons of the kings of the earth	Mt 17:25-26*	NIV§89 NASB§126	The issue was whether Peter and Jesus should pay a tax	Ministry around Galilee

Summary	Scripture	Harmony Sec. Nos.	Comment	Period of Christ's Ministry
The disciples disputed about greatness in the kingdom	Mt 18:1-4*	NIV§90 NASB§127	Childlike humility determines greatness	Ministry around Galilee
The parable of the unmerciful servant offers a lesson about the kingdom	Mt 18:23-35*	NIV§92 NASB§129	Forgiveness is available only to the forgiving	Ministry around Galilee
Renouncing marriage for the sake of the kingdom	Mt 19:12*	NIV§122 NASB§176	Jesus' no-divorce policy makes remaining single an option so as to enter the kingdom	Ministry in and around Perea
The King says the kingdom belongs to such as children	Mt 19:14	NIV§123 NASB§177	The disciples tried to hinder children from coming to Jesus	Ministry in and around Perea
The difficulty for the rich in entering the kingdom	Mt 19:23-24	NIV§124a NASB§178	The disciples equated entering the kingdom with being saved	Ministry in and around Perea
The disciples will sit on twelve thrones when the Son of Man establishes his kingdom	Mt 19:28*	NIV§124a NASB§178	This is their reward for leaving everything and following Jesus	Ministry in and around Perea
The King emphasizes God's sovereignty in rewarding people in the kingdom	Mt 20:1-16*	NIV§124b NASB§179	Laborers who were hired late received the same wages as those who labored all day	Ministry in and around Perea
James's and John's mother requests for them to sit on Jesus' right and left	Mt 20:21	NIV§125b NASB§181	Only Matthew specifically mentions the kingdom	Ministry in and around Perea
Two blind men address Jesus as the "Son of David"	Mt 20:30	NIV§126 NASB§182	These men recognized Jesus' kingly office	Ministry in and around Perea
Key verse in Matthew: "See [Behold], your king comes to you"	**Mt 21:5, 9**	NIV§128b NASB§187	Only Matthew calls him the Son of David, a fact the Jewish leaders pick up on (Mt 21:15)	Formal Presentation of Christ to Israel
The King takes the kingdom away from rejecters in favor of a future repentant nation	Mt 21:43*	NIV§132b NASB§194	The King looks for the fruit of repentance	Formal Presentation of Christ to Israel
The parable of the king who gave a wedding banquet for his son	Mt 22:1-14*	NIV§132b NASB§194	The invited guests were not worthy, so others took their place	Formal Presentation of Christ to Israel
Jesus' question about the Messiah, the son of David	Mt 22:42	NIV§136 NASB§198	Jesus asked how he could be both David's son and David's Lord	Formal Presentation of Christ to Israel
Scribes and Pharisees not entering the kingdom and denying entrance to others	Mt 23:13*	NIV§137a NASB§199	The first of seven woes of Jesus the King against this group	Formal Presentation of Christ to Israel
The King likens the kingdom to ten virgins, five prepared and five unprepared	Mt 25:1-13*	NIV§139f NASB§207	Preparedness for the institution of the future kingdom is the lesson	Prophecies in Preparation for the Death of Christ
The King likens the kingdom to a man on a journey who left his servants in charge of his possessions	Mt 25:14-30*	NIV§139f NASB§207	The lesson is to be busy about the master's business while he is gone	Prophecies in Preparation for the Death of Christ
In the kingdom the King will judge from the throne of his glory	Mt 25:31-34*	NIV§139g NASB§208	The King will admit some to his kingdom; others he will exclude	Prophecies in Preparation for the Death of Christ

Summary	Scripture	Harmony Sec. Nos.	Comment	Period of Christ's Ministry
The King will drink the fruit of the vine in the kingdom with the disciples	Mt 26:29	NIV§148 NASB§217	The Last Supper was the last time he did so before that time	Prophecies in Preparation for the Death of Christ
Jesus said yes to the question of whether he was the Christ, the Son of God	Mt 26:63-64	NIV§155 NASB§229	The high priest accused him of blasphemy for claiming to be the King	The Death of Christ
Jesus said yes to the question of whether he was the King of the Jews	Mt 27:11	NIV§159 NASB§233	This was at his first appearance before Pilate	The Death of Christ
The soldiers mockingly put a crown of thorns on his head and called him "King of the Jews"	Mt 27:29	NIV§162 NASB§236	This was after he had been condemned to die by crucifixion	The Death of Christ
"THE KING OF THE JEWS" was on the inscription of his cross	Mt 27:37	NIV§164 NASB§238	The inscription was composed by the Roman soldiers	The Death of Christ

#28—Mark's Emphasis on Jesus as Servant

(Key Verse: See Mark 10:45 below.)

* Scriptures marked by an asterisk have no exact parallels in the other three Gospels.

Summary	Scripture	Harmony Sec. Nos.	Comment	Period of Christ's Ministry
Knowing a servant's ancestors is not important	–	NIV§3 NASB§3	Mark's Gospel tells nothing of Jesus' genealogy or background	A Preview of Who Jesus Is
A Gospel of action: "immediately" occurs repeatedly	Mk 1:10*	NIV§24 NASB§27	A servant is busy and constantly on the move	End of John's Ministry and the Beginning of Christ's
"Immediately" the Spirit sent, not led, Jesus into the desert	Mk 1:12*	NIV§25 NASB§28	Matthew and Luke say the Spirit led him into the desert; a king or a man is led, but a servant is sent	End of John's Ministry and the Beginning of Christ's
Jesus and his disciples went "immediately" from the synagogue to the house of Simon and Andrew	Mk 1:29*	NIV§43 NASB§49	No time for leisure in a servant's schedule	Ministry in Galilee
Simon and Andrew spoke to Jesus "immediately" about Simon's mother-in-law	Mk 1:30*	NIV§43 NASB§49	As soon as Jesus arrived in the house he had a task to perform	Ministry in Galilee
Before daybreak in the morning Jesus was up and alone praying	Mk 1:35*	NIV§44 NASB§50	A servant needs to arise early to have enough time to complete his tasks	Ministry in Galilee
Jesus invited his disciples to accompany him to other towns to preach	Mk 1:38*	NIV§44 NASB§50	Jesus' purpose for coming was to remain busy in preaching	Ministry in Galilee
Jesus "immediately" sent away the cured leper	Mk 1:43*	NIV§45 NASB§52	A servant does not waste time basking in the glory of his accomplishments	Ministry in Galilee
After healing the leper, Jesus stayed out of the public eye	Mk 1:45*	NIV§45 NASB§52	A servant works behind the scenes	Ministry in Galilee
Jesus knew "immediately" what his critics were thinking	Mk 2:8*	NIV§46 NASB§53	He even hurried to his task of healing the paralytic	Ministry in Galilee
The paralytic "immediately" took up his pallet and walked	Mk 2:12*	NIV§46 NASB§53	The servant wasted no time in performing his miracles	Ministry in Galilee
A servant is often not appreciated even by his own family	Mk 3:21*	NIV§61 NASB§79	Jesus' family thought he was out of his mind	Ministry in Galilee
The farmer "immediately" puts his sickle to the grain after it ripens	Mk 4:29*	NIV§64c NASB§84	A servant realizes the necessity of prompt action at the earliest possible moment	Ministry in Galilee
"Immediately" after leaving the boat, Jesus was met by the man with an unclean spirit	Mk 5:2*	NIV§66 NASB§94	Very little rest for the servant as he moves from one task to another	Ministry in Galilee

Summary	Scripture	Harmony Sec. Nos.	Comment	Period of Christ's Ministry
Mark portrays most graphically the danger faced by the servant	Mk 5:3-5*	NIV§66 NASB§94	The servant had to deal with a demon-possessed person that no one else could handle	Ministry in Galilee
Jesus perceived "immediately" that power had gone out of him	Mk 5:30*	NIV§67 NASB§95	The servant wastes no time in dealing with people	Ministry in Galilee
The response of those who witnessed the raising of Jairus's daughter was "immediate"	Mk 5:42*	NIV§67 NASB§95	The action in any of the servant's activities is fast-moving	Ministry in Galilee
The servant invites his disciples to take a break in the strenuous action	Mk 6:31*	NIV§72b NASB§104	Jesus and his disciples went to a lonely place, away from the people	Ministry around Galilee
Jesus spoke to the frightened disciples "immediately" to calm their fears	Mk 6:50	NIV§74 NASB§107	While they were in the boat, Jesus had come to them in the dark, walking on the water	Ministry around Galilee
The people of Gennesaret recognized Jesus "immediately"	Mk 6:54*	NIV§75 NASB§108	As soon as Jesus' boat landed, he was swamped by crowds again	Ministry around Galilee
For his Roman readers Mark explained the traditions of the elders	Mk 7:3-4*	NIV§77 NASB§111	The detailed requirements of tradition would interest Romans, who were a people more interested in actions than in teachings	Ministry around Galilee
The Gentile woman came "immediately" after hearing of Jesus' arrival	Mk 7:25*	NIV§78 NASB§112	Jesus could not escape notice for long because a servant has to keep busy	Ministry around Galilee
Healing the deaf man who could hardly speak required special emotional output	Mk 7:33-34*	NIV§79a NASB§113	Jesus looked up to heaven "with a deep sigh" in performing this private miracle	Ministry around Galilee
Jesus entered the boat with his disciples "immediately" after feeding the 4,000	Mk 8:10*	NIV§80 NASB§115	The heavy schedule demands and opposition of the Pharisees brought another deep sigh (Mk 8:12)	Ministry around Galilee
A two-stage miracle calls attention to the servant's extra effort expended	Mk 8:22-25*	NIV§81b NASB§117	Jesus healed the man's blindness in two stages	Ministry around Galilee
"Immediately" after Jesus' transfiguration a crowd came to meet him	Mk 9:14-15*	NIV§87 NASB§124	The servant hardly had time to catch his breath	Ministry around Galilee
The demon attacked the boy "immediately" after he was brought to Jesus	Mk 9:20*	NIV§87 NASB§124	The servant had to act immediately	Ministry around Galilee
Once again the servant had to control the uncontrollable	Mk 9:22, 26-27*	NIV§87 NASB§124	The spirit had thrown the boy into the fire and water to destroy him	Ministry around Galilee
The servant emphasizes service to others	Mk 9:41*	NIV§91 NASB§128	Giving a cup of water in Christ's name deserves a reward	Ministry around Galilee
The servant mentions the hardness of heart of Moses' generation	Mk 10:3-5*	NIV§122 NASB§176	Moses' provision for divorce in Dt 24:1-4 was a concession to Israel's disobedience	Ministry in and around Perea

Summary	Scripture	Harmony Sec. Nos.	Comment	Period of Christ's Ministry
The servant emphasizes the difficulty of entering the kingdom	Mk 10:24*	NIV§124a NASB§178	Three times in consecutive verses Jesus spoke of how hard it is for a rich man to enter the kingdom	Ministry in and around Perea
Faithful service will be rewarded	Mk 10:30	NIV§124a NASB§178	Peter asked about rewards for following Christ	Ministry in and around Perea
The servant promises James and John the same sufferings he experiences	Mk 10:39*	NIV§125b NASB§181	James and John asked for places of honor but were told about suffering for their service	Ministry in and around Perea
Key verse in Mark: "The Son of Man did not come to be served, but to serve"	**Mk 10:45**	NIV§125b NASB§181	Mark highlights Jesus' acts of service rather than his teaching ministry	Ministry in and around Perea
Bartimaeus regained his sight "immediately"	Mk 10:52	NIV§126 NASB§182	The servant completes his tasks rapidly	Ministry in and around Perea
The disciples of the servant get "immediate" results too	Mk 11:2-3	NIV§128b NASB§187	The two disciples found the colt right away and the owner released it right away	Formal Presentation of Christ to Israel
The servant recognizes God as the only Lord	Mk 12:29*	NIV§135 NASB§197	Only Mark cites Dt 6:4: "the LORD our God is one LORD"	Formal Presentation of Christ to Israel
The servant recognizes the sacrifice of the widow who gave all she had	Mk 12:41-44	NIV§138 NASB§201	The size of the gift is less important than what one has left after giving	Formal Presentation of Christ to Israel
Judas arrived "immediately" after Jesus finished his agonizing prayer in Gethsemane	Mk 14:43*	NIV§153 NASB§227	The servant had no ease between his difficult time in the garden and his arrest by Roman officials	The Death of Christ
Judas "immediately" went to Jesus and kissed him	Mk 14:45*	NIV§153 NASB§227	The servant had no lull before his betrayal	The Death of Christ
Everyone, including "a young man," forsook the servant	Mk 14:50-52*	NIV§153 NASB§227	According to tradition that young man was Mark	The Death of Christ
The servant was convicted through false testimony	Mk 14:57-59	NIV§155 NASB§229	Mark highlights the inconsistency of the testimony	The Death of Christ
The Council met "immediately" after daybreak to condemn the servant officially	Mk 15:1*	NIV§157 NASB§231	They wasted no time, just as the servant wasted no time throughout his ministry	The Death of Christ

#29—Luke's Emphasis on Jesus as Man

(Key Verse: See Luke 19:10 below.)

* Scriptures marked by an asterisk have no parallels in the other three Gospels.

Summary	Scripture	Harmony Sec. Nos.	Comment	Period of Christ's Ministry
Jesus' lineage traced to the first human, Adam	Lk 3:23, 38*	NIV§3 NASB§3	Matthew traced Jesus' Jewish lineage to Abraham through David	A Preview of Who Jesus Is
The circumstances of the supernatural conception of Jesus' forerunner and cousin John is told	Lk 1:13, 24*	NIV§4 NASB§4	The child promised to Zechariah and Elizabeth would prepare the people for the coming of the Lord	Early Years of John the Baptist
The human origin of Jesus through the virgin birth foretold to Mary	Lk 1:31, 34-35*	NIV§5 NASB§5	Mary was also told of the miraculous conception by Elizabeth her relative	Early Years of John the Baptist
The two expectant mothers, Mary and Elizabeth, meet	Lk 1:39-45*	NIV§6 NASB§6	The baby in Elizabeth's womb responds to the baby in Mary's womb	Early Years of John the Baptist
Mary stayed with Elizabeth about 3 months and then returned home	Lk 1:56*	NIV§7 NASB§7	By the end of 3 months Mary's pregnancy was becoming obvious	Early Years of John the Baptist
The birth and naming of John the Baptist	Lk 1:57, 60, 63*	NIV§8a NASB§8	The baby was named John in accord with the angel's instructions (Lk 1:13)	Early Years of John the Baptist
The human development of John the Baptist	Lk 1:80*	NIV§8c NASB§10	John's development paralleled that of Jesus (Lk 2:40)	Early Years of John the Baptist
Luke dates the birth of Jesus in relation to events of human history	Lk 2:1-2*	NIV§10 NASB§12	Jesus' birth came at the time of a decree from Caesar Augustus while Quirinius was governor of Syria	Early Years of Jesus Christ
Mary gave birth to Jesus in Bethlehem	Lk 2:4-5*	NIV§10 NASB§12	Joseph took his pregnant wife-to-be to Bethlehem with himself to register	Early Years of Jesus Christ
Shepherds were witnesses to the birth that had just happened	Lk 2:16-17*	NIV§11 NASB§13	An angel of the Lord told the shepherds where to find the baby	Early Years of Jesus Christ
Jesus was circumcised on the eighth day just like every other newborn baby	Lk 2:21*	NIV§12 NASB§14	At this time he received the name Jesus in accord with the angel's instructions	Early Years of Jesus Christ
Jesus was presented in the temple just like every other newborn baby	Lk 2:22-23*	NIV§13 NASB§15	Mary also received the prescribed purification at this time	Early Years of Jesus Christ
Jesus' human development followed the pattern of his cousin John (Lk 1:80)	Lk 2:40*	NIV§17 NASB§20	Luke's attention to Jesus' humanity is seen as clearly here as anywhere	Early Years of Jesus Christ
According to custom Jesus attended his first Passover at age 12	Lk 2:42*	NIV§18 NASB§21	Jesus' parents were concerned about him, as they would have been about any other 12-year-old	Early Years of Jesus Christ

Summary	Scripture	Harmony Sec. Nos.	Comment	Period of Christ's Ministry
Luke describes Jesus' adolescence and early manhood	Lk 2:52*	NIV§19 NASB§22	Luke describes Jesus' continued human development and submission to his parents	Early Years of Jesus Christ
Luke places the ministry of John, Jesus' cousin, solidly in the stream of human history	Lk 3:1-2*	NIV§20 NASB§23	Roman rulers and Jewish high priests are Luke's means of dating John's advent to preach	Public Ministry of John the Baptist
Luke specifies responses from different groups to John's call for repentance	Lk 3:10-14*	NIV§22 NASB§25	This is another way Luke has of emphasizing Jesus' humanity through John	Public Ministry of John the Baptist
John imprisoned by Herod the tetrarch	Lk 3:19-20*	NIV§34 NASB§38	This encounter of Jesus' cousin with a human ruler accents Jesus' humanity again	End of John's Ministry and Beginning of Christ's
Jesus' teaching praised by all in the synagogues	Lk 4:15*	NIV§37 NASB§43	Jesus began his Galilean ministry as any man would have	Ministry in Galilee
Jesus recognized as the son of Joseph	Lk 4:22-24*	NIV§39 NASB§45	To the people of Nazareth Jesus was a hometown boy	Ministry in Galilee
Jesus joined in the fishing expedition with other fishermen	Lk 5:4-11*	NIV§41 NASB§51	Jesus helped other human beings in earning a living	Ministry in Galilee
Luke includes the title "Son of Man" here and in 25 other places	Lk 5:24	NIV§46 NASB§53	"Son of Man" indicates Jesus' true humanity as well as his Messiahship	Ministry in Galilee
Luke brings out Jesus' emphasis on having compassion for others and helping them	Lk 6:29-30, 34-36, 38*	NIV§54e, 54g NASB§68, 70	This is part of the Sermon on the Plain (Mount) omitted by Matthew	Ministry in Galilee
As a fellow human being, Jesus felt compassion for the widow whose son had died	Lk 7:13*	NIV§56 NASB§74	Jesus felt compassion for a fellow human being and raised her son from the dead	Ministry in Galilee
Jesus showed compassion by healing many people	Lk 7:21*	NIV§57 NASB§75	Jesus' acts of compassion were also signs of his Messiahship	Ministry in Galilee
Compassionate Jesus forgave the sins of a sinful but contrite woman	Lk 7:47-50*	NIV§59 NASB§77	Jesus' Pharisaic host despised the sinful woman	Ministry in Galilee
Several women followed Jesus as a result of his compassionate help	Lk 8:2-3*	NIV§60 NASB§78	These women and others contributed to supporting Jesus and the Twelve	Ministry in Galilee
Luke tells the subject of Jesus' discussion with Moses and Elijah: his physical death	Lk 9:31*	NIV§85 NASB§121	Jesus' "departure" from this world was necessitated by his humanity	Ministry around Galilee
Jesus showed his compassion in sending out the 72 and telling them to pray for more laborers	Lk 10:1-2*	NIV§102a NASB§139	Jesus had a concern for fellow human beings and wanted them to hear about the kingdom	Later Judean Ministry
Jesus had concern for the lower classes	Lk 10:21, 23-24*	NIV§102b NASB§140	Jesus thanked the Father for revealing truth to the less privileged and not to the wise	Later Judean Ministry

Summary	Scripture	Harmony Sec. Nos.	Comment	Period of Christ's Ministry
Jesus commends the Samaritan who helped the man who had been robbed and beaten	Lk 10:30-37*	NIV§103 NASB§141	Jesus would have us show mercy to fellow human beings regardless of race	Later Judean Ministry
Commendably Mary was more concerned about personal relationships than about physical preparations	Lk 10:38-42*	NIV§104 NASB§142	Martha was the hostess but was upset with Mary for not helping prepare for their guest	Later Judean Ministry
The case of the friend at midnight indicates an understanding of how human nature responds	Lk 11:8*	NIV§105 NASB§143	The neighbor came after everyone was in bed to ask for help and received it because of his shamelessness	Later Judean Ministry
A woman remarked, "Blessed is the mother who gave you birth and nursed you"	Lk 11:27*	NIV§106 NASB§144	Jesus' contemporaries were well aware of his full humanity	Later Judean Ministry
Jesus was aware of the human tendency toward greed	Lk 12:15*	NIV§108b ASB§147	As a man, Jesus fully appreciated the tests of life that humans face	Later Judean Ministry
Jesus used accountability on a human level to illustrate our accountability to God	Lk 12:36, 47*	NIV§108c NASB§148	The Lord's ability to capture human situations so effectively is a reminder of his humanity	Later Judean Ministry
Luke illustrated Jesus' compassion for others in healing a woman who had been sick for 18 years	Lk 13:11-13*	NIV§110 NASB§152	The woman was bent over and could not straighten up because of being afflicted by a spirit	Later Judean Ministry
Jesus laments over the failure of his fellow Jews to repent	Lk 13:34*	NIV§113b NASB§163	Jesus' sadness demonstrates his strong compassion for others once again	Ministry in and around Perea
Jesus showed compassion for the poor, the crippled, the lame, and the blind who could not repay him	Lk 14:13*	NIV§114 NASB§164	In healing a man with dropsy on the Sabbath (Lk 14:5), Jesus reminded his critics of what they would do for animals	Ministry in and around Perea
Jesus used human family ties to illustrate the primacy of a call to discipleship	Lk 14:26*	NIV§115 NASB§165	As a man, Jesus well knew that family ties are the strongest that exist	Ministry in and around Perea
The parable of the lost son illustrates the compassion of the Father and the Son	Lk 15:32*	NIV§116 NASB§166	Divine compassion for the lost stands in contrast to Pharisaic disdain for sinners	Ministry in and around Perea
God's compassion extended to poor Lazarus, not to the rich man	Lk 16:22-24*	NIV§117b NASB§168	A love for money precluded the compassion that Jesus showed	Ministry in and around Perea
Jesus responded to the plea for mercy from the ten leprous men by healing them	Lk 17:13-14*	NIV§120a NASB§173	Only one of the ten who were cleansed returned to express gratitude	Ministry in and around Perea
The tax collector was justified before God because he asked for mercy	Lk 18:13-14*	NIV§121 NASB§175	The tax collector admitted his sin, but the Pharisee expressed his self-righteous pride	Ministry in and around Perea
In compassion Jesus responded to the blind man's plea for mercy	Lk 18:39, 42-43	NIV§126 NASB§182	The blind man's faith allowed Jesus to heal him	Ministry in and around Perea

Summary	Scripture	Harmony Sec. Nos.	Comment	Period of Christ's Ministry
Key verse in Luke: "The Son of Man came to seek and to save what was lost"	**Lk 19:10***	NIV§127a NASB§183	Because he is a true member of the human race, Jesus fulfills the role of a kinsman-redeemer for lost mankind (Lev 25:47-49)	Ministry in and around Perea
Jesus wept over the city of Jerusalem, once again illustrating his compassion	Lk 19:41*	NIV§128b NASB§187	God must judge sin, but that does not prevent him from having compassion for men	Formal Presentation of Christ to Israel
Jesus evidenced his compassion for the poor widow	Lk 21:3-4	NIV§138 NASB§201	God's compassion shows no respect of persons	Formal Presentation of Christ to Israel
Jesus said in anticipation of his death, "The Son of Man will go as it has been decreed"	Lk 22:22*	NIV§146 NASB§214	Jesus anticipated the end of his human sojourn on earth	Prophecies in Preparation for the Death of Christ
Luke portrays graphically Jesus' anguish in the Garden of Gethsemane and his need of help	Lk 22:43-44*	NIV§152 NASB§226	Only Luke mentions the angel's help and Jesus' sweatlike drops of blood	Prophecies in Preparation for the Death of Christ
Jesus asked Judas if he was betraying "the Son of Man" with a kiss	Lk 22:48*	NIV§153 NASB§227	Luke continues to emphasize the manhood of Jesus	Prophecies in Preparation for the Death of Christ
Pilate said, "I find no basis for a charge against this man"	Lk 23:4	NIV§159 NASB§233	Only the Gospel of Luke calls Jesus "this man"	The Death of Christ
Pilate asked whether "the man" was a Galilean	Lk 23:6*	NIV§160 NASB§234	Another of Luke's notices about the full humanity of Jesus	The Death of Christ
Pilate twice more refers to Jesus as "this man"	Lk 23:14*	NIV§161 NASB§235	Luke is careful to capitalize on Pilate's language	The Death of Christ
Pilate asked, "What crime has this man committed?"	Lk 23:22	NIV§161 NASB§235	Luke repeatedly emphasizes Jesus' humanity	The Death of Christ
Luke notices the sorrow of the people who mourned as Jesus was led away	Lk 23:27*	NIV§163 NASB§237	The people regretted the loss of Jesus' human companionship	The Death of Christ
Jesus showed compassion for the repentant criminal hanging beside him	Lk 23:43*	NIV§164 NASB§238	In those moments of severe suffering it would have been easy for Jesus not to think of others	The Death of Christ
At the moment of Jesus' death the centurion noted the innocence of "this man"	Lk 23:47	NIV§166 NASB§240	Only one who is truly human can experience a human death	The Death of Christ
Only one who is fully human could need to have his body buried	Lk 23:52-53	NIV§167b NASB§242	Joseph of Arimathea placed Jesus' body in a special tomb	The Death of Christ
The men at the tomb spoke of the necessity for "the Son of Man" to be crucified and rise again	Lk 24:7	NIV§171 NASB§246	This is the last occurrence of "the Son of Man" in Luke's Gospel	The Resurrection and Ascension of Christ

#30—John's Emphasis on Jesus as God

(Key Verse: See John 20:31 below.)

* Scriptures marked by an asterisk have no parallels in the other three Gospels.

Summary	Scripture	Harmony Sec. Nos.	Comment	Period of Christ's Ministry
Jesus the Word existed in the beginning with God and was God	Jn 1:1, 14*	NIV§2 NASB§2	As God, Jesus was also the Creator of all things (Jn 1:3)	A Preview of Who Jesus Is
Jesus is "God the One and Only, who is at the Father's side"	Jn 1:18*	NIV§2 NASB§2	No one has ever seen God, but Jesus has made him known	A Preview of Who Jesus Is
John the Baptist identified Jesus as the one who would baptize with the Holy Spirit	Jn 1:33*	NIV§27 NASB§30	Only God can baptize with the Holy Spirit	End of John's Ministry and the Beginning of Christ's
Andrew identified Jesus as the Messiah	Jn 1:41*	NIV§28 NASB§31	The Old Testament portrays the Messiah as God	End of John's Ministry and the Beginning of Christ's
Nathanael identified Jesus as the Son of God and the King of Israel	Jn 1:49*	NIV§28 NASB§31	These were titles for deity	End of John's Ministry and the Beginning of Christ's
Jesus called God his Father in speaking of his Father's house	Jn 2:16*	NIV§31 NASB§34	Later Jesus' critics took this as a claim of equality with the Father (Jn 5:18)	End of John's Ministry and the Beginning of Christ's
Jesus stated that he had descended from heaven	Jn 3:13*	NIV§32b NASB§36	God is the only one who preexisted and whose origin is heaven	End of John's Ministry and the Beginning of Christ's
John the Baptist spoke of the Father's love for the Son	Jn 3:35*	NIV§33 NASB§37	John knew Jesus was the Son of God into whose hands God had given all things	End of John's Ministry and the Beginning of Christ's
Jesus identified himself to the woman of Samaria as the Messiah	Jn 4:26*	NIV§35a NASB§39	The woman recognized Jesus as a prophet first	End of John's Ministry and the Beginning of Christ's
The woman of Samaria eventually introduced Jesus to her city as the Messiah	Jn 4:29*	NIV§35b NASB§40	The woman phrased her suggestion cautiously as a question but made her point, many from her city eventually coming to believe in Jesus	End of John's Ministry and the Beginning of Christ's
Jesus defends himself for calling God his Father and making himself equal with God	Jn 5:19-47*	NIV§49c NASB§58	Jesus has the authority to judge and raise the dead and has the witness of John, his works, and the Scriptures	Ministry in Galilee
After feeding the 5,000, Jesus was recognized by the people as the Prophet who was to come into the world	Jn 6:14*	NIV§73 NASB§106	The Messiah was the Prophet to whom they referred, one like Moses (Dt 18:15)	Ministry around Galilee
Jesus calls himself the bread from heaven, the only one who has seen the Father	Jn 6:46, 51*	NIV§76a NASB§109	Only God could make such claims as these	Ministry around Galilee

Summary	Scripture	Harmony Sec. Nos.	Comment	Period of Christ's Ministry
Peter calls Jesus "the Holy One of God"	Jn 6:69*	NIV§76b NASB§110	This is the title of the Messiah-King and of God himself (Ps 16:10; 71:22; 78:41; 89:18; Isa 1:4)	Ministry around Galilee
The people wondered whether the rulers knew that Jesus was the Messiah	Jn 7:26, 41*	NIV§96a, 96b NASB§133, 134	Much confusion prevailed in Jerusalem, and the people were amazed that no one halted Jesus' public ministry	Later Judean Ministry
Jesus said he existed before Abraham	Jn 8:58*	NIV§99b NASB§138	To claim preexistence is to claim to be God	Later Judean Ministry
The healed blind man believed in Jesus as the Son of Man	Jn 9:35-38*	NIV§100d NASB§156	The Son of Man was the promised Messiah	Later Judean Ministry
Jesus tells the Jewish people that he is the Messiah	Jn 10:24-25*	NIV§111 NASB§160	The Messiah is the God-man	Later Judean Ministry
"I and the Father are one"	Jn 10:30*	NIV§111 NASB§160	To claim to be of one essence with the Father is to claim to be God	Later Judean Ministry
Martha expressed her belief in Jesus as the Messiah, the Son of God	Jn 11:27*	NIV§118b NASB§171	Jesus accepted Martha's confession without correcting her	Ministry in and around Perea
Jesus raised Lazarus from the dead	Jn 11:43-44*	NIV§118b NASB§171	Only God can raise someone from the dead	Ministry in and around Perea
Jesus knew that the Father had put all things into his hands and that he had come from and was going back to the Father	Jn 13:3*	NIV§145 NASB§213	Only God could possess such power and prerogatives as these	Prophecies in Preparation for the Death of Christ
Jesus spoke of his ascension to the Father's house and his return to take disciples there	Jn 14:2-3*	NIV§149 NASB§218	Only God could characterize his activities in this way	Prophecies in Preparation for the Death of Christ
"Anyone who has seen me has seen the Father.... I am in the Father and the Father is in me"	Jn 14:9, 11*	NIV§149 NASB§218	Jesus must be God to make statements like these	Prophecies in Preparation for the Death of Christ
Jesus spoke of sending the Holy Spirit to the disciples	Jn 15:26; 16:7*	NIV§150b, 150c NASB§220, 221	Only a person of the Godhead can send the Holy Spirit	Prophecies in Preparation for the Death of Christ
Jesus spoke of the glory he had with the Father before the world existed	Jn 17:5*	NIV§151 NASB§224	To be preexistent Jesus had to be God	Prophecies in Preparation for the Death of Christ
The Jews told Pilate that Jesus called himself the Son of God	Jn 19:7*	NIV§161 NASB§235	The unique Son of God must himself be God	The Death of Christ
Eight days after Jesus' resurrection he appeared to Thomas, who addressed him, "My Lord and my God"	Jn 20:28*	NIV§179 NASB§254	Skeptical Thomas gave the strongest confession of all of Jesus' deity by putting him on the same plane as the Father	Resurrection and Ascension of Christ
Key verse in John: "These are written that you may believe that Jesus is the Christ, the Son of God"	**Jn 20:31**	NIV§179 NASB§254	John's purpose in writing his Gospel was to prove the Messiahship and deity of Christ	Resurrection and Ascension of Christ

#31—Jesus' Miracles in Capernaum

Miracle	Scripture	Harmony Section Numbers	Jesus' Location	Time
healing royal official's son	Jn 4:46-54	NIV§38, NASB§44	Cana in Galilee, away from Capernaum	shortly after arrival in Galilee to begin Galilean ministry
healing a demoniac	Mk 1:23-26; Lk 4:33-35	NIV§42, NASB§48	in the synagogue of Capernaum	right after the call of Peter, Andrew, James, and John
healing Peter's mother-in-law	Mt 8:14; Mk 1:29-30; Lk 4:38-39	NIV§43, NASB§49	in Peter's house in Capernaum	just after healing a demoniac in the synagogue in Capernaum
healing a paralytic	Mt 9:1-8; Mk 2:1-12; Lk 5:17-26	NIV§46, NASB§53	inside a house in Cana	shortly after arrival in Galilee to begin Galilean ministry
healing a centurion's servant	Mt 8:5-13; Lk 7:1-10	NIV§55, NASB§73	on his way to the centurion's house	well into the Galilean ministry period, just after the Sermon on the Mount and just before the first public rejection by Israel's leaders
raising Jairus's daughter from death	Mt 9:18-19, 23-26; Mk 5:21-24, 35-43; Lk 8:40-42, 49-56	NIV§67, NASB§95	in a room with the daughter, her parents, Peter, James, and John	just after the first public rejection by Israel's leaders and the beginning of Jesus' parabolic teaching
healing a woman with bleeding for 12 years	Mt 9:20-22; Mk 5:25-34; Lk 8:43-48	NIV§67, NASB§95	passing by the woman in a crowd	just before the raising of Jairus's daughter
sight restored for two blind men	Mt 9:28-30	NIV§68, NASB§96	somewhere indoors	just after the healing of Jairus's daughter
healing of a deaf-mute	Mt 9:32-33	NIV§68, NASB§96	somewhere indoors	just after the healing of two blind men
coin in fish's mouth	Mt 17:27	NIV§89, NASB§126	near the Sea of Galilee	after Peter's confession and the Transfiguration

Means	Results	Response	Additional Conditions	Timing of Miracles
spoken word	royal official and his household convinced of Jesus' authority	father and his household believed	rebuke of people for lack of faith	same time as Jesus spoke the word
a command	the demon left without injuring the man	people amazed at Jesus' authority	news about Jesus spread throughout the whole region of Galilee	immediate healing
touched her hand, rebuked the fever	she rose and began to serve	people brought many other sick and demon-possessed	Peter, James, and John were witnesses to the miracle	immediate healing
spoken word	crowd convinced of Jesus' authority	crowd's amazement and praise to God	(1) faith of the friends who lowered him through the roof, (2) accusation of blasphemy for claiming to forgive sins	immediate healing
spoken word	centurion's household convinced of Jesus' authority	[unknown]	(1) centurion a friend of Israel, (2) centurion's faith commended in advance, (3) healing in response to centurion's faith	immediate healing
taking her hand and spoken word	Jairus, his wife, Peter, James, and John convinced of Jesus' authority	astonishment of her parents and the three disciples	(1) Jesus the object of laughter by the mourners, (2) instructions that the witnesses tell no one, (3) spreading fame	immediate healing
a touch of Jesus' cloak	the healed woman convinced of Jesus' authority	woman relieved of suffering	(1) Jesus unaware that a miracle had happened, (2) healed woman hid at first, (3) woman's faith commended	immediate healing
Jesus touched their eyes	their sight restored	the two spread the news about Jesus all over the region	Jesus instructed the healed men to tell no one, but they disregarded his instructions	immediate healing
[not specified]	a demon driven out	the crowd was amazed at his authority	Jesus' opponents claimed he had performed the miracle through the power of the prince of demons	immediate healing
Peter told to look into the mouth of the first fish he catches	temple tax paid	[not specified]	miracle performed in response to Peter's encounter with tax collectors	after Peter followed instructions

#32—Jesus' Activities in or near Capernaum, other than Miracles

Activity	Scripture	Harmony Section Numbers	Location	Season and Year
Departure from Nazareth, arrival in Capernaum	Mt 4:13-16	NIV§40 NASB§46	By the sea, in the region of Zebulun and Naphtali	winter, A.D. 28
First call of four disciples	Mt 4:18-22	NIV§41 NASB§47	By the Sea of Galilee	winter, A.D. 28
Second call of the four	Lk 5:1-11	NIV§41 NASB§51	By the Lake of Gennesaret	winter, A.D. 28
Call of Matthew	Mt 9:9; Mk 2:13-14; Lk 5:27-28	NIV§47a NASB§54	Capernaum	summer, A.D. 28
Banquet at Matthew's house	Mt 9:10-13; Mk 2:15-17; Lk 5:29-32	NIV§47b NASB§55	Capernaum	summer, A.D. 28
Three illustrations explain changed conditions	Mt 9:14-17; Mk 2:18-22; Lk 5:33-39	NIV§48 NASB§56	Capernaum	summer, A.D. 28
Woes on three cities for their failure to repent	Mt 11:20-30	NIV§58 NASB76	Capernaum, Chorazin, Bethsaida	fall, A.D. 28
Discourse on the bread of life	Jn 6:22-59	NIV§76a NASB§109	In the synagogue of Capernaum	spring, A.D. 29
Defection among the disciples	Jn 6:60-71	NIV§76b NASB§110	In the synagogue of Capernaum	spring, A.D. 29
Conflict over the tradition of ceremonial defilement	Mt 15:1-20; Mk 7:1-23; Jn 7:1	NIV§77 NASB§111	Galilee, perhaps Capernaum	spring, A.D. 29
Rivalry over greatness dispelled	Mt 18:1-5; Mk 9:33-37; Lk 9:46-48	NIV§90 NASB§127	In a house in Capernaum	summer, A.D. 29
Warning against causing believers to stumble	Mt 18:6-14; Mk 9:38-50; Lk 9:49-50	NIV§91 NASB§128	In a house in Capernaum	summer, A.D. 29
Treatment and forgiveness of a sinning brother	Mt 18:15-35	NIV§92 NASB§129	In a house in Capernaum	summer, A.D. 29

1. Or, seventy times seven times.

Occasion	Results	Additional Comments
After Jesus' rejection in Nazareth	Capernaum became Jesus' new home	The fulfillment of Isa 9:1-2
While two pairs of brothers were fishing	Peter, Andrew, James, and John left their nets and followed Jesus	Jesus promised to make them fishers of men
After Jesus had taught the crowd from a boat	Peter, James, John, and companions left everything and followed Jesus	At Jesus' bidding they put down their nets and brought in many fish
Jesus passed by Matthew sitting at his tax booth	Jesus summoned Matthew to follow, and he did	Matthew's other name was Levi
Matthew hosted a great banquet for Jesus	Jesus dined with tax collectors and sinners	The Pharisees and the scribes criticized Jesus for eating with tax collectors and sinners
John's disciples and the Pharisees inquired why they should fast when Jesus' disciples did not	Jesus explained that fasting was inappropriate while the bridegroom was present	Three illustrations: the bridegroom, the patched garment, the wineskins
Lack of repentance by three cities where many miracles were performed	Jesus pronounced woes on these cities	Jesus' thanks to the Father for revealing spiritual truths to little children
The day after Jesus fed the 5,000	Jesus spoke of being the living bread that came down from heaven	The Jews had difficulty accepting his claims
Disciples were grumbling about Jesus' claim to be the bread that came down from heaven	Many disciples withdrew from following Jesus	Peter confessed Jesus to be the Holy One of God
The Pharisees and scribes criticized Jesus' disciples for not observing the tradition of the elders	Jesus rebuked the critics for neglecting the command of God for the sake of holding to the tradition of men	Jesus revealed that defilement comes from outside, not inside
The disciples were arguing about who was the greatest	Jesus used a little child to teach the importance of humility	Jesus taught that the disciple who is least is the one who is great
John saw someone driving out demons in Jesus' name	Jesus warned against causing people to sin	Principle established: Whoever is not against us is for us
Peter asked how often he should forgive a brother sinning against him	Jesus replied not just seven times but seventy-seven times[1]	Jesus illustrated by the story of a servant forgiven by the king but unwilling to forgive a fellow servant

#33—Gospel Activities in Jerusalem before Passion Week

(All activities during Passion Week took place in Jerusalem.)

Event	Location	Time	Scripture	Harmony Section Numbers
John's birth foretold to Zechariah	in the temple	6 B.C.	Lk 1:5-25	NIV§4 NASB§4
Jesus presented in the temple	in the temple	5 B.C.	Lk 2:22-38	NIV§13 NASB§15
Visit of the Magi	Jerusalem, then Bethlehem	3-2 B.C.	Mt 2:1-12	NIV§14 NASB§17
Jesus' first Passover in Jerusalem	in the temple	A.D. 8-9	Lk 2:41-50	NIV§18 NASB§21
First cleansing of the temple	in the temple	spring, A.D. 27	Jn 2:13-22	NIV§31 NASB§34
An early response to Jesus' miracles	throughout Jerusalem	summer, A.D. 27	Jn 2:23-25	NIV§32a NASB§35
Nicodemus's interview with Jesus	somewhere in Jerusalem	summer, A.D. 27	Jn 3:1-21	NIV§32b NASB§36
A lame man healed on the Sabbath	a pool by the Sheep Gate	fall, A.D. 28	Jn 5:1-9	NIV§49a NASB§57
Effort to kill Jesus	somewhere in Jerusalem	fall, A.D. 28	Jn 5:10-18	NIV§49b NASB§58
Discourse defending the Son's equality with the Father	somewhere in Jerusalem	fall, A.D. 28	Jn 5:19-47	NIV§40c NASB§59
Mixed reaction to Jesus' teaching and miracles	in the temple	fall, A.D. 29	Jn 7:11-31	NIV§96a NASB§133
Frustrated attempt to arrest Jesus	in the temple	fall, A.D. 29	Jn 7:32-52	NIV§96b NASB§134
Conflict over Jesus' claim to be the light of the world	in the temple	fall, A.D. 29	Jn 8:12-20	NIV§98 NASB§136

Persons Involved	Activity	Circumstances	Results
Zechariah, an angel of the Lord	Zechariah burning incense in the temple	The angel promised Zechariah a son	Zechariah unable to speak
Jesus, Joseph, Mary, Simeon, Anna	Presentation of Jesus, purification of Mary, song of Simeon, prophecies of Simeon and Anna	Direct revelation to Simeon and Anna regarding the future salvation of Israel through Jesus	Joseph and Mary were amazed at the things said about their child
Magi, Herod the Great, chief priests, scribes, Jesus, Mary	Discovery of Jesus and gifts presented to him by the Magi	Long journey by the Magi to Jerusalem, then to Bethlehem	Magi warned in a dream not to return to Herod, returned home another way
Jesus, his parents, temple teachers	Jesus in dialogue with temple teachers while his parents searched for him	Without his parents' knowledge Jesus stayed in temple when they left	Parents perplexed over his statement that he had to be in his Father's house
Jesus; sellers of cattle, sheep, and doves; money changers; the Jews	Jesus drove out the merchants for turning his Father's house into a market	The Jews resented Jesus' action and his claim of ability to raise the temple in 3 days	His disciples later understood him to speak of raising his own body from the dead
Jesus, many people in Jerusalem	People were impressed with Jesus' many miracles	Jesus knew the depravity of mankind	Jesus did not entrust himself to the people
Jesus, Nicodemus	Jesus told Nicodemus about his need to be born again and believe in God's Son	Nicodemus was impressed with the miracles done by Jesus	Nicodemus did not understand Jesus' words about a new birth
Jesus, a lame man	Jesus healed the lame man	The man had been sick for 38 years	The miracle occurred on the Sabbath
Jesus, the healed lame man, the Jews	Since Jesus told the man to take his mat and walk, the Jews condemned Jesus for breaking the Sabbath	The Jews scolded the healed lame man for carrying his mat on the Sabbath	Jesus proceeded to defend his claim of equality with the Father
Jesus, his Jewish listeners	Jesus cites the Son's role in judgment and resurrection, the witness of John the Baptist, his own works, and the Scriptures	Jesus defends his role in unfriendly surroundings	No recorded response
Jesus, the Jews, the multitude, the people of Jerusalem	Jesus' enemies were seeking to seize him, but many believed in him	The occasion was the Feast of Tabernacles	The debate about Jesus continued
Jesus, the Jews, the Pharisees, the chief priests, the multitude, Nicodemus, the officers	Debate about whether Jesus was the Messiah	The occasion was the Feast of Tabernacles	The officers failed to carry out the arrest
Jesus, the Pharisees	The Pharisees challenged the truthfulness of Jesus' witness	Jesus was defending his truthfulness in the treasury	No one arrested Jesus

Event	Location	Time	Scripture	Harmony Section Numbers
Invitation to believe in Jesus	in the temple	fall, A.D. 29	Jn 8:21-30	NIV§99a NASB§137
Relationship to Abraham, and attempted stoning	in the temple	fall, A.D. 29	Jn 8:31-59	NIV§99b NASB§138
Jesus' visit with Mary and Martha	Bethany near Jerusalem	fall, A.D. 29	Lk 10:38-42	NIV§104 NASB§142
Healing a man born blind	somewhere in Jerusalem	fall, A.D. 29	Jn 9:1-7	NIV§100a NASB§153
Reaction of a healed blind man's neighbors	somewhere in Jerusalem	fall, A.D. 29	Jn 9:8-12	NIV§100b NASB§154
Examination and excommunication of the blind man by the Pharisees	somewhere in Jerusalem	fall, A.D. 29	Jn 9:13-34	NIV§100c NASB§155
Jesus' identification of himself to the blind man	somewhere in Jerusalem	fall, A.D. 29	Jn 9:35-38	NIV§100d NASB§156
Spiritual blindness of the Pharisees	somewhere in Jerusalem	fall, A.D. 29	Jn 9:39-41	NIV§100e NASB§157
Allegory of the good shepherd and the sheep	somewhere in Jerusalem	fall, A.D. 29	Jn 10:1-18	NIV§101a NASB§158
Further division among the Jews	somewhere in Jerusalem	fall, A.D. 29	Jn 10:19-21	NIV§101b NASB§159
Another attempt to stone or arrest Jesus for blasphemy	somewhere in Jerusalem	fall, A.D. 29	Jn 10:22-39	NIV§111 NASB§160
Sickness and death of Lazarus	Bethany near Jerusalem	winter, A.D. 30	Jn 11:1-16	NIV§118a NASB§170
Lazarus raised from the dead	Bethany near Jerusalem	winter, A.D. 30	Jn 11:17-44	NIV§118b NASB§171
Decision of the Sanhedrin to put Jesus to death	somewhere in Jerusalem	winter, A.D. 30	Jn 11:45-54	NIV§119 NASB§172

Persons Involved	Activity	Circumstances	Results
Jesus, the Jews	Jesus tells his listeners they will die in their sins	Listeners did not realize that Jesus claimed to be from the Father	Many came to believe in him
Jesus, the Jews	Jesus tells his listeners their father is the devil; they accuse Jesus of having a demon	Jesus claimed preexistence	They tried to stone Jesus, but he escaped
Jesus, Mary, Martha	Mary listening to Jesus, Martha busy with the meal	Martha wanted Mary to help prepare to serve their guest	Jesus said Mary had chosen the good part
Jesus, a man blind from birth	Jesus made clay, applied it to the man's eyes, and told him to go wash	The purpose of the man's blindness was to display the works of God	The man obeyed and received his sight
The blind man, his neighbors	The man gives an account of being healed by Jesus	The neighbors wondered whether this could be the blind beggar	The blind man did not know Jesus' whereabouts
The blind man, his neighbors, the Pharisees, the man's parents	The man tells how Jesus healed him, and the Pharisees refused to believe him	The man's parents refused to get involved for fear of being excommunicated	The Pharisees put the man out of the synagogue
Jesus, the blind man	Jesus led the man to faith in Jesus	Jesus heard about the man's excommunication and sought him out	The man worshiped Jesus
Jesus, the Pharisees	The Pharisees recognized Jesus' accusation that they were blind	The Pharisees were unwilling to admit their spiritual need	The Pharisees' sin remained unforgiven
Jesus, the Pharisees	Jesus compared himself to the good shepherd and the Pharisees to thieves	Jesus' role was to lead the godly remnant from Israel and give them life	Jesus was ready to obey the Father's command to lay down his life for the sheep
Two groups of Jews	The allegory of the good shepherd caused division among the listeners	Some said Jesus had a demon, others said he did not	The Jewish people were split further
Jesus, the Jews	Jesus tells his listeners that they do not believe because they are not among his sheep	The Jews accused Jesus of blasphemy for claiming to be God	The Jews tried to seize Jesus but couldn't
Lazarus, Jesus, the disciples, Didymus (Thomas)	Jesus declined to go to Bethany until after Lazarus died	The disciples advised against going back to Jerusalem for fear of the Jews	The disciples grudgingly agreed to go, expecting to die with Jesus when they went
Martha, Mary, Jesus, the Jews, Lazarus	Jesus consoled Martha and Mary and called Lazarus from the tomb	Lazarus had been dead for four days when the stone was removed from the tomb	Lazarus's grave clothes were removed
Pharisees, chief priests, Caiaphas, the Jews, Jesus	The Jewish leaders convened a council to determine how to keep people from believing in Jesus	The raising of Lazarus and other signs made the leaders fearful of Roman action against the nation of Israel	The Council planned to kill Jesus, and Jesus withdrew from the Jerusalem area

#34—Crises in the Life of Christ

Event	Scripture	Harmony Sec. Numbers	Place	Time	Occasion, Issue
Birth	Lk 2:1-7	NIV§10, NASB§12	Bethlehem	6-5 B.C.	Mankind's need for a kinsman-redeemer (2Co 5:19)
Baptism	Mt 3:13-17; Mk 1:9-11; Lk 3:21-23a	NIV§24, NASB§27	Bethany beyond Jordan	summer, A.D. 26	Divided between 30 years of private life and 3 years of public ministry
Temptation	Mt 4:1-11; Mk 1:12-13; Lk 4:1-13	NIV§25, NASB§28	Judean desert	summer, A.D. 26	Beginning of Jesus' public ministry
Sabbath Controversies	Mt 12 9-14; Mk 3:6; Lk 6:11; Jn 5:1-47	NIV§49a-51, NASB§57-61	Jerusalem and Galilee	fall, A.D. 28	Lame man, disciples' hunger, man with shriveled hand
Apostles appointed, and Sermon on the Mount	Mt 5:1–7:29; Mk 3:13-19; Lk 6:12-49	NIV§53-54i, NASB§63-72	a mountain near the Sea of Galilee	fall, A.D. 28	Need for leadership help, clarification of prerequisites for entering the kingdom
Public rejection by leaders and parabolic mysteries about the kingdom	Mt 12:22–13:52; Mk 3:20–4:34; Lk 8:4-21	NIV§61-64k, NASB§79-92	Galilee	winter, A.D. 29	Healing of a demon-possessed man who was blind and dumb
Peter's confession and the Transfiguration	Mt 16:13–17:9; Mk 8:27–9:10; Lk 9:18-36	NIV§182a-186, NASB§118-122	near Caesarea Philippi	summer, A.D. 29	Climax of 6 months of training of the Twelve: awareness of Jesus' Messiahship
Raising of Lazarus and Sanhedrin's decision to kill Jesus	Jn 11:1-54	NIV§118a-119, NASB§170-172	Bethany near Jerusalem	spring, A.D. 30	Sickness and death of Lazarus
Formal offer of Christ to Israel	Mt 21:1-17; Mk 11:1-18; Lk 19:19-48; Jn 12:12-19	NIV§128b-129b, NASB§187-189	Jerusalem	spring, A.D. 30	Great expectation that the King would establish his kingdom

Purpose or Result	Witnesses	Jesus' Response	Opponents and Their Part	Other Conditions
Complete deity combined with complete humanity in one person	Shepherds, Magi, Mary, Joseph	n/a	Herod the Great's attempt to destroy	God's response: star in the east, angelic song
Jesus identified with repenting sinners who awaited the kingdom	John the Baptist and others being baptized	Insisted on being baptized over John's protest	John insisted that the leaders repent	God's response: opened heavens, descending Spirit, voice from heaven
Settle the issue of who is Lord	Jesus and the devil	Threefold use of the Word of God	Satan challenged Jesus' loyalty to the will of God	God's response: sent angels to minister to Jesus
Overturning of unbiblical tradition	Jews, Pharisees, and others in a synagogue	Claimed to be God and Lord of the Sabbath	Objected to Jesus' use of the Sabbath and threatened to destroy him	Jesus performed two miracles of healing, disciples picked grain
Exposing superficial righteousness of the scribes and Pharisees	The Twelve and great crowds from widely scattered areas, including Jerusalem	All-night prayer in preparation	No stated response	Crowd's response: amazed at Jesus' authoritative teaching
Kingdom takes on additional form, one unforeseen in the OT	The crowds and the Twelve	Labels opponents' response as unpardon- able and eternal sin; launches parabolic ministry	Scribes and Pharisees from Jerusalem blinded to parabolic teaching	Crowd's response: ready to declare Jesus the promised son of David
Direct disclosure of Jesus' coming death, disclosure of the church's establish- ment, preview of 2nd coming	The Twelve; then the Twelve and the crowd; then Peter, James, and John	Reveals his own future suffering and that of his disciples	Peter challenged Jesus' prediction of future suf- fering and death	God's response: provision of visible glory, sending of Moses and Elijah, voice from heaven
Many Jews believed, great popularity for Jesus, God and Jesus glorified	Mary, Martha, the Twelve, some Jews	Waited and then went to Lazarus after he died	Chief priests and Phar- isees plan to kill Jesus	Danger in going to Jerusalem: stoning
2nd cleansing of the temple	The crowds, Pharisees, the Twelve, those buying and selling in the temple	Wept for Jerusalem	Resentment over the warm reception for Jesus, desire to kill Jesus	Jerusalem's problem: spiritual blindness

Event	Scripture	Harmony Sec. Numbers	Place	Time	Occasion, Issue
Official challenges to Jesus' authority	Mt 21:23–23:39; Mk 11:27–12:40; Lk 20:1-47	NIV§132a-137b; NASB§193-200	Jerusalem	spring, A.D. 30	Source of authority, taxes to Caesar, resurrection, greatest commandment, the Messiah and David, corrupt leadership
Crucifixion	Mt 27:35-50; Mk 15:24-37; Lk 23:33b-46; Jn 19:18-30	NIV§164-165, NASB§238-239	Golgotha in Jerusalem	spring, A.D. 30	Verdict pronounced by Pilate
Resurrection	Mt 28:5-8; Mk 16:2-8; Lk 24:1-11; Jn 20:1-10	NIV§171-172, NASB§246-247	garden tomb of Golgotha	spring, A.D. 30	Third day after crucifixion as Jesus had predicted
Ascension	Lk 24:50-53; Ac 1:9-12	NIV§184, NASB§259	Bethany and the Mount of Olives	spring, A.D. 30	Jesus' need to return to the Father

Purpose or Result	Witnesses	Jesus' Response	Opponents and Their Part	Other Conditions
To entrap Jesus	The disciples, Jesus' antagonists	Cites John's authority, render to both Caesar and God, no marriage after resurrection, love the Lord your God, Messiah both Lord and son of David, pronounces woes	Chief priests, scribes, elders, Pharisees, Herodians, Sadducees, a lawyer	The occasion: Jesus' arrival in the temple
To satisfy the demands of chief priests, rulers, and people	Centurion, soldiers, two malefactors, Mary Magdalene, Mary the mother of James and Joseph, Mary the mother of James and John, Salome, other women and acquaintances from Galilee, chief priests, elders, crowds, disciples	Prayer for forgiveness of his enemies, promise to the repentant criminal, provision for his mother, cry of separation from the Father, acknowledgment of thirst, cry of accomplishment, cry of resignation	Physical cruelty, taunts	Response of Jesus' followers: sorrow and despondency, Joseph and Nicodemus handled the burial
To prove God had accepted Jesus' sacrifice for sin (Ro 4:25)	The empty tomb: Mary Magdalene, Mary the mother of James, Salome, other women, Peter, John	Appeared to Mary Magdalene, other women, two disciples on road to Emmaus, ten assembled disciples, eleven assembled disciples, seven disciples, the Eleven again, James, disciples for a third time	Claimed Jesus' disciples had stolen the body	Response of Jerusalem: 3,000 became Christians at Pentecost
To allow the coming of the Spirit	The apostles, two men in white clothing	Ministry of intercession begun	n/a	Disciples' response: an extended prayer meeting

#35—Seven Lessons of Jesus on Discipleship

1. Valuing Eternal Realities over Temporal Matters

The Challenge	Scripture	Harmony Sec. Nos.	Audience	Occasion	Period of Christ's Ministry	The Result or Lesson
"Come . . . Follow me"	Jn 1:39, 43, 46	NIV§28 NASB§31	Andrew, Philip	Two disciples of John the Baptist followed Jesus	End of John's Ministry and Beginning of Christ's	Result: Andrew, Peter, Philip, and Nathanael become Jesus' followers
"Follow me, and I will make you fishers of men"	Mt 4:19; Mk 1:17	NIV§41 NASB§47	Peter, Andrew James, and John	Jesus walking by the Sea of Galilee	Ministry of Christ in Galilee	Result: the four fishermen left their nets and boats and followed Jesus
"From now on you will catch men"	Lk 5:10	NIV§41 NASB§51	Peter, James, John, and their companions	Jesus got into Peter's boat to teach and instructed the fishermen to let down their nets	Ministry of Christ in Galilee	Result: they left everything and followed Jesus
"Follow me"	Mt 9:9; Mk 2:14; Lk 5:27	NIV§47a NASB§54	Matthew	Jesus saw Matthew sitting at the tax collector's booth	Ministry in Galilee	Result: Matthew followed Jesus and gave him a great banquet in his house
Jesus sent the twelve disciples out to proclaim the kingdom	Mt 10:1; Mk 6:7; Lk 9:1-2	NIV§70b NASB§99	The twelve apostles	The need to spread the good news about the kingdom more rapidly	Ministry of Christ in Galilee	Result: the Twelve went throughout Galilee two by two
"Whoever loses his life for my sake will find it"	Mt 10:39	NIV§70b NASB§99	The twelve apostles	The need to spread the good news about the kingdom more rapidly	Ministry of Christ in Galilee	Lesson: valuing eternal life more than temporal life
"Whoever loses his life for me will find it"	Mt 16:25; Mk 8:35; Lk 9:24	NIV§83 NASB§119	The disciples and the crowd	Preparing his followers for the suffering that awaits them	Ministry around Galilee	Lesson: valuing eternal life more than temporal life
"Follow me . . . go and proclaim the kingdom of God"	Mt 8:22; Lk 9:60	NIV§93 NASB§132	A scribe and two others	On the road toward Jerusalem	Ministry around Galilee	Lesson: complete commitment required of followers
"Only one thing is needed"	Lk 10:42	NIV§104 NASB§142	Martha	Martha's complaint that Mary was not helping to serve	Later Judean Ministry	Lesson: listening to Jesus is more important than temporal duties
"I came to bring . . . division"	Lk 12:51	NIV§108d NASB§149	The disciples	Warning the disciples about coming family divisions	Later Judean Ministry	Lesson: a disciple can expect his family to alienate him for following Jesus
"Anyone who does not carry his cross and follow me cannot be my disciple"	Lk 14:27	NIV§115 NASB§165	Large crowds	Emphasizing to large crowds their need to count the cost of following Jesus	Ministry in and around Perea	Lesson: giving up everything temporal is necessary in following Jesus

The Challenge	Scripture	Harmony Sec. Nos.	Audience	Occasion	Period of Christ's Ministry	The Result or Lesson
A disciple is to serve, not be served	Lk 17:7-10	NIV§117c NASB§169	The disciples	One of four lessons on discipleship	Ministry in and around Perea	Lesson: a disciple is an unworthy servant
"Whoever loses his life will preserve it"	Lk 17:33	NIV§120b NASB§174	The disciples	Teaching about preparedness for Jesus' return	Ministry in and around Perea	Lesson: valuing of eternal life more than temporal life
"The man who hates his life in this world will keep it for eternal life"	Jn 12:25	NIV§130a NASB§190	Andrew and Philip	The desire of some Greeks to see Jesus	Formal Presentation of Christ to Israel	Lesson: valuing of eternal life more than temporal life
"This poor widow has put more into the treasury than all the others"	Mk 12:43	NIV§138 NASB§201	The disciples	Jesus watching the crowd putting their contributions into the temple treasury	Formal Presentation of Christ to Israel	Lesson: "she . . . put in everything—all she had to live on"
"Anyone who kills you will think he is offering a service to God"	Jn 16:2	NIV§150b NASB§220	The eleven disciples	Jesus' words to the disciples the night before his crucifixion	Prophecies in Preparation for the Death of Christ	Lesson: "If they persecuted me, they will persecute you also" (Jn 15:20)
"Do you truly love me more than these?"	Jn 21:15	NIV§180 NASB§255	Peter	Peter and six other disciples had gone back to their fishing after Jesus' resurrection	Resurrection and Ascension of Christ	Lesson: the follower must always keep Jesus in first place among his priorities

2. Faith in and Dependence on God

The Challenge	Scripture	Harmony Sec. Nos.	Audience	Occasion	Period of Christ's Ministry	The Result or Lesson
"Bring them [the five loaves and two fish] here to me"	Mt 14:18	NIV§72c NASB§105	The twelve disciples	The feeding of the 5,000	Ministry around Galilee	Result: the five loaves and two fish miraculously fed 5,000 with plenty left over
"You of little faith, why did you doubt?"	Mt 14:31	NIV§74 NASB§107	Peter, with the other disciples watching	Peter, walking on the water, began to sink	Ministry around Galilee	Result: Jesus rescued Peter, and the rest in the boat proclaimed him the Son of God
"Woman, you have great faith! Your request is granted"	Mt 15:28	NIV§78 NASB§112	A Canaanite woman with the disciples present	A Gentile woman's request to Jesus to heal her daughter	Ministry around Galilee	Result: the woman's daughter was healed
Jesus broke the loaves and fish and gave them to the disciples, and they in turn gave them to the people	Mt 15:36	NIV§79b NASB§114	The disciples	Jesus' compassion for a crowd without food for three days	Ministry around Galilee	Result: the seven loaves and few small fish fed 5,000 with plenty left over
"If you have faith as small as a mustard seed, you can say to this mountain, 'Move from here to there' and it will move. Nothing will be impossible for you"	Mt 17:20	NIV§87 NASB§124	The apostles	Jesus exorcised the demon from a boy that the 9 disciples were unable to exorcise	Ministry around Galilee	Result: the boy was healed, and the disciples saw their need for faith and prayer

The Challenge	Scripture	Harmony Sec. Nos.	Audience	Occasion	Period of Christ's Ministry	The Result or Lesson
"Go to the lake and throw out your line. Take the first fish you catch; open its mouth and you will find a four-drachma coin"	Mt 17:27	NIV§89 NASB§126	Peter	The need to pay the temple tax	Ministry around Galilee	Result: Peter found the coin and paid the tax
"Seek his kingdom, and these things will be given to you as well"	Lk 12:31	NIV§108b NASB§147	The disciples	Part of a warning against greed and trust in wealth	Later Judean Ministry	Lesson: God will provide for Jesus' followers more than he does for ravens, lilies, and grass
"If you have faith as small as a mustard seed, you can say to this mulberry tree, 'Be uprooted and planted in the sea,' and it will obey you"	Lk 17:6	NIV§117c NASB§169	The apostles	Jesus' response to his apostles' request that he increase their faith	Ministry in and around Perea	Lesson: the responsibility for increasing one's faith falls on the follower himself or herself
"Don't I have the right to do what I want with my own money?"	Mt 20:15	NIV§124b NASB§179	The disciples	Parable of the landowner's sovereignty	Ministry in and around Perea	Lesson: the follower is dependent on the sovereign choice of God
"Have faith in God"	Mk 11:22	NIV§131 NASB§192	The disciples	Seeing the withered fig tree	Formal Presentation of Christ to Israel	Lesson: through faith the follower can accomplish the impossible
"I will ask the Father, and he will give you another Counselor to be with you forever"	Jn 14:16	NIV§149 NASB§218	The eleven disciples	Jesus' parting words the night before his crucifixion	Prophecies in Preparation for the Death of Christ	Lesson: the disciple is dependent on the Holy Spirit for help
"No branch can bear fruit by itself; it must remain in the vine. Neither can you bear fruit unless you remain in me"	Jn 15:4	NIV§150a NASB§219	The eleven disciples	Jesus' parting words the night before his crucifixion	Prophecies in Preparation for the Death of Christ	Lesson: the disciple must abide in Christ to be fruitful
"If I go, I will send him [the Counselor] to you"	Jn 16:7	NIV§150c NASB§221	The eleven disciples	Jesus' parting words the night before his crucifixion	Prophecies in Preparation for the Death of Christ	Lesson: the disciple is dependent on the Spirit for guidance into all truth
"Protect them by the power of your name"	Jn 17:11	NIV§151 NASB§224	The eleven disciples	Jesus' parting prayer the night before his crucifixion	Prophecies in Preparation for the Death of Christ	Lesson: the disciple is dependent on the Father for protection
"Watch and pray so that you will not fall into temptation"	Mt 26:41; Mk 14:38; Lk 22:46	NIV§152 NASB§226	Peter, James, and John	The disciples slept while Jesus agonized in prayer	Prophecies in Preparation for the Death of Christ	Lesson: "The spirit is willing, but the body is weak"

The Challenge	Scripture	Harmony Sec. Nos.	Audience	Occasion	Period of Christ's Ministry	The Result or Lesson
"Why do doubts rise in your minds?"	Lk 24:38	NIV§178 NASB§253	The disciples except for Thomas	Jesus appeared to ten disciples after his resurrection	Resurrection and Ascension of Christ	Lesson: the disciples were slow to believe Jesus had risen
"Blessed are those who have not seen and yet have believed"	Jn 20:29	NIV§179 NASB§254	Thomas	Jesus appeared to the eleven disciples	Resurrection and Ascension of Christ	Lesson: the blessed disciple is one who believes without seeing
"If I want him to remain alive until I return, what is that to you? You must follow me"	Jn 21:22	NIV§180 NASB§255	Peter	After Jesus predicted Peter's death, Peter asked about John	Resurrection and Ascension of Christ	Lesson: the disciple must focus on the Lord, not on a fellow disciple
"You will receive power when the Holy Spirit comes on you"	Ac 1:8	NIV§183 NASB§258	The eleven apostles	Jesus' final appearance before his ascension	Resurrection and Ascension of Christ	Lesson: the disciple's power to witness comes from the Holy Spirit

3. Spread the Good News

The Challenge	Scripture	Harmony Sec. Nos.	Audience	Occasion	Period of Christ's Ministry	The Result or Lesson
"Open your eyes and look at the fields! They are ripe for harvest"	Jn 4:35	NIV§35b NASB§40	The disciples	Just after Jesus' conversation with a Samaritan woman	End of John's Ministry and the Beginning of Christ's	Result: many Samaritans believed because of Jesus' words
"Let your light shine before men, that they may see your good deeds and praise your Father in heaven"	Mt 5:16	NIV§54c NASB§66	The disciples	Part of the Sermon on the Mount	Ministry of Christ in Galilee	Lesson: Jesus' followers are the light shining in a dark world
"He sent them out to preach the kingdom of God"	Lk 9:2; cf. Mt 10:7	NIV§70b NASB§99	The twelve apostles	Commissioning the disciples to reach Galilee	Ministry of Christ in Galilee	Result: they reported to Jesus all they had done and taught (Mk 6:30; Lk 9:10a)
"Tell them, 'The kingdom of God is near you'"	Lk 10:9	NIV§102a NASB§139	The seventy-two disciples	Commissioning the disciples in Judea	Later Judean Ministry	Result: even the demons were subject to the disciples in Jesus' name
"Put this money to work . . . until I come back"	Lk 19:13	NIV§127b NASB§184	Those who supposed the kingdom was to appear immediately	Parable of the nobleman who went to a distant country	Ministry in and around Perea	Lesson: disciples must be busy fulfilling their responsibilities
Unfaithfulness of the Jewish leadership a wrong example to follow	Mt 21:28–22:14; Mk 12:1-12; Lk 20:9-19	NIV§132b NASB§194	Disciples, chief priests, scribes, and elders	A challenge of Jesus' authority by Jewish officials	Formal Presentation of Christ to Israel	Lesson: unfaithful discharge of responsibility has tragic consequences

The Challenge	Scripture	Harmony Sec. Nos.	Audience	Occasion	Period of Christ's Ministry	The Result or Lesson
"Keep watch, because you do not know on what day your Lord will come"	Mt 24:42; Mk 13:33; Lk 21:34	NIV§139f NASB§207	The twelve disciples	Part of the Olivet Discourse	Prophecies in Preparation for the Death of Christ	Lesson: stay busy so that the Lord will find you in service whenever he returns
"As the Father has sent me, I am sending you"	Jn 20:21	NIV§178 NASB§253	Ten of the disciples	Jesus' first postresurrection appearance to the assembled group	Resurrection and Ascension of Christ	Lesson: disciples must reach out to others just as Jesus did
"Make disciples of all nations"	Mt 28:19	NIV§181 NASB§256	Eleven disciples	Jesus' appearance to the disciples in Galilee	Resurrection and Ascension of Christ	Lesson: a disciple must multiply himself by making disciples
"You will be my witnesses in Jerusalem, and in all Judea and Samaria, and to the ends of the earth"	Ac 1:8; cf. Lk 24:47	NIV§183 NASB§258	Eleven disciples	Jesus' appearance to the disciples in Jerusalem	Resurrection and Ascension of Christ	Lesson: spread the good news far and wide

4. Humility and Consideration for Others

The Challenge	Scripture	Harmony Sec. Nos.	Audience	Occasion	Period of Christ's Ministry	The Result or Lesson
"So that we may not offend them, go to the lake and throw out your line"	Mt 17:27	NIV§89 NASB§126	Peter	Meeting with those who were collecting the temple tax	Ministry around Galilee	Result: Peter found a coin miraculously and paid the tax
"Whoever humbles himself like this child is the greatest in the kingdom of heaven"	Mt 18:4	NIV§90 NASB§127	The disciples	A discussion among the disciples about who was the greatest	Ministry around Galilee	Lesson: humility like that of a child is of highest value in the kingdom
"Woe to the world because of the things that cause people to sin!"	Mt 18:7	NIV§91 NASB§128	The disciples	An outsider driving out demons in Jesus' name	Ministry around Galilee	Lesson: the follower must be sensitive to any action that may cause others to stumble
Peter told to forgive a sinning brother seventy-seven times	Mt 18:21-22	NIV§92 NASB§129	The disciples	Jesus has just taught how to deal with a sinning brother in the church	Ministry around Galilee	Lesson: unwillingness to forgive from the heart will bring severe punishment from the Father
"Do not rejoice that the spirits submit to you, but rejoice that your names are written in heaven"	Lk 10:20	NIV§102b NASB§140	The seventy-two disciples	The report of the seventy-two returning from their mission	Later Judean Ministry	Lesson: having one's name written in heaven, not power over demons, is a cause for rejoicing
Prove yourself to be a neighbor by your merciful treatment of others	Lk 10:36-37	NIV§103 NASB§141	An expert in the law	The question, "Who is my neighbor?"	Later Judean Ministry	Lesson: a despised Samaritan proves himself to be a neighbor by his acts of mercy
"Be on your guard against the yeast of the Pharisees, which is hypocrisy"	Lk 12:1	NIV§108a NASB§146	The disciples	Gathering of a crowd of many thousands who were stepping on one another	Later Judean Ministry	Lesson: only humility can overcome a guise of greatness

The Challenge	Scripture	Harmony Sec. Nos.	Audience	Occasion	Period of Christ's Ministry	The Result or Lesson
"Things that cause people to sin are bound to come, but woe to that person through whom they come"	Lk 17:1	NIV§117c NASB§169	The disciples	One of four short lessons on discipleship given by Jesus	Ministry in and around Perea	Lesson: actions that cause others to stumble should be carefully avoided
"If your brother sins, rebuke him, and if he repents, forgive him"	Lk 17:3	NIV§117c NASB§169	The disciples	One of four short lessons on discipleship given by Jesus	Ministry in and around Perea	Lesson: God puts a high premium on willingness to forgive a repentant sinner
"Anyone who will not receive the kingdom of God like a little child will never enter it"	Lk 18:17; cf. Mt 19:14; Mk 10:15	NIV§123 NASB§177	The disciples	The disciples were forbidding people to bring children to Jesus	Ministry in and around Perea	Lesson: humility exemplified in the life of a child will characterize those who receive the kingdom
"Whoever wants to become great among you must be your servant"	Mt 20:26; Mk 10:43	NIV§125b NASB§181	Mary, the mother of James and John, and all the disciples	James and John requested the seats at Jesus' right and left in the kingdom	Ministry in and around Perea	Lesson: ambitious pride prevails among rulers of the Gentiles, but humility among Jesus' followers
"When you stand praying, if you hold anything against anyone, forgive him, so that your Father in heaven may forgive you your sins"	Mk 11:25	NIV§131 NASB§192	The disciples	The disciples had just seen the withered fig tree Jesus had cursed, and they received a lesson on faith	Formal Presentation of Christ to Israel	Lesson: forgiveness of others is necessary for answered prayer and forgiveness by the Father
"Whatever you did for one of the least of these brothers of mine, you did for me"	Mt 25:40	NIV§139g NASB§208	The disciples	Part of the Olivet Discourse on Tuesday of Passion Week	Prophesies in Preparation for the Death of Christ	Lesson: deeds of kindness done for Jesus' brothers in need are done also for Jesus himself
"You also should wash one another's feet"	Jn 13:14	NIV§145 NASB§213	The disciples	Jesus washed the disciples' feet the night before his death	Prophecies in Preparation for the Death of Christ	Lesson: a slave should practice the same humility as his Master
"The greatest among you should be like the youngest, and the one who rules like the one who serves"	Lk 22:26	NIV§144 NASB§215	The twelve apostles	The Passover meal the night before Jesus' death	Prophecies in Preparation for the Death of Christ	Lesson: disciples are different from kings of the Gentiles who lord it over their subjects

5. Discernment

The Challenge	Scripture	Harmony Sec. Nos.	Audience	Occasion	Period of Christ's Ministry	The Result or Lesson
"Destroy this temple, and I will raise it again in three days"	Jn 2:19	NIV§31 NASB§34	Jesus' Jewish opponents in Jerusalem	Jesus' response to his opponents' questioning of his authority to cleanse the temple	End of John's Ministry and Beginning of Christ's	Result: after Jesus' resurrection his disciples realized he was talking about the temple of his body (Jn 2:21)

The Challenge	Scripture	Harmony Sec. Nos.	Audience	Occasion	Period of Christ's Ministry	The Result or Lesson
"Watch out for false prophets. They come to you in sheep's clothing, but inwardly they are ferocious wolves"	Mt 7:15	NIV§54h NASB§71	The disciples and the crowds	Part of the Sermon on the Mount	Ministry of Christ in Galilee	Lesson: "every good tree bears good fruit, but a bad tree bears bad fruit" (Mt 7:17)
"Every teacher of the law who has been instructed about the kingdom of heaven is like the owner of a house who brings out of his storeroom new treasures as well as old"	Mt 13:52	NIV§64k NASB§92	The disciples	Part of Jesus' parabolic mysteries of the kingdom	Ministry of Christ in Galilee	Lesson: the disciples are challenged to understand the new parabolic truths about the kingdom along with the OT teaching about the kingdom
"The things that come out of the mouth come from the heart, and these make a man 'unclean'"	Mt 15:18; cf. Mk 7:20	NIV§77 NASB§111	The disciples	Just after Jesus' conflict with the Pharisees and scribes over ceremonial defilement	Ministry of Christ in Galilee	Lesson: a person's depraved heart, not unclean food, is what makes him unclean
"Be on your guard against the yeast of the Pharisees and Sadducees [and the yeast of Herod]"	Mt 16:6; Mk 8:15	NIV§81a NASB§116	The disciples	The disciples thought Jesus was scolding them for forgetting to bring bread	Ministry around Galilee	Lesson: Jesus is more concerned about correcting error than about bread for the body, which he can provide miraculously, as he did for the 5,000 and 4,000
"This was not revealed to you by man, but by my Father in heaven"	Mt 16:17	NIV§82 NASB§118	Peter and the rest of the disciples	Just after Peter's confession at Caesarea Philippi	Ministry around Galilee	Lesson: only the Father can reveal Jesus' true identity to people
Revelation concerning Jesus' coming death and resurrection	Mk 9:31-32; Lk 9:44-45	NIV§88 NASB§125	The disciples	Jesus' second direct prediction of his resurrection	Ministry around Galilee	Result: the disciples did not have enough discernment to understand what Jesus was talking about
"Blessed are the eyes that see what you see"	Lk 10:23	NIV§102b NASB§140	The seventy-two disciples	After the seventy-two returned from their mission to Judea	Later Judean Ministry	Lesson: the Father has chosen to reveal to disciples matters that were hidden from prophets and kings

6. Prayer

The Challenge	Scripture	Harmony Sec. Nos.	Audience	Occasion	Period of Christ's Ministry	The Result or Lesson
"This, then, is how you should pray"	Mt 6:9	NIV§54f NASB§69	The disciples and the crowds	Jesus' warning against praying as the hypocrites did	Ministry of Christ in Galilee	Lesson: pray in secret and without meaningless repetition; also pray for God's glory and your needs
"Ask, and it will be given to you; seek, and you will find; knock, and the door will be opened to you"	Mt 7:7	NIV§54h NASB§71	The disciples and the crowds	The conclusion to the Sermon on the Mount	Ministry of Christ in Galilee	Lesson: pray persistently, for the Father knows how to give what is good to those who ask him

The Challenge	Scripture	Harmony Sec. Nos.	Audience	Occasion	Period of Christ's Ministry	The Result or Lesson
"Ask the Lord of the harvest . . . to send out workers into his harvest field"	Mt 9:38	NIV§70a NASB§98	The disciples	Jesus' observing of the crowds, and his compassion for them	Ministry of Christ in Galilee	Lesson: pray for more workers to spread the good news; result: those praying ended up going
"When you pray, say"	Lk 11:2	NIV§105 NASB§143	The disciples	A request from the disciples that Jesus teach them to pray	Later Judean Ministry of Christ	Lesson: pray persistently to the Father, who gives the Holy Spirit
"Will not God bring about justice for his chosen ones, who cry out to him day and night?"	Lk 18:7	NIV§121 NASB§175	The disciples	A parable to show the disciples they should always pray and not give up	Ministry of Christ in and around Perea	Lesson: if persistence gets results with an unrighteous judge, it will surely produce justice for the elect
"Ask and you will receive, and your joy will be complete"	Jn 16:24	NIV§150e NASB§223	The eleven disciples	Part of Jesus' parting instructions the night before his death	Prophecies in Preparation for the Death of Christ	Lesson: an invitation to come directly to the Father, asking in Jesus' name
"Watch and pray so that you will not fall into temptation"	Mt 26:41; Mk 14:38; cf. Lk 22:46	NIV§152 NASB§226	Peter, James, and John	While Jesus was agonizing in prayer in Gethsemane	Prophecies in Preparation for the Death of Christ	Lesson: avoid the temptation to sleep when you should be praying

7. Watchfulness

The Challenge	Scripture	Harmony Sec. Nos.	Audience	Occasion	Period of Christ's Ministry	The Result or Lesson
"It will be good for those servants whose master finds them watching when he comes"	Lk 12:37	NIV§108c NASB§148	The disciples	Jesus has just spoken to his "little flock" about being prepared for the kingdom	Later Judean Ministry	Lesson: doing God's will consistently and without interruption is the best preparation for Jesus' return
"How is it that you don't know how to interpret this present time?"	Lk 12:56	NIV§108e NASB§150	The crowd	Those familiar with weather signs should have recognized the signs of the times	Later Judean Ministry	Lesson: understanding signs of the kingdom's nearness should be as easy as recognizing changing weather patterns
"Just as it was in the days of Noah, so also will it be in the days of the Son of Man"	Lk 17:26	NIV§120b NASB§174	The disciples	On the eve of Jesus' final journey to Jerusalem	Ministry in and around Perea	Lesson: Jesus' return will be unexpected and will send some away to judgment
"When you see these things happening, you know that it is near, right at the door"	Mk 13:29; cf. Mt 24:33; Lk 21:31	NIV§139e NASB§206	The disciples	Part of the Olivet Discourse on Tuesday of Passion Week	Prophecies in Preparation for the Death of Christ	Lesson: foreshadowing of the future tribulation will signal the nearness of Jesus' return to earth
"Be on guard! Be alert! You do not know when that time will come"	Mk 13:33; cf. Mt 24:42; Lk 21:34	NIV§139f NASB§207	The disciples	Part of the Olivet Discourse on Tuesday of Passion Week	Prophecies in Preparation for the Death of Christ	Lesson: there is no way to predict when the events of the future tribulation will begin, so constant readiness is vital

Phase	Subject	Scripture	Harmony Sec. Nos.	Period of Ministry
kingdom future	eternal reign of Mary's son	Lk 1:30-33	NIV§5 NASB§5	Early Years of John the Baptist
kingdom future	John's message of repentance	Mt 3:2	NIV§21 NASB§24	Public Ministry of John the Baptist
kingdom future	Nicodemus told how to see and enter the kingdom	Jn 3:3, 5	NIV§32b NASB§36	End of John's Ministry and Beginning of Christ's
kingdom future	nearness of the kingdom	Mt 4:17; Mk 1:15	NIV§37 NASB§43	Ministry in Galilee
kingdom future	gospel of the kingdom preached	Mt 4:23; Lk 4:43	NIV§44 NASB§50	Ministry in Galilee
kingdom future	blessedness of the poor in spirit, those persecuted for righteousness sake	Mt 5:3, 10; Lk 6:20	NIV§54b NASB§65	Ministry in Galilee
kingdom future	observance of the law and unhypocritical righteousness	Mt 5:19-20	NIV§54d NASB§67	Ministry in Galilee
kingdom future	prayer for the coming kingdom on earth	Mt 6:9-10	NIV§54f NASB§69	Ministry in Galilee
kingdom future	the primacy of God's kingdom	Mt 6:33	NIV§54g NASB§70	Ministry in Galilee
kingdom future	access to the kingdom denied	Mt 7:21	NIV§54h NASB§71	Ministry in Galilee
kingdom future	many Gentiles will inhabit the kingdom	Mt 8:11	NIV§55 NASB§73	Ministry in Galilee
kingdom future	the kingdom suffers violence[1]	Mt 11:12; Lk 7:28	NIV§57 NASB§75	Ministry in Galilee
kingdom future	proclaiming and preaching the kingdom throughout Galilee	Lk 8:1	NIV§60 NASB§78	Ministry in Galilee

1. Or, forcefully advances.

Method of Teaching	Opportunity	Response Expected	Other Factors
through the angel Gabriel	for Mary to give birth to the Son of the Most High	that Mary would cherish her role as Jesus' mother	Mary's son was to occupy the throne of David, reigning over Israel forever
through the preaching of John	for Israel to repent in preparation for her kingdom	water baptism for those willing to repent	Pharisees and Sadducees were unwilling to submit to John's baptism
direct instruction	seeing and entering the kingdom	new birth, faith in God's Son	Nicodemus recognized that Jesus came from God but was unaware of the new birth
direct instruction	receiving the kingdom	repentance	Jesus preached the same message John the Baptist had preached earlier
direct instruction	to hear the gospel authenticated by miracles, signs, and wonders	repentance	teaching, proclaiming the gospel, and healing characterized the general nature of Jesus' Galilean ministry
direct instruction	possession of the kingdom	cultivation of a humble spirit and a strong stand for righteousness	Jesus introduced his Sermon on the Mount (Plain) by relating his subject to the OT kingdom
direct instruction	greatness in and entering the kingdom	exceeding the righteousness of the scribes and Pharisees	Jesus required obedience to every detail of the law regarding pure motivation
direct instruction	to pray for the kingdom	that Israelites would pray for the institution of the Messianic kingdom	a model prayer in contrast to the hypocritical prayers of the Pharisees
direct instruction	to have temporal needs met through putting the kingdom first	that Israelites would seek God's kingdom and righteousness first	this priority sets Jesus' followers in contrast to the Gentiles
direct instruction	warning to those who do not heed Jesus' words	that listeners would obey the words of Jesus	related to Jesus' admonition to discern a prophet's genuineness by his fruits
direct instruction	follow the pattern of the centurion's faith	that Israel would respond in faith as the centurion did	warning that many Israelites would be denied access to the kingdom because of a lack of faith
direct instruction	for the one who is least in the kingdom to be greater than John the Baptist	respond to John's command to repent	tax collectors had received John's baptism of repentance, but Pharisees and lawyers had not
direct instruction	for people to ready themselves for the kingdom	that people would repent in preparation for the coming kingdom	Jesus was accompanied by his disciples and other followers on this mission that attracted attention of the Jewish leadership

Phase	Subject	Scripture	Harmony Sec. Nos.	Period of Ministry
kingdom present	the kingdom has come upon you	Mt 12:28	NIV§61 NASB§79	Ministry in Galilee
kingdom present	the mysteries of the kingdom begun in light of rejection earlier in the day	Mt 13:11; Mk 4:11; Lk 8:10	NIV§64b NASB§83	Ministry in Galilee
kingdom present	the parable of the soils	Mt 13:3-9, 18-23; Mk 4:3-9, 14-20; Lk 8:5-9, 11-15	NIV§64b NASB§83	Ministry in Galilee
kingdom present	the parable of the seed's spontaneous growth	Mk 4:26-29	NIV§64c NASB§84	Ministry in Galilee
kingdom present	the parable of the weeds (tares)	Mt 13:24-30, 36-43	NIV§64d NASB§85, NIV§64g NASB§88	Ministry in Galilee
kingdom present	the parable of the mustard tree	Mt 13:31-32; Mk 4:30-32	NIV§64e NASB§86	Ministry in Galilee
kingdom present	the parable of the leavened loaf	Mt 13:33-35; Mk 4:33-34	NIV§64f NASB§87	Ministry in Galilee
kingdom present	the parable of the hidden treasure	Mt 13:44	NIV§64h NASB§89	Ministry in Galilee
kingdom present	the parable of the pearl of great price	Mt 13:45-46	NIV§64i NASB§90	Ministry in Galilee
kingdom present	the parable of the net	Mt 13:47-50	NIV§64j NASB§91	Ministry in Galilee
kingdom present	the parable of the house owner	Mt 13:51-52	NIV§64k NASB§92	Ministry in Galilee
kingdom future	nearness of the kingdom	Mt 10:7; Lk 9:2	NIV§70b NASB§99	Ministry in Galilee
kingdom future	speaking to a large crowd about the kingdom	Lk 9:11	NIV§72b NASB§104	Ministry around Galilee

Method of Teaching	Opportunity	Response Expected	Other Factors
direct instruction	warning against blaspheming against the Holy Spirit	an inner condition that will produce good speech	Jesus' enemies, by saying he had an unclean spirit, committed the unforgivable or eternal sin
parabolic instruction begun	to gain understanding of a new phase of the kingdom	receptivity by the faithful, blindness by the rejecters	Jesus began to use parables in order to impart new truths to the receptive and to hide truths from the unreceptive
parabolic instruction	new understanding of the kingdom regarding unreceptive hearers	that listeners would understand new conditions necessitated by rejection	earlier in the day the Jewish leadership had openly rejected Jesus' Messianic credentials
parabolic instruction	new understanding of spontaneous growth in the kingdom	that the loyal would continue sowing seed in spite of no outward signs of growth	the disciples could have been discouraged by the first parable's revelation that 3/4 of the soils were unreceptive
parabolic instruction	new understanding of the presence of evil in the kingdom	that the righteous would understand the final punishment of the wicked	the time for removing the weeds does not come until institution of the kingdom future
parabolic instruction	new understanding of the disproportionate final size of the kingdom	that the disciples would understand the presence of evil in the kingdom	the small beginning of Jesus' band of 12 disciples corresponds to the smallness of the mustard seed
parabolic instruction	new understanding of evil within the kingdom[2]	that the disciples would understand the hiddenness of evil[3]	main character in this parable is a woman instead of a man
parabolic instruction	new understanding of the hiddenness and value of the new truths about the kingdom[4]	that the disciples would grasp and treasure hidden truths about the kingdom[5]	the parable of the house owner equates the treasure with an understanding of things new and old
parabolic instruction	new understanding of the value of new truths about the kingdom[6]	that the disciples would value truths about the new form of the kingdom[7]	Jesus earlier used a pearl as a symbol for spiritual understanding
parabolic instruction	new understanding of the end of the age	that the disciples would understand the judgment of the wicked at the beginning of the kingdom future	the angels will cast the wicked into a furnace of fire
parabolic instruction	to understand the hidden truths in the parables	that the disciples would distinguish the OT kingdom truths from the new truths just taught in parables	a disciple of the kingdom should share his understanding with others
direct instruction	sharing the proclamation of the kingdom with Jesus	some would repent and others would not	the message was to go to the people of Israel throughout Galilee
direct instruction	to witness Jesus' miracles and learn about the kingdom	that people would repent in preparation for the kingdom	Jesus had compassion on the large crowd and miraculously fed 5,000 men plus women and children

2. Or, new understanding of the gradual growth of the kingdom.
3. Or, the growth of the spiritual kingdom.
4. Or, new understanding of the value of the kingdom.
5. Or, that the disciples would appreciate the value of the kingdom.
6. Or, new understanding of the value of the kingdom.
7. Or, that the disciples would value the kingdom.

Phase	Subject	Scripture	Harmony Sec. Nos.	Period of Ministry
kingdom future	a popular attempt to make Jesus King	Jn 6:15	NIV§73 NASB§106	Ministry around Galilee
kingdom present	promise to Peter of the keys of the kingdom	Mt 16:19	NIV§82 NASB§118	Ministry around Galilee
kingdom future	preview of the coming kingdom	Mt 16:28; Mk 9:1; Lk 9:27	NIV§84-85 NASB§120-121	Ministry around Galilee
kingdom present	greatness in the kingdom	Mt 18:1-5; Mk 9:33-37; Lk 9:46-48	NIV§90 NASB§127	Ministry around Galilee
kingdom future	eliminating causes of sin	Mk 9:43	NIV§91 NASB§128	Ministry around Galilee
kingdom present	willingness to forgive	Mt 18:23	NIV§92 NASB§129	Ministry around Galilee
kingdom future	encouragement to proclaim the kingdom	Lk 9:60, 62	NIV§93 NASB§132	Ministry around Galilee
kingdom future	nearness of the kingdom	Lk 10:9, 11	NIV§102a NASB§139	Later Judean Ministry
kingdom future	prayer for the coming kingdom on earth	Lk 11:2	NIV§105 NASB§143	Later Judean Ministry
kingdom present	the kingdom has come upon you	Lk 11:20	NIV§106 NASB§144	Later Judean Ministry
kingdom future	the primacy of God's kingdom	Lk 12:31-32	NIV§108b NASB§147	Later Judean Ministry
kingdom present	the parable of the mustard tree	Lk 13:18-19	NIV§110 NASB§152	Later Judean Ministry
kingdom present	the parable of the leavened loaf	Lk 13:20-21	NIV§110 NASB§152	Later Judean Ministry
kingdom future	how many are to be saved?	Lk 13:23, 28-29	NIV§113a NASB§162	Ministry in and around Perea

Method of Teaching	Opportunity	Response Expected	Other Factors
implication of Jesus' actions	to understand that Jesus would not be King of morally unprepared subjects	that people would quit craving the miracle, such as feeding the 5,000	after feeding the 5,000, Jesus withdrew to a mountain alone
direct instruction	for Peter to admit new peoples to the invisible kingdom	that Peter and the other disciples would understand the church as a new phase of the kingdom	the opportunity came to Peter after his climactic confession of Jesus as Christ, the Son of the living God
direct instruction and experience	seeing Jesus transfigured	reassuring the disciples that the present phase of the kingdom does not nullify the OT promises of a future kingdom	Peter, James, and John witnessed the transfiguration of Jesus and the appearance of Moses and Elijah
direct instruction, using a little child as an example	to achieve greatness in the kingdom	becoming humble like a little child	Jesus settled the dispute among the Twelve regarding greatness
direct instruction	to enter the kingdom	removing causes of sin in one's own life	in the context Jesus condemns causes for sin in one's own life as well as in the lives of others
parabolic instruction	to forgive as God has forgiven us	that the disciples would develop a forgiving spirit	an unwillingness to forgive will result in retribution from the Father
direct instruction	for would-be disciples to escape distraction	that these men would leave other duties to follow Jesus	Jesus required complete commitment from those who wanted to follow him
direct instruction	to reach Judea and other areas with the message about the kingdom	some would receive the message and others would not	Jesus sent out the 72 with a message similar to that of the Twelve in Galilee
direct instruction	to pray for the kingdom	that Israelites would pray for the institution of the Messianic kingdom	a model prayer in response to the disciples' request for one such as John had given his disciples
direct instruction	to hear the word of God and obey it	to recognize Jesus' exorcism of demons as God's authentication	Jesus responded to the accusation that he drive out demons by the power of the prince of demons
direct instruction	to receive the kingdom by putting it first	that Israelites would seek God's kingdom first	this priority contrasts Jesus' followers with the pagan world
parabolic instruction	new understanding of the disproportionate final size of the kingdom	that the disciples would understand the presence of evil in the kingdom	the small beginning was Jesus' band of 12 disciples
parabolic instruction	new understanding of evil within the kingdom[8]	that the disciples would understand the hiddenness of evil[9]	the main character in this parable is a woman instead of a man
direct instruction	to enter by the narrow door	a few will enter, but most will not	some outside Israel will be saved, but many Israelites will be excluded from the kingdom

8. Or, new understanding of the gradual growth of the kingdom.

9. Or, the growth of the spiritual kingdom.

Phase	Subject	Scripture	Harmony Sec. Nos.	Period of Ministry
kingdom future	blessedness of those who eat in the kingdom	Lk 14:15	NIV§114 NASB§164	Ministry in and around Perea
kingdom future	forcing one's way into the kingdom	Lk 16:16	NIV§117b NASB§168	Ministry around Perea
kingdom present	the presence of the kingdom	Lk 17:20-21	NIV§120a NASB§173	Ministry in and around Perea
kingdom future	renouncing marriage for the sake of the kingdom	Mt 19:12	NIV§122 NASB§176	Ministry in and around Perea
kingdom future	receiving the kingdom like a little child	Mt 19:13-15; Mk 10:13-16; Lk 18:15-17	NIV§123 NASB§177	Ministry in and around Perea
kingdom future	difficulty for the rich in entering the kingdom	Mt 19:23-24; Mk 10:23-25; Lk 18:24-25	NIV§124a NASB§178	Ministry in and around Perea
kingdom future	rewards for following Jesus	Mt 19:27-29; Mk 10:28-30; Lk 18:28-30	NIV§124a NASB§178	Ministry in and around Perea
kingdom present	the landowner's sovereignty in paying his laborers	Mt 20:1	NIV§124b NASB§179	Ministry in and around Perea
kingdom future	occupancy of the thrones on Jesus' right and left	Mt 20:20-23; Mk 10:35-40	NIV§125b NASB§181	Ministry in and around Perea
kingdom future	lesson on the delay of the kingdom	Lk 19:11-28	NIV§127b NASB§184	Ministry in and around Perea
kingdom future	the King offers himself to Israel	Mt 21:5; Mk 11:9-10; Lk 19:38; Jn 12:15	NIV§128b NASB§187	Formal Presentation of Christ to Israel
kingdom present	chief priests, scribes, and elders rebuked for leadership failures	Mt 21:31, 43	NIV§132b NASB§194	Formal Presentation of Christ to Israel

Method of Teaching	Opportunity	Response Expected	Other Factors
through the lips of a fellow diner	to learn the danger of ignoring an invitation to the kingdom	that listeners would respond eagerly to the opportunity to enter the kingdom	Jesus had just healed a man on the Sabbath, creating friction with the lawyers and Pharisees
direct teaching	to learn that wealth is not the way into the kingdom	that the Pharisees would be convicted over their love for money	Jesus followed up these words with the story of the rich man and Lazarus
answer to a question from the Pharisees	to realize the kingdom is already here	skepticism by the Pharisees	the Pharisees looked for outward kingdom and were unaware of the new kingdom necessitated by their rejection of Jesus
explaining to his disciples his "no-divorce" standard	to renounce marriage in order to seek the kingdom without distraction	that the disciples and others would not follow the Pharisee's low standards of divorce and remarriage	Jesus cited the institution of marriage (Ge 2:24) to refute the Pharisaic interpretation of Dt 24:1-4
direct instruction, using little children as an example	to see the exemplary qualities of little children	allowing little children access to Jesus	the disciples tried to hinder people from bringing their babies to Jesus
direct instruction prompted by the question of the rich young ruler	to see the danger of materialism	the rich man should have sold all his possessions and given to the poor	the cost for following Jesus and entering the kingdom is high
direct instruction prompted by the question of the rich young ruler	to be motivated toward faithful service	sacrificial service in following Jesus	Jesus promised the Twelve they would sit on 12 thrones judging the 12 tribes of Israel
parabolic instruction	for insight into God's sovereignty in rewarding his servants	that the disciples would be content with their roles in the future kingdom	the laborers who started work late in the day received the same wages as those who worked all day
direct instruction prompted by a request from James and John	to serve rather than being served	follow Jesus' example of serving rather than being served	the other ten disciples were indignant with James and John
illustrative story	for the disciples to fulfill their mission while Jesus is away	that the disciples produce spiritual profit while awaiting the kingdom	the master in the story gave each servant a certain amount and expected them to earn a profit
obvious fulfillment of Zec 9:9	for Israel to embrace her King	rejection by the nation's leadership	the crowds that welcomed Jesus recognized the fulfillment of Zec 9:9 on the occasion of the Triumphal Entry
parabolic instruction	for Israel's leaders to repent	continued rejection of Jesus' Messiahship	the leaders understood the parables to teach the withdrawal of the kingdom from themselves in favor of a repentant nation of the future

Phase	Subject	Scripture	Harmony Sec. Nos.	Period of Ministry
kingdom future	commendation to a scribe for his wise answer	Mk 12:34	NIV§135 NASB§197	Formal Presentation of Christ to Israel
kingdom future	exclusion from the kingdom	Mt 23:13	NIV§137a NASB§199	Formal Presentation of Christ to Israel
kingdom future	gospel of the kingdom preached to all nations	Mt 24:14	NIV§139b NASB§203	Prophecies in Preparation for the Death of Christ
kingdom present	nearness of the future kingdom during the present	Lk 21:31	NIV§139e NASB§206	Prophecies in Preparation for the Death of Christ
kingdom future	judgment by the King on the throne of his glory	Mt 25:31-34	NIV§139g NASB§208	Prophecies in Preparation for the Death of Christ
kingdom future	joining Christ in his rule over the kingdom	Lk 22:29-30	NIV§144 NASB§215	Prophecies in Preparation for the Death of Christ
kingdom future	resumption of fellowship with the disciples	Mt 26:29; Mk 14:25	NIV§148 NASB§217	Prophecies in Preparation for the Death of Christ
kingdom future	the origin of Jesus' kingdom	Jn 18:36	NIV§159 NASB§233	Death of Christ
kingdom future	verdict to crucify the King of the Jews	Mk 15:9; Jn 18:39; 19:14-15	NIV§161 NASB§235	Death of Christ
kingdom future	request of the thief on the cross	Lk 23:42	NIV§164 NASB§238	Death of Christ
kingdom future	Joseph of Arimathea as one waiting for the kingdom	Mk 15:43; Lk 23:51	NIV§167a NASB§241	Death of Christ
kingdom future	the future redemption of Israel	Lk 24:21, 25-27	NIV§176 NASB§251	Resurrection and Ascension of Christ
kingdom future	the time of restoration for Israel's kingdom	Ac 1:6-7	NIV§183 NASB§258	Resurrection and Ascension of Christ

Method of Teaching	Opportunity	Response Expected	Other Factors
direct instruction	to be close to entering the kingdom	that listeners would see love for God and neighbor as more important than offerings and sacrifices	through his questioner's response to his answer, Jesus recognized an inner condition that qualified this man to enter the kingdom
direct instruction	to see the danger of scribal and Pharisaic hypocrisy	that the Jewish leaders would react against Jesus' condemnation of them	this was the first of seven woes pronounced by Jesus against the scribes and Pharisees
direct instruction	to understand the widespread dissemination of the good news about the kingdom	that the disciples would see the continuing spread of the gospel of the kingdom in the period before Jesus' return	Jesus predicted severe persecution of his followers as they spread the gospel
parable of the fig tree	to discern the signs of the times and the nearness of the kingdom	that followers would be watchful and faithful	Jesus pointed to the destruction of Jerusalem and other foreshadowings of end-time events to indicate nearness of the future kingdom
direct instruction	to evaluate one's treatment of Jesus' brothers	that followers would demonstrate the fruit of repentance	the faithful inherit the kingdom promised them
direct instruction	for the Twelve to eat and drink at Christ's table in the kingdom and sit on twelve thrones	that the Twelve would learn to serve and quit arguing about who was the greatest	the lesson was prompted by another argument over who was the greatest
direct instruction	to commemorate the Lord's death until he returns	that the church would continue this commemorative ordinance	Jesus promises to partake again with the disciples in the future kingdom
direct instruction	for Pilate to release Jesus	that Pilate would yield to pressure from the religious leaders and the crowds	Pilate found Jesus not guilty
through the lips of Pilate	for Pilate to release Jesus	that Pilate would yield to pressure from the religious leaders and the crowds and deliver him to be crucified	under the persuasion of the chief priests and elders the crowd asked for the release of Barabbas rather than Jesus
through the lips of the thief on the cross	for the thief to join Jesus in paradise	that Jesus would honor the faith of the thief on the cross	the thief evidenced his faith in Jesus by defending him against the abuse of the other thief
writers' description of Joseph	for Joseph to give Jesus an honorable burial	that Pilate would release Jesus' body to Joseph	to wait for the kingdom is equivalent to being a disciple in the true sense according to Matthew's and John's account of the event (Mt 27:47; Jn 19:38)
Jesus' dialogue with two disciples on the road to Emmaus	to have hope revived through Jesus' resurrection	that the two would believe the OT and tell the others about Jesus' resurrection	the two did not recognize who Jesus was at first
direct instruction	for the eleven disciples to ask when Israel's future kingdom would come	only the Father knows when this will happen	Jesus' parting words to the Eleven before his ascension

#37—Similar Events in the Gospels

Points of Similarity	Harmony Sec. Nos.	Scripture	Section Topic	Period of Christ's Ministry	Season and Date
Foretelling a miraculous birth	NIV§4 NASB§4	Lk 1:7, 13	John's birth foretold to Zechariah	Early Years of John the Baptist	6 B.C.
	NIV§5 NASB§5	Lk 1:31, 35	Jesus' birth foretold to Mary	Early Years of John the Baptist	6 B.C.
	NIV§9 NASB§11	Mt 1:20, 21, 23	Circumstances of Jesus' birth explained to Joseph	Early Years of Jesus Christ	6 B.C.
Song because of a miraculous birth	NIV§6 NASB§6	Lk 1:42-45	Mary's visit to Elizabeth	Early Years of John the Baptist	6 B.C.
	NIV§7 NASB§7	Lk 1:46-55	Mary's song of joy	Early Years of John the Baptist	6 B.C.
	NIV§8b NASB§9	Lk 1:68-79	Zechariah's prophetic song	Early Years of John the Baptist	5 B.C.
	NIV§13 NASB§15	Lk 2:29-32	Jesus presented in the temple	Early Years of Jesus Christ	5 B.C.
A voice in the desert	NIV§21 NASB§24	Mt 3:3; Mk 1:3; Lk 3:4	John's person, proclamation, and baptism	Public Ministry of John the Baptist	winter, A.D. 26
	NIV§26 NASB§29	Jn 1:23	John's self-identification to the priests and Levites	End of John's Ministry and the Beginning of Christ's	summer, A.D. 26
Preparatory nature of John's ministry	NIV§23 NASB§26	Mt 3:11; Mk 1:7; Lk 3:16	John's description of Jesus	Public Ministry of John the Baptist	winter, A.D. 26
	NIV§26 NASB§29	Jn 1:26-27	John's self-identification to the priests and Levites	End of John's Ministry and the Beginning of Christ's	summer, A.D. 26
Spirit's descent on Jesus	NIV§24 NASB§27	Mt 3:16; Mk 1:10; Lk 3:21-22	Jesus' baptism by John	End of John's Ministry and the Beginning of Christ's	summer, A.D. 26
	NIV§27 NASB§30	Jn 1:32	John's identification of Jesus as the Son of God	End of John's Ministry and the Beginning of Christ's	summer, A.D. 26
Identification of the Son by the Father	NIV§24 NASB§27	Mt 3:17; Mk 1:11; Lk 3:22	Jesus' baptism by John	End of John's Ministry and the Beginning of Christ's	summer, A.D. 26
	NIV§85 NASB§121	Mt 17:5; Mk 9:7; Lk 9:35	Transfiguration of Jesus	Ministry around Galilee	summer, A.D. 29
Cleansing the temple	NIV§31 NASB§34	Jn 2:14-16	First cleansing of the temple at the Passover	End of John's Ministry and the Beginning of Christ's	spring, A.D. 27

Points of Similarity	Harmony Sec. Nos.	Scripture	Section Topic	Period of Christ's Ministry	Season and Date
	NIV§129b NASB§189	Mt 21:12; Mk 11:15-16; Lk 19:45	Second cleansing of the temple	Formal Presentation of Christ to Israel	Monday of Passion Week, spring, A.D. 30
John's imprisonment	NIV§34 NASB§38	Lk 3:19-20	Jesus' departure from Judea	End of John's Ministry and the Beginning of Christ's	fall, A.D. 27
	NIV§71b NASB§102	Mt 14:3; Mk 6:17	Earlier imprisonment and beheading of John the Baptist	Ministry of Christ in Galilee	winter, A.D. 29
Healing at a distance	NIV§38 NASB§44	Jn 4:46-50	Child at Capernaum healed by Jesus while at Cana	Ministry of Christ in Galilee	winter, A.D. 28
	NIV§55 NASB§73	Mt 8:5-8, 13; Lk 7:1-2, 7, 10	A certain centurion's faith and the healing of his servant	Ministry of Christ in Galilee	fall, A.D. 28
Sabbath controversies	NIV§49a-49b NASB§57-58	Jn 5:8-9, 16	Lame man healed on the Sabbath in Jerusalem	Ministry of Christ in Galilee	fall, A.D. 28
	NIV§50 NASB§60	Mt 12:1-2; Mk 2:23-24; Lk 6:1-2	Controversy over disciples' picking grain on the Sabbath	Ministry of Christ in Galilee	fall, A.D. 28
	NIV§51 NASB§61	Mt 12:10-14; Mk 3:2-6; Lk 6:6-11	Healing of a man's withered hand on the Sabbath	Ministry of Christ in Galilee	fall, A.D. 28
	NIV§110 NASB§152	Lk 13:10-13	Opposition from a synagogue official for healing a woman on the Sabbath	Later Judean Ministry	fall, A.D. 29
	NIV§100c NASB§155	Jn 9:13-16	Examination and excommunication of a blind man by the Pharisees	Later Judean Ministry	fall, A.D. 29
	NIV§114 NASB§164	Lk 14:1-6	Healing of a man with dropsy while eating with a Pharisaic leader on the Sabbath	Ministry in and around Perea	winter, A.D. 30
Twelve apostles listed	NIV§53 NASB§63	Mk 3:16-19; Lk 6:13-16	Twelve apostles named	Ministry of Christ in Galilee	fall, A.D. 28
	NIV§70b NASB§99	Mt 10:2-4	Commissioning of the Twelve	Ministry of Christ in Galilee	winter, A.D. 29
	- - -	Ac 1:13	Immediately after Jesus' parting blessing and departure	Resurrection and Ascension of Christ	spring, A.D. 30
Raising the dead	NIV§56 NASB§74	Lk 7:12-15	A widow's son raised at Nain	Ministry of Christ in Galilee	fall, A.D. 28
	NIV§67 NASB§95	Mt 9:18, 23-25; Mk 5:22-23, 39-42; Lk 8:41-42, 52-55	Return to Galilee, healing of a woman who touched Jesus' cloak, and raising of Jairus's daughter	Ministry of Christ in Galilee	winter, A.D. 29

Points of Similarity	Harmony Sec. Nos.	Scripture	Section Topic	Period of Christ's Ministry	Season and Date
	NIV§118b NASB§171	Jn 11:38-44	Lazarus raised from the dead	Ministry in and around Perea	winter, A.D. 30
Anointing with perfume	NIV§59 NASB§77	Lk 7:37-38	Jesus' feet anointed by a sinful but contrite woman	Ministry of Christ in Galilee	winter, A.D. 29
	NIV§141 NASB§186	Mt 26:7; Mk 14:3; Jn 12:3	Mary's anointing of Jesus for burial	Formal Presentation of Christ to Israel	Sunday of Passion Week, spring, A.D. 30
Healing the blind	NIV§68 NASB§96	Mt 9:28-30	Three miracles of healing and another blasphemous accusation	Ministry of Christ in Galilee	winter, A.D. 29
	NIV§100a NASB§153	Jn 9:1-7	Healing of a man born blind	Later Judean Ministry	fall, A.D. 29
	NIV§126 NASB§182	Mt 20:30-34; Mk 10:46-52; Lk 18:35-43	Healing Bartimaeus and his companion	Ministry in and around Perea	winter, A.D. 30
Feeding the multitudes	NIV§72c NASB§105	Mt 14:17-21; Mk 6:38-44; Lk 9:13-17; Jn 6:9-13	Feeding the five thousand	Ministry around Galilee	spring, A.D. 29
	NIV§79b NASB§114	Mt 15:34-38; Mk 8:5-9	Feeding the four thousand in Decapolis	Ministry around Galilee	summer, A.D. 29
Confessions of Jesus' identity	NIV§76b NASB§110	Jn 6:68-69	Defection among the disciples	Ministry around Galilee	spring, A.D. 29
	NIV§82 NASB§118	Mt 16:16; Mk 8:29; Lk 9:20	Peter's identification of Jesus as the Christ, and first prophecy of the church	Ministry around Galilee	summer, A.D. 29
	NIV§118b NASB§171	Jn 11:27	Lazarus raised from the dead	Ministry in and around Perea	winter, A.D. 30
Peter's denials	NIV§147 NASB§216	Lk 22:34; Jn 13:38	First prediction of Peter's denial	Prophecies in Preparation for the Death of Christ	Thursday of Passion Week, spring, A.D. 30
	NIV§147 NASB§225	Mt 26:34; Mk 14:30	Second prediction of Peter's denial	Prophecies in Preparation for the Death of Christ	Thursday of Passion Week, spring, A.D. 30
	NIV§154 NASB§228	Jn 18:17	First Jewish phase of Jesus' trial, before Annas	Death of Christ	Friday of Passion Week, spring, A.D. 30

Points of Similarity	Harmony Sec. Nos.	Scripture	Section Topic	Period of Christ's Ministry	Season and Date
	NIV§156 NASB§230	Mt 26:69-74; Mk 14:66-71; Lk 22:56-60; Jn 18:25-27	Peter's denials	Death of Christ	Friday of Passion Week, spring, A.D. 30
Postresurrection appearances to the disciples	NIV§176 NASB§251	Lk 24:15-31	Appearance to two disciples traveling to Emmaus	Resurrection and Ascension of Christ	spring, A.D. 30
	NIV§178 NASB§253	Lk 24:36-38; Jn 20:19-20	Appearance to the ten assembled disciples	Resurrection and Ascension of Christ	spring, A.D. 30
	NIV§181 NASB§256	Mt 28:16-20; 1 Co 15:6	Appearance to the Eleven in Galilee	Resurrection and Ascension of Christ	spring, A.D. 30
	NIV§183 NASB§258	Lk 24:44-49; Ac 1:3-8	Appearance to the disciples in Jerusalem	Resurrection and Ascension of Christ	spring, A.D. 30
	NIV§184 NASB§259	Lk 24:50-51; Ac 1:9	Jesus' parting blessing departure	Resurrection and Ascension of Christ	spring, A.D. 30

#38—Sayings Jesus and Others Repeated
on More Than One Occasion

Points of Similarity	Harmony Sec. Nos.	Scripture	Section Topic	Period of Christ's Ministry	Season and Date
All things are possible, nothing impossible with God	NIV§5 NASB§5	Lk 1:37	Jesus' birth foretold to Mary	Early Years of John the Baptist	5 B.C.
	NIV§87 NASB§124	Mk 9:23	Healing of a demoniac boy, and faithlessness rebuked	Ministry around Galilee	summer, A.D. 29
	NIV§87 NASB§124	Mt 17:20	Healing of a demoniac boy, and faithlessness rebuked	Ministry around Galilee	summer, A.D. 29
	NIV§124a NASB§178	Mt 19:26; Mk 10:27	Riches and the kingdom	Ministry in and around Perea	winter, A.D. 30
	NIV§152 NASB§226	Mk 14:36	Jesus' three agonizing prayers in Gethsemane	Prophecies in Preparation for the Death of Christ	Friday of Passion Week, spring, A.D. 30
A prophet without honor in his own country	NIV§36 NASB§42	Jn 4:44	Jesus' arrival in Galilee	Galilean Ministry	fall, A.D. 27
	NIV§39 NASB§43	Lk 4:24	Early rejection in Nazareth	Galilean Ministry	winter, A.D. 28
	NIV§69 NASB§97	Mt 13:57; Mk 6:4	Final visit to Nazareth	Galilean Ministry	winter, A.D. 29
Call for disciples to follow	NIV§28 NASB§31	Jn 1:43	Jesus' first followers	Transition from John the Baptist to Jesus	winter, A.D. 27
	NIV§41 NASB§47	Mt 4:19; Mk 1:17	First call of the four	Galilean Ministry	winter, A.D. 28
	NIV§41 NASB§47	Mt 4:21; Mk 1:20	First call of the four	Galilean Ministry	winter, A.D. 28
	NIV§41 NASB§51	Lk 5:11	Second call of the four	Galilean Ministry	winter, A.D. 28
	NIV§47a NASB§54	Mt 9:9; Mk 2:14; Lk 5:27	Call of Matthew	Galilean Ministry	winter, A.D. 28
Lighting a lamp	NIV§54c NASB§66	Mt 5:15	Responsibility while awaiting the kingdom	Galilean Ministry	fall, A.D. 28
	NIV§64b NASB§83	Mk 4:21; Lk 8:16	Parable of the soils	Galilean Ministry	winter, A.D. 29
	NIV§106 NASB§144	Lk 11:33	Third blasphemous accusation and second debate with enemies	Later Judean Ministry	fall, A.D. 29

Points of Similarity	Harmony Sec. Nos.	Scripture	Section Topic	Period of Christ's Ministry	Season and Date
Salt of the earth	NIV§54c NASB§66	Mt 5:13	Responsibility while awaiting the kingdom	Galilean Ministry	fall, A.D. 28
	NIV§91 NASB§128	Mk 9:50	Warning against causing believers to stumble	Ministry around Galilee	summer, A.D. 29
	NIV§115 NASB§165	Lk 14:34	Cost of discipleship	Ministry in and around Perea	winter, A.D. 30
Permanence of the law	NIV§54d NASB§67	Mt 5:18	Law, righteousness, and the kingdom	Galilean Ministry	fall, A.D. 28
	NIV§117b NASB§168	Lk 16:17	Story to teach the danger of wealth	Ministry in and around Perea	winter, A.D. 30
Loss of hand or eye	NIV§54e NASB§68	Mt 5:29-30	Six contrasts in interpreting the law	Galilean Ministry	fall, A.D. 28
	NIV§91 NASB§128	Mt 18:8-9; Mk 9:43-47	Warning against causing believers to stumble	Ministry around Galilee	summer, A.D. 29
Reconciliation with another person	NIV§54e NASB§68	Mt 5:24-26	Six contrasts in interpreting the law	Galilean Ministry	fall, A.D. 28
	NIV§108e NASB§150	Lk 12:58-59	Warning against failing to discern the times	Later Judean Ministry	fall, A.D. 29
Divorce and remarriage	NIV§54e NASB§68	Mt 5:31-32	Six contrasts in interpreting the law	Galilean Ministry	fall, A.D. 28
	NIV§117b NASB§168	Lk 16:18	Story to teach the danger of wealth	Ministry in and around Perea	winter, A.D. 30
	NIV§122 NASB§176	Mt 19:9; Mk 10:11	Conflict with Pharisees about divorce	Ministry in and around Perea	winter, A.D. 30
Taking an oath	NIV§54e NASB§68	Mt 5:34-37	Six contrasts in interpreting the law	Galilean Ministry	fall, A.D. 28
	NIV§137a NASB§199	Mt 23:20-22	Woes against scribes and Pharisees	Formal Presentation to Israel	Sunday of Passion Week, spring, A.D. 30
The disciple's prayer	NIV§54f NASB§69	Mt 6:9-13	Three hypocritical practices to be avoided	Galilean Ministry	fall, A.D. 28
	NIV§105 NASB§143	Lk 11:2-4	Lesson on how to pray	Later Judean Ministry	fall, A.D. 29
Unhypocritical prayer	NIV§54f NASB§69	Mt 6:5	Three hypocritical practices to be avoided	Galilean Ministry	fall, A.D. 28
	NIV§121 NASB§175	Lk 18:9-14	Final journey to Jerusalem	Ministry in and around Perea	winter, A.D. 30
Forgiveness of men and forgiveness by God	NIV§54f NASB§69	Mt 6:14-15	Three hypocritical practices to be avoided	Galilean Ministry	fall, A.D. 28

Points of Similarity	Harmony Sec. Nos.	Scripture	Section Topic	Period of Christ's Ministry	Season and Date
	NIV§131 NASB§192	Mk 11:25	Withered fig tree and a lesson on faith	Formal Presentation to Israel	Sunday of Passion Week, spring, A.D. 30
Measuring out	NIV§54g NASB§70	Lk 6:38	Prohibitions against avarice, harsh judgment, unwise exposure of sacred things	Galilean Ministry	fall, A.D. 28
	NIV§64b NASB§83	Mk 4:24	Parable of the soils	Galilean Ministry	winter, A.D. 29
Anxieties of life	NIV§54g NASB§70	Mt 6:31-34	Prohibitions against avarice, harsh judgment, unwise exposure of sacred things	Galilean Ministry	fall, A.D. 28
	NIV§64b NASB§83	Mt 13:22; Mk 4:19; Lk 8:14	Parable of the soils	Galilean Ministry	winter, A.D. 29
	NIV§108b NASB§147	Lk 12:22-23	Warning about greed and trust in riches	Later Judean Ministry	fall, A.D. 29
Follower not above his leader	NIV§54g NASB§70	Lk 6:40	Prohibitions against avarice, harsh judgment, unwise exposure of sacred things	Galilean Ministry	fall, A.D. 28
	NIV§70b NASB§99	Mt 10:24	Commissioning of the Twelve	Galilean Ministry	winter, A.D. 29
	NIV§145 NASB§213	Jn 13:14-15	Washing the disciples' feet	Prophecies in Preparation for the Death of Christ	Thursday of Passion Week, spring, A.D. 30
	NIV§150b NASB§220	Jn 15:20	Opposition from the world	Prophecies in Preparation for the Death of Christ	Thursday of Passion Week, spring, A.D. 30
Lamp of the body	NIV§54g NASB§70	Mt 6:22	Prohibitions against avarice, harsh judgment, unwise exposure of sacred things	Galilean Ministry	fall, A.D. 28
	NIV§106 NASB§144	Lk 11:34	Third blasphemous accusation and second debate with enemies	Later Judean Ministry	fall, A.D. 29
Value of sparrows	NIV§54g NASB§70	Mt 6:26	Prohibitions against avarice, harsh judgment, unwise exposure of sacred things	Galilean Ministry	fall, A.D. 28
	NIV§108a NASB§146	Lk 12:6	Warning the disciples about hypocrisy	Later Judean Ministry	fall, A.D. 29
Danger of riches	NIV§54g NASB§70	Mt 6:19	Prohibitions against avarice, harsh judgment, unwise exposure of sacred things	Galilean Ministry	fall, A.D. 28

Points of Similarity	Harmony Sec. Nos.	Scripture	Section Topic	Period of Christ's Ministry	Season and Date
	NIV§108b NASB§147	Lk 12:15, 34	Warning about greed and trust in riches	Later Judean Ministry	fall, A.D. 29
Impossibility of being a slave to two masters	NIV§54g NASB§70	Mt 6:24	Prohibitions against avarice, harsh judgment, unwise exposure of sacred things	Galilean Ministry	fall, A.D. 28
	NIV§117a NASB§167	Lk 16:13	Parable to teach the proper use of money	Ministry in and around Perea	winter, A.D. 30
Recognition by fruit	NIV§54h NASB§71	Mt 7:20	Application and conclusion of the Sermon on the Mount	Galilean Ministry	fall, A.D. 28
	NIV§61 NASB§79	Mt 12:33	Blasphemous accusation by scribes and Pharisees	Galilean Ministry	winter, A.D. 29
Ask, seek, knock	NIV§54h NASB§71	Mt 7:7-8	Application and conclusion of the Sermon on the Mount	Galilean Ministry	fall, A.D. 28
	NIV§105 NASB§143	Lk 11:9-10	Lesson on how to pray and parable of the importunate friend	Later Judean Ministry	fall, A.D. 29
Narrow entrance	NIV§54h NASB§71	Mt 7:13-14	Application and conclusion of the Sermon on the Mount	Galilean Ministry	fall, A.D. 28
	NIV§113a NASB§162	Lk 13:24	Question about salvation and entering the kingdom	Ministry in and around Perea	winter, A.D. 30
Many coming from east and west	NIV§55 NASB§73	Mt 8:11	Healing of centurion's servant	Galilean Ministry	fall, A.D. 29
	NIV§113a NASB§162	Lk 13:29	Question about salvation and entering the kingdom	Ministry in and around Perea	winter, A.D. 30
Weeping and gnashing of teeth	NIV§55 NASB§73	Mt 8:12	Healing of centurion's servant	Galilean Ministry	fall, A.D. 28
	NIV§64g NASB§88	Mt 13:42	Parable of the weeds (tares) explained	Galilean Ministry	winter, A.D. 29
	NIV§64j NASB§91	Mt 13:50	Parable of the net	Galilean Ministry	winter, A.D. 29
	NIV§113a NASB§162	Lk 13:28	Question about salvation and entering the kingdom	Ministry in and around Perea	winter, A.D. 30
	NIV§132b NASB§194	Mt 22:13	Official challenge of Jesus' authority	Formal Presentation to Israel	Tuesday of Passion Week, spring, A.D. 30
	NIV§139f NASB§207	Mt 25:30	Five parables to teach watchfulness and faithfulness	Prophecies in Preparation for the Death of Christ	Tuesday of Passion Week, spring, A.D. 30

Points of Similarity	Harmony Sec. Nos.	Scripture	Section Topic	Period of Christ's Ministry	Season and Date
Woes to the cities	NIV§58 NASB§76	Mt 11:21	Woes for failure to repent	Galilean Ministry	winter, A.D. 29
	NIV§102a NASB§139	Lk 10:13	Commissioning of the Seventy-two	Later Judean Ministry	fall, A.D. 29
Driving out demons, being for and against	NIV§61 NASB§79	Mt 12:24, 30	Blasphemous accusation by the scribes and Pharisees	Galilean Ministry	winter, A.D. 29
	NIV§91 NASB§128	Mk 9:38-40; Lk 9:49-50	Warning against causing believers to stumble	Ministry around Galilee	summer, A.D. 29
	NIV§106 NASB§144	Lk 11:14, 23	Third blasphemous accusation by the scribes and Pharisees	Later Judean Ministry	fall, A.D. 29
Blasphemy against Jesus for driving out demons and against the Holy Spirit	NIV§61 NASB§79	Mt 12:31; Mk 3:29	Blasphemous accusation by the scribes and Pharisees	Galilean Ministry	winter, A.D. 29
	NIV§68 NASB§96	Mt 9:34	Three miracles of healing	Galilean Ministry	winter, A.D. 29
	NIV§106 NASB§144	Lk 11:15	Third blasphemous accusation by the scribes and Pharisees	Later Judean Ministry	fall, A.D. 29
	NIV§108a NASB§146	Lk 12:10	Warning about hypocrisy	Later Judean Ministry	fall, A.D. 29
No sign given	NIV§62 NASB§80	Mt 12:39	Request for a sign refused	Galilean Ministry	winter, A.D. 29
	NIV§80 NASB§115	Mt 16:4	Encounter with the Pharisees and Sadducees after a return to Galilee	Ministry around Galilee	summer, A.D. 29
	NIV§106 NASB§144	Lk 11:29	Third blasphemous accusation by the scribes and Pharisees	Later Judean Ministry	fall, A.D. 29
Hardened hearts and blinded eyes	NIV§64b NASB§83	Mt 13:14	Parable of the soils	Galilean Ministry	winter, A.D. 29
	NIV§130b NASB§191	Jn 12:40	Departure from an unbelieving multitude	Formal Presentation of Christ to Israel	Monday of Passion Week, A.D. 30
Mustard tree	NIV§64e NASB§86	Mt 13:31-32; Mk 4:31-32	Parable of the mustard tree	Galilean Ministry	winter, A.D. 29
	NIV§110 NASB§152	Lk 13:19	Healing a woman on the Sabbath	Later Judean Ministry	fall, A.D. 29
Yeast (leaven)	NIV§64f NASB§87	Mt 13:33	Parable of the leavened loaf	Galilean Ministry	winter, A.D. 29
	NIV§81a NASB§116	Mt 16:6, 11, 12; Mk 8:15	Warning about error of the Pharisees, Sadducees, and Herodians	Ministry around Galilee	summer, A.D. 29
	NIV§108a NASB§146	Lk 12:1	Warning about hypocrisy	Later Judean Ministry	fall, A.D. 29
	NIV§110 NASB§152	Lk 13:21	Healing a woman on the Sabbath	Later Judean Ministry	fall, A.D. 29

Points of Similarity	Harmony Sec. Nos.	Scripture	Section Topic	Period of Christ's Ministry	Season and Date
Sending out workers	NIV§70a NASB§98	Mt 9:38	Shortage of workers	Galilean Ministry	winter, A.D. 29
	NIV§70b NASB§99	Mt 10:5	Commissioning of the Twelve	Galilean Ministry	winter, A.D. 29
	NIV§102a NASB§139	Lk 10:1-3	Commissioning of the Seventy-two	Later Judean Ministry	fall, A.D. 29
Cost of discipleship	NIV§70b NASB§99	Mt 10:39	Commissioning of the Twelve	Galilean Ministry	winter, A.D. 29
	NIV§83 NASB§119	Mt 16:24-25; Mk 8:34-35; Lk 9:23-24	First prediction of rejection, crucifixion, and resurrection	Ministry around Galilee	summer, A.D. 29
	NIV§115 NASB§165	Lk 14:27	Cost of discipleship	Ministry in and around Perea	winter, A.D. 30
	NIV§120b NASB§174	Lk 17:33	Instructions regarding the Son of Man's coming	Ministry in and around Perea	winter, A.D. 30
	NIV§130a NASB§190	Jn 12:25-26	Request of some Greeks	Formal Presentation of Christ to Israel	Monday of Passion Week, A.D. 30
A cup of water	NIV§70b NASB§99	Mt 10:42	Commissioning of the Twelve	Galilean Ministry	winter, A.D. 29
	NIV§91 NASB§128	Mk 9:41	Warning against causing believers to stumble	Ministry around Galilee	summer, A.D. 29
Confession before men	NIV§70b NASB§99	Mt 10:32	Commissioning of the Twelve	Galilean Ministry	winter, A.D. 29
	NIV§108a NASB§146	Lk 12:8	Warning about hypocrisy	Later Judean Ministry	fall, A.D. 29
Divided households	NIV§70b NASB§99	Mt 10:35-36	Commissioning of the Twelve	Galilean Ministry	winter, A.D. 29
	NIV§108d NASB§149	Lk 12:52-53	Warning about coming division	Later Judean Ministry	fall, A.D. 29
	NIV§139b NASB§203	Mk 13:12	Beginning of birth pains (Olivet Discourse)	Prophecies in Preparation for Death of Christ	Tuesday of Passion Week, A.D. 30
Trials before courts and rulers	NIV§70b NASB§99	Mt 10:17-18	Commissioning of the Twelve	Galilean Ministry	winter, A.D. 29
	NIV§108a NASB§146	Lk 12:11	Warning about hypocrisy	Later Judean Ministry	fall, A.D. 29
	NIV§139b NASB§203	Mk 13:9; Lk 21:12	Beginning of birth pains (Olivet Discourse)	Prophecies in Preparation for the Death of Christ	Tuesday of Passion Week, spring, A.D. 30

Points of Similarity	Harmony Sec. Nos.	Scripture	Section Topic	Period of Christ's Ministry	Season and Date
Loving and hating life	NIV§70b NASB§99	Mt 10:39	Commissioning of the Twelve	Galilean Ministry	winter, A.D. 29
	NIV§83 NASB§119	Mt 16:25; Mk 8:35; Lk 9:24	First direct prediction of rejection, crucifixion, and resurrection	Ministry around Galilee	summer, A.D. 29
	NIV§130a NASB§190	Jn 12:25	Request of some Greeks and necessity of Son of Man's being lifted up	Formal Presentation to Israel	Monday of Passion Week, spring, A.D. 30
Prophecies of death and resurrection	NIV§83 NASB§119	Mt 16:21; Mk 8:31; Lk 9:22	First direct prediction of rejection, crucifixion, and resurrection	Ministry around Galilee	summer, A.D. 29
	NIV§86 NASB§122	Mt 17:9; Mk 9:9	Command to keep the Transfiguration secret	Ministry around Galilee	summer, A.D. 29
	NIV§88 NASB§125	Mt 17:22-23; Mk 9:31	Second direct prediction of resurrection	Ministry around Galilee	summer, A.D. 29
	NIV§125a NASB§180	Mt 20:19; Mk 10:34; Lk 18:33	Third direct prediction of resurrection	Ministry in and around Perea	winter, A.D. 30
Faith as a mustard seed	NIV§87 NASB§124	Mt 17:20	Healing of a demoniac boy and faithlessness rebuked	Ministry around Galilee	summer, A.D. 29
	NIV§117cN ASB§169	Lk 17:6	Four lessons on discipleship	Ministry in and around Perea	winter, A.D. 30
Example of little children	NIV§90 NASB§127	Mt 18:2-3; Mk 9:36-37; Lk 9:47-48	Rivalry over greatness	Ministry around Galilee	summer, A.D. 29
	NIV§123 NASB§177	Mt 19:14; Mk 10:14-15; Lk 18:16-17	Example of little children	Ministry of Christ in and around Perea	winter, A.D. 30
Receiving the Son is receiving the Father	NIV§90 NASB§127	Mk 9:37; Lk 9:48	Rivalry over greatness	Ministry around Galilee	summer, A.D. 29
	NIV§145 NASB§213	Jn 13:20	Washing the disciples' feet	Prophecies Preparing for the Death of Christ	Thursday of Passion Week, spring, A.D. 30
The ninety-nine	NIV§91 NASB§128	Mt 18:12-13	Warning against causing believers to stumble	Ministry around Galilee	summer, A.D. 29
	NIV§116 NASB§166	Lk 15:4-7	Parables in defense of association with sinners	Ministry in and around Perea	winter, A.D. 30
Warning against stumbling blocks	NIV§91 NASB§128	Mt 18:6-9	Warning against causing believers to stumble	Ministry in and around Perea	winter, A.D. 30
	NIV§117c NASB§169	Lk 17:1-2	Four lessons on discipleship	Ministry in and around Perea	winter, A.D. 30

Points of Similarity	Harmony Sec. Nos.	Scripture	Section Topic	Period of Christ's Ministry	Season and Date
Where I am, you cannot come	NIV§96b NASB§134	Jn 7:34	Spoken to the officers sent by chief priests and Pharisees	Later Judean Ministry	fall, A.D. 29
	NIV§99a NASB§137	Jn 8:22	Spoken to the Jews	Later Judean Ministry	fall, A.D. 29
	NIV§147 NASB§216	Jn 13:36	Spoken to Simon Peter	Prophecies in Preparation for the Death of Christ	Thursday of Passion Week, spring, A.D. 30
Greatest commandment in the law	NIV§103 NASB§141	Lk 10:25-27	Story of the good Samaritan	Later Judean Ministry	fall, A.D. 29
	NIV§135 NASB§197	Mt 22:36-38	Question by a Pharisaic scribe	Formal Presentation to Israel	Tuesday of Passion Week, spring, A.D. 30
Persistent prayer	NIV§105 NASB§143	Lk 11:5-8	Lesson on how to pray and parable of the persistent friend	Later Judean Ministry	fall, A.D. 29
	NIV§121 NASB§175	Lk 18:1-5	Two parables on prayer: the persistent widow and the Pharisee and the publican	Ministry in and around Perea	winter, A.D. 30
Woes against scribes and Pharisees	NIV§107 NASB§145	Lk 11:42-52	Woes against scribes and Pharisees while eating with a Pharisee	Later Judean Ministry	fall, A.D. 29
	NIV§137a NASB§199	Mt 23:13-36	Seven woes against the scribes and Pharisees	Formal Presentation to Israel	Tuesday of Passion Week, spring, A.D. 30
Readiness for Christ's return	NIV§108c NASB§148	Lk 12:35-48	Warning against being unprepared for the Son of Man's coming	Later Judean Ministry	fall, A.D. 29
	NIV§139f NASB§207	Mt 24:42– 25:13; Mk 13:33-37; Lk 21:34-36	Five parables to teach watchfulness and faithfulness	Prophecies in Preparation for the Death of Christ	Tuesday of Passion Week, spring, A.D. 30
Last first and first last	NIV§113a NASB§162	Lk 13:30	Question about salvation and entering the kingdom	Ministry in and around Perea	winter, A.D. 30
	NIV§124a NASB§178	Mt 19:30; Mk 10:31	Riches and the kingdom	Ministry in and around Perea	winter, A.D. 30
	NIV§124b NASB§179	Mt 20:16	Parable of the landowner's sovereignty	Ministry in and around Perea	winter, A.D. 30
Lament over Jerusalem	NIV§113b NASB§163	Lk 13:34-35	Anticipation of Jesus' coming death and lament over Jerusalem	Ministry in and around Perea	winter, A.D. 30

Points of Similarity	Harmony Sec. Nos.	Scripture	Section Topic	Period of Christ's Ministry	Season and Date
	NIV§137b NASB§200	Mt 23:37-38	Lament over Jerusalem	Formal Presentation to Israel	Tuesday of Passion Week, spring, A.D. 30
Signs of Christ's return	NIV§120b NASB§174	Lk 17:23-24, 26-27, 31, 34-35	Instructions regarding the Son of Man's coming	Ministry in and around Perea	winter, A.D. 30
	NIV§139c-139e NASB, 204-206	Mt 24:17-18, 23, 27, 37-41; Mk 13:15-16, 21	Abomination of desolation, coming of the Son of Man, and signs of nearness (Olivet Discourse)	Prophecies in Preparation for the Death of Christ	Tuesday of Passion Week, spring, A.D. 30
Rivalry over greatness	NIV§125b NASB§181	Mt 20:25-26; Mk 10:42-43	Warning against ambitious pride	Ministry in and around Perea	winter, A.D. 30
	NIV§144 NASB§215	Lk 22:25-26	Dissension among the disciples over greatness	Prophecies in Preparation for the Death of Christ	Thursday of Passion Week, spring, A.D. 30
Faithful handling of the Lord's possessions	NIV§127B NASB§184	Lk 19:12-27	Parable of the minas	Ministry in and around Perea	winter, A.D. 30
	NIV§139f NASB§207	Mt 25:14-30	Parable of the talents	Preparation for the Death of Christ	Tuesday of Passion Week, spring, A.D. 30

#39—Growing Opposition to Jesus

Scripture	Scripture Reference	Harmony Sec. Nos.	Period of Jesus' Ministry	Time	Occasion	Outcome
"Herod is going to search for the child to kill him.... [He] gave orders to kill all the boys"	Mt 2:13, 16	NIV§15 NASB§18	Early Years of Jesus Christ	5-3 B.C.	The birth of Jesus	Jesus' family escaped into Egypt
"Then the Jews demanded of him, 'What miraculous sign can you show us to prove your authority to do all this?'"	Jn 2:18	NIV§31 NASB§34	Beginning of Christ's Ministry	A.D. 27	First cleansing of the temple	Jesus promised to raise the temple of his body in three days
"The Pharisees heard that Jesus was gaining and baptizing more disciples than John"	Jn 4:1	NIV§34 NASB§38	Beginning of Christ's Ministry	A.D. 27	Jesus' baptizing of disciples provoked jealousy on the part of the Pharisees	Jesus left Judea and went to Galilee to escape from the Pharisees' stronghold
"When Jesus heard that John had been put in prison, he returned to Galilee"	Mt 4:12; cf. Mk 1:14a	NIV§34 NASB§38	Beginning of Christ's Ministry	A.D. 27	Imprisonment of John was in essence opposition to Jesus' ministry	Jesus went into Galilee to pick up where John had left off
"All the people in the synagogue ... drove him out of the town, and took him to the brow of the hill on which the town was built, in order to throw him down the cliff"	Lk 4:28-29	NIV§39 NASB§45	Early in Christ's Galilean Ministry	late A.D. 27	Jesus' claim of fulfilling the prophecy of Isa 61:1-2 to people of his hometown of Nazareth	Jesus walked right through the crowd and left town
"At this, some of the teachers of the law said to themselves, 'This fellow is blaspheming!'"	Mt 9:3; cf. Mk 2:7; Lk 5:21	NIV§46 NASB§53	Christ's Ministry in Galilee	A.D. 28	Jesus' claim of possessing the authority to forgive the paralytic's sins	Jesus cured the paralytic in proof of his God-given authority
"But the Pharisees and the teachers of the law who belonged to their sect complained to [Jesus'] disciples, 'Why do you eat and drink with tax collectors and "sinners"?'"	Lk 5:30; cf. Mt 9:11; Mk 2:16	NIV§47b NASB§55	A little later during Christ's Galilean Ministry	A.D. 28	Jesus attended a dinner at Matthew's house where despised tax collectors and sinners were present	Jesus responded that healthy people do not need a doctor, but sick people do
"So, because Jesus was doing these things on the Sabbath, the Jews persecuted him.... The Jews tried all the harder to kill him"	Jn 5:16, 18	NIV§49b NASB§58	A visit to Jerusalem during Christ's Galilean Ministry	fall, A.D. 28	Jesus healed a long-time invalid on the Sabbath and called God his own Father	Jesus validated the truthfulness of the accusation that he considered himself equal to God
"You refuse to come to me to have life"	Jn 5:40	NIV§49c NASB§59	Same visit to Jerusalem during Christ's Galilean Ministry	fall, A.D. 28	Part of Jesus' response to those who persecuted him and sought to kill him	Declares his listeners to be in opposition to Moses
"When the Pharisees saw this, they said to him, 'Look! Your disciples are doing what is unlawful on the Sabbath'"	Mt 12:2; cf. Mk 2:24; Lk 6:2	NIV§50 NASB§60	Back in Galilee during Christ's Galilean Ministry	fall, A.D. 28	Disciples were picking grain on the Sabbath	After pointing out the examples of David and the priests, Jesus declares himself to be Lord of the Sabbath

Scripture	Scripture Reference	Harmony Sec. Nos.	Period of Jesus' Ministry	Time	Occasion	Outcome
"The Pharisees and the teachers of the law were looking for a reason to accuse Jesus, so they watched him closely to see if he would heal on the Sabbath"	Lk 6:7; cf. Mk 3:2; Mt 12:10	NIV§51 NASB§61	A little later in Christ's Galilean Ministry	fall, A.D. 28	The presence of a man with a shriveled hand in a synagogue	Jesus healed the man's hand in front of everyone, so "the Pharisees . . . began to plot with the Herodians how they might kill Jesus" (Mk 3:6)
Of John the Baptist, the Pharisees and experts in the law said, "He has a demon"; of Jesus, they said, "Here is a glutton and a drunkard, a friend of tax collectors and 'sinners'"	Lk 7:33-34; cf. Mt 11:18-19	NIV§57 NASB§75	Still in Christ's Galilean Ministry	winter, A.D. 29	Delegation from John the Baptist, and Jesus' resulting discussion of John's relationship to the kingdom	Jesus illustrates the fickleness of the generation of Israel that had accepted neither himself nor John
"When the Pharisee who had invited him saw this, he said to himself, 'If this man were a prophet, he would know who is touching him and what kind of woman she is—that she is a sinner'"	Lk 7:39	NIV§59 NASB§77	Christ's Galilean Ministry	winter, A.D. 29	Jesus' invitation to a meal at a Pharisee's home, where a sinful woman bathed his feet with her tears	Jesus reprimanded the Pharisee for his lack of devotion and forgave the woman's sins because of her faith
"When his family heard about this, they went to take charge of him, for they said, 'He is out of his mind'"	Mk 3:21	NIV§61 NASB§79	Latter part of Christ's Galilean Ministry	winter, A.D. 29	Healing of a demon-possessed man who was blind and mute	Jesus gave higher priority to spiritual family ties than those of a physical family
"The teachers of the law who came down from Jerusalem said, 'He is possessed by Beelzebub! By the prince of demons he is driving out demons'"	Mk 3:22; cf. Mt 12:24	NIV§61 NASB§ 79	Latter part of Christ's Galilean Ministry	winter, A.D. 29	Healing of a demon-possessed man who was blind and mute	Jesus labels their accusation as blasphemy against the Holy Spirit, an unforgivable and eternal sin
"Some of the Pharisees and teachers of the law said to him, 'Teacher, we want to see a miraculous sign from you'"	Mt 12:38	NIV§62 NASB§79	Latter part of Christ's Galilean Ministry	winter, A.D. 29	Response to Jesus' strong words regarding the unforgivable and eternal sin	Jesus promised no further signs except the sign of his coming resurrection from the dead
"The Pharisees said, 'It is by the prince of demons that he drives out demons'"	Mt 9:34	NIV§68 NASB§96	Latter part of Christ's Galilean Ministry	winter, A.D. 29	Healing of a demon-possessed man who could not talk	[no response recorded]
"'Where then did this man get all these things?' And they took offense at him"	Mt 13:56-57; cf. Mk 6:2-3	NIV§69 NASB§97	Latter part of Christ's Galilean Ministry	winter, A.D. 29	Jesus' last visit to his hometown of Nazareth	The people's lack of faith limited Jesus' miracles; "Only in his hometown and in his own house is a prophet without honor" (Mt 13:57)
"[The Jews] said, 'Is this not Jesus, the son of Joseph, whose father and mother we know? How can he now say, "I came down from heaven"?'"	Jn 6:42	NIV§76a NASB§109	A visit to Capernaum during Christ's Ministry around Galilee	spring, A.D. 29	Jesus' discourse on the bread of life, in which he stated he had come down from heaven	Jesus commanded his listeners to stop grumbling and recognize his claim to be the bread of life

Scripture	Scripture Reference	Harmony Sec. Nos.	Period of Jesus' Ministry	Time	Occasion	Outcome
"'Have I not chosen you, the Twelve? Yet one of you is a devil!' (He meant Judas, the son of Simon Iscariot, who, though one of the Twelve, was later to betray him.)"	Jn 6:70-71	NIV§76b NASB§110	A visit to Capernaum during Christ's Ministry around Galilee	spring, A.D. 29	Grumbling over Jesus' statement about eating his flesh and drinking his blood	Jesus continued ministering to the Twelve without specifying which one was a devil
"Pharisees and teachers of the law came to Jesus from Jerusalem and asked, 'Why do your disciples break the tradition of the elders? They don't wash their hands before they eat!'"	Mt 15:2; cf. Mk 7:5	NIV§77 NASB§111	Middle of Christ's Ministry around Galilee	summer, A.D. 29	A group of religious leaders confronted Jesus regarding habits of his disciples that broke the traditions they advocated	Jesus condemned the traditions of the elders that necessitated a breaking of God's word, "purposely staying away from Judea because the Jews there were waiting to take his life" (Jn 7:1)
"The Pharisees and Sadducees came to Jesus and tested him by asking him to show them a sign from heaven"	Mt 16:1; cf. Mk 8:11	NIV§80 NASB§115	Middle of Christ's Ministry around Galilee	summer, A.D. 29	After the feeding of the 4,000 and a boat ride across the Sea of Galilee	Jesus said, "A wicked and adulterous generation looks for a miraculous sign, but none will be given it except the sign of Jonah" (Mt 16:4)
"Peter took him aside and began to rebuke him. 'Never, Lord!' he said. 'This shall never happen to you!'"	Mt 16:22; cf. Mk 8:32	NIV§83 NASB§119	Latter part of Christ's Ministry around Galilee	late summer, A.D. 29	After Peter's confession and Jesus' first prediction of his coming death and resurrection, Peter challenged Jesus' prediction	Jesus rebuked Peter, "Get behind me, Satan! You are a stumbling block to me; you do not have in mind the things of God, but the things of men" (Mt 16:23)
"At this they tried to seize him, but no one laid a hand on him, because his time had not yet come"	Jn 7:30	NIV§96a NASB§133	Christ's Later Judean Ministry	early fall, A.D. 29	Jesus' arrival in Jerusalem for the Feast of Tabernacles prompted mixed reactions among the people	Jesus eluded his opponents because his time for execution had not yet come
"Then the chief priests and the Pharisees sent temple guards to arrest him"	Jn 7:32	NIV§96b NASB§134	Christ's Later Judean Ministry	early fall, A.D. 29	Jewish leaders reacted to whisperings by the crowd regarding Jesus' identity and role	The temple guards reported to the chief priests and Pharisees: "No one ever spoke the way this man does" (Jn 7:46)
"The Pharisees challenged him, 'Here you are, appearing as your own witness; your testimony is not valid'"	Jn 8:13	NIV§98 NASB§136	Christ's Later Judean Ministry	early fall, A.D. 29	Jewish leaders were responding to Jesus' claim to be the light of the world	"He spoke these words while teaching in the temple area. Yet no one seized him, because his time had not yet come" (Jn 8:20)
"The Jews answered him, 'Aren't we right in saying that you are a Samaritan and demon-possessed?'. . . they picked up stones to stone him. . . ."	Jn 8:48, 59	NIV§99b NASB§138	Christ's Later Judean Ministry	early fall, A.D. 29	Jesus called his opponents children of the devil and questioned their spiritual lineage from Abraham	"They picked up stones to stone him, but Jesus hid himself, slipping away from the temple grounds" (Jn 8:59)

Scripture	Scripture Reference	Harmony Sec. Nos.	Period of Jesus' Ministry	Time	Occasion	Outcome
"But some of them said, 'By Beelzebub, the prince of demons, he is driving out demons.' Others tested him by asking for a sign from heaven"	Lk 11:15	NIV§106 NASB§144	Christ's Later Judean Ministry	fall, A.D. 29	Jesus drove out a demon that was mute so that the man who had been mute spoke	The crowd was amazed; Jesus replied that Satan cannot be divided against himself.
"When Jesus left there, the Pharisees and the teachers of the law began to oppose him fiercely and to besiege him with questions, waiting to catch him in something he might say"	Lk 11:53-54	NIV§107 NASB§146	Christ's Later Judean Ministry	fall, A.D. 29	Jesus pronounced woes on the Pharisees and experts in the law because of their surprise that Jesus did not wash first before a meal and because of their hypocrisy	Jesus left their presence after denouncing their practices
"Indignant because Jesus had healed on the Sabbath, the synagogue ruler said to the people, 'There are six days for work. So come and be healed on those days, not on the Sabbath'"	Lk 13:14	NIV§110 NASB§152	Christ's Later Judean Ministry	fall, A.D. 29	On the Sabbath, Jesus healed a woman crippled by a spirit for eighteen years	Jesus censured his critics for not allowing for such acts of mercy on the Sabbath
"The Jews had decided that anyone who acknowledged that Jesus was the Christ would be put out of the synagogue"	Jn 9:22	NIV§100c NASB§155	Christ's Later Judean Ministry	late fall, A.D. 29	The Pharisees had threatened the blind man and his parents if they confessed Jesus as the Christ	Jesus said, "If you [Pharisees] were blind, you would not be guilty of sin; but now that you claim you can see, your guilt remains" (Jn 9:41)
"Many . . . said, 'He is demon-possessed and raving mad. Why listen to him?' . . . The Jews picked up stones to stone him. . . . They tried to seize him"	Jn 10:20, 31, 39	NIV§101b NIV§111, NASB§159, NASB§160	Christ's Later Judean Ministry	late fall, A.D. 29	Jesus gave the allegory of the good shepherd and claimed power to lay down his life and take it up again, and he called himself God's Son	Jesus responded to each of the allegations and "escaped their grasp" (Jn 10:39)
"At that time some Pharisees came to Jesus and said to him, 'Leave this place and go somewhere else. Herod wants to kill you'"	Lk 13:31	NIV§113b NASB§163	Christ's Ministry in and around Perea	winter, A.D. 30	Jesus was traveling through Herod Antipas's domain, probably through Perea	Jesus sent word back to Herod that he would continue healing and proceed to Jerusalem, the appropriate city for a prophet to die in
"One Sabbath, when Jesus went to eat in the house of a prominent Pharisee, he was being carefully watched"	Lk 14:1	NIV§114 NASB§164	Christ's Ministry in and around Perea	winter, A.D. 30	On the Sabbath Jesus healed a man suffering with dropsy	Jesus asked his critics whether it was lawful to heal on the Sabbath or not, to which they gave no answer
"The Pharisees and the teachers of the law muttered, 'This man welcomes sinners and eats with them'"	Lk 15:1	NIV§116 NASB§166	Christ's Ministry in and around Perea	winter, A.D. 30	Jesus was the center of attention of a gathering of tax collectors and "sinners"	Jesus responded to his critics by telling three parables to emphasize the importance in God's sight of the repentance of one sinner

Scripture	Scripture Reference	Harmony Sec. Nos.	Period of Jesus' MInistry	Time	Occasion	Outcome
"The Pharisees, who loved money, heard all this and were sneering at Jesus"	Lk 16:14	NIV§117b NASB§168	Christ's Ministry in and around Perea	winter, A.D. 30	Jesus told his disciples a parable about the proper use of money that offended lovers of money such as the Pharisees	Jesus replied by telling the story of the rich man and Lazarus and what happened to them after death
"So from that day on [the Sanhedrin] plotted to take his life"	Jn 11:53	NIV§119 NASB§172	Late in Christ's Ministry in and around Perea	late winter, A.D. 30	The chief priests and Pharisees feared that Jesus' increasing popularity would cause the Romans to take away the degree of autonomy they enjoyed	Jesus withdrew to an area near the desert with his disciples and did not circulate publicly any longer
"Some Pharisees came and tested him by asking, 'Is it lawful for a man to divorce his wife?'"	Mk 10:2; cf. Mt 19:3	NIV§122 NASB§176	Late in Christ's Ministry in and around Perea	late winter, A.D. 30	Upon his return to Judea, Jesus attracted large crowds, so the Pharisees tried once again to catch him in a verbal mistake	Jesus taught that divorce was not in God's original plan when he instituted marriage
"All the people began to mutter, 'He has gone to be the guest of a "sinner"'"	Lk 19:7	NIV§127a NASB§183	Late in Christ's Ministry in and around Perea	early spring, A.D. 30	Jesus invited himself to be a guest in Zacchaeus's home	After Zacchaeus promised to repay four times the amount he had taken from people unfairly, Jesus pronounced him to be a true son of Abraham
"But the chief priests, the teachers of the law and the leaders among the people were trying to kill [Jesus]"	Lk 19:47; cf. Mk 11:18	NIV§129b NASB§189	The Formal Presentation of Christ to Israel	Sunday of Passion Week, spring, A.D. 30	Jesus cleansed the temple a second time, this time during the last week before crucifixion	The opponents could not find a way to carry out their plan because Jesus was so popular with the people
"Jesus entered the temple courts, and, while he was teaching, the chief priests and the elders of the people came to him. 'By what authority are you doing these things?' they asked. 'And who gave you this authority?'"	Mt 21:23; cf. Mk 11:27-28; Lk 20:1-2	NIV§132a NASB§193	The Formal Presentation of Christ to Israel	Tuesday of Passion Week, spring, A.D. 30	Jesus was teaching and preaching in the temple courts	Jesus answered with a question regarding the source of John's baptism, leaving his antagonists with no way to answer
"The teachers of the law and the chief priests looked for a way to arrest him immediately, because they knew he had spoken this parable against them"	Lk 20:19; cf. Mt 21:45-46; Mk 12:12	NIV§132b NASB§194	The Formal Presentation of Christ to Israel	Tuesday of Passion Week, spring, A.D. 30	Jesus told a parable that plainly charged the chief priests, Pharisees, and teachers of the law with unfaithfulness to their God-given responsibility	The leaders feared the people, so they left Jesus and went away
"Later they sent some of the Pharisees and Herodians to Jesus to catch him in his words"	Mk 12:13; cf. Mt 22:15-16; Lk 20:20	NIV§133 NASB§195	The Formal Presentation of Christ to Israel	Tuesday of Passion Week, spring, A.D. 30	During this day of confrontation, members of the Pharisaic and Herodian parties "hoped to catch Jesus in something he said so that they might hand him over to the power and authority of the governor" (Lk 20:20)	Jesus noted that the issue was not tribute to *either* Caesar *or* God, but rather tribute to *both* Caesar *and* to God. His critics were silenced and went away

Scripture	Scripture Reference	Harmony Sec. Nos.	Period of Jesus' Ministry	Time	Occasion	Outcome
"Finally, the woman died. Now then, at the resurrection, whose wife will she be of the seven, since all of them were married to her?"	Mt 22:27-28; cf. Mk 12:22-23; Lk 20:32-33	NIV§134 NASB§196	The Formal Presentation of Christ to Israel	Tuesday of Passion Week, spring, A.D. 30	The Sadducees who said there was no resurrection tried to trip Jesus up with a question they thought he couldn't answer	Jesus corrected his opponents' view regarding life after resurrection by pointing out that there is no marriage or giving in marriage in that state. His response silenced his questioners
"One of them, an expert in the law, tested him with this question: 'Teacher, which is the greatest commandment in the Law?'"	Mt 22:35-36; cf. Mk 12:28	NIV§135 NASB§197	The Formal Presentation of Christ to Israel	Tuesday of Passion Week, spring, A.D. 30	After seeing how Jesus silenced the Sadducees with his answer from the law, the Pharisees posed another question they thought he couldn't answer	Jesus picked the two greatest commandments: the most important from Dt 6:4-5 and the next greatest from Lev 19:18. His response silenced his critics once again
"The chief priests and the teachers of the law were looking for some sly way to arrest Jesus and kill him"	Mk 14:1; cf. Mt 26:4; Lk 22:2	NIV§140 NASB§209	Prophecies in Preparation for Christ's Death	Wednesday of Passion Week, spring, A.D. 30	Passover was two days away, so the leaders were plotting how they could get rid of Jesus after the Feast	The strategy was to wait until the end of the Feast to keep the people from rioting when they arrested and killed Jesus
"Judas Iscariot, one of the Twelve, went to the chief priests to betray Jesus to them"	Mk 14:10; cf. Mt 26:14-15; Lk 22:3-4	NIV§142 NASB§210	Prophecies in Preparation for Christ's Death	Wednesday of Passion Week, spring, A.D. 30	Judas unexpectedly provided Jesus' opponents an opportunity to rid themselves of him before the Passover Feast	The chief priests and the temple guard gave Judas 30 silver coins in exchange for his cooperation, so Judas watched for an opportunity to betray Jesus
"Now the betrayer had arranged a signal with them: 'The one I kiss is the man; arrest him.' Going at once to Jesus, Judas said, 'Greetings, Rabbi!' and kissed him."	Mt 26:48-49; cf. Mk 14:44-45; Lk 22:47-53	NIV§153 NASB§227	The Death of Christ	before daylight, Friday morning of Passion Week, spring, A.D. 30	Judas led a large contingent of Roman soldiers to the Garden of Gethsemane, where Jesus had gone with the Eleven	The soldiers and Jewish officials arrested Jesus, causing all his followers to desert him and flee
"Meanwhile, the high priest questioned Jesus about his disciples and his teaching"	Jn 18:19	NIV§154 NASB§228	The Death of Christ	before daylight, Friday morning of Passion Week, spring, A.D. 30	The first phase of Jesus' trial before Jewish authorities afforded Annas, the father-in-law of Caiaphas, an opportunity to question Jesus and find a basis for convicting him	Jesus reminded Annas that he had spoken openly, so his teachings were not a secret. An official struck Jesus in the face
"The high priest tore his clothes. 'Why do we need any more witnesses? You have heard the blasphemy. What do you think?' They all condemned him as worthy of death"	Mk 14:63-64; cf. Mt 26:65-66	NIV§155 NASB§229	The Death of Christ	before daylight, Friday morning of Passion Week, spring, A.D. 30	The second phase of Jesus' trial before Jewish authorities gave Caiaphas his chance to find a reason to condemn Jesus	The Sanhedrin unofficially condemned Jesus for blasphemy because he allegedly said that he would destroy the temple and raise it in three days

Scripture	Scripture Reference	Harmony Sec. Nos.	Period of Jesus' Ministry	Time	Occasion	Outcome
"Very early in the morning, the chief priests, with the elders, the teachers of the law and the whole Sanhedrin, reached a decision"	Mk 15:1a; cf. Mt 27:1; Lk 22:71	NIV§157 NASB§231	The Death of Christ	daybreak, Friday morning of Passion Week, spring, A.D. 30	Daylight hours provided the Sanhedrin its opportunity to make official their condemnation of Jesus, this time for claiming to be the Son of God	In answer to their question of whether he was the Son of God, Jesus responded, "You are right in saying I am" (Lk 22:70)
"And [the whole assembly] began to accuse him, saying, 'We have found this man subverting our nation. He opposes payment of taxes to Caesar and claims to be Christ, a king'"	Lk 23:2; cf. Lk 23:5	NIV§159 NASB§233	The Death of Christ	early Friday morning of Passion Week, spring, A.D. 30	The Sanhedrin led Jesus to Pilate, the Roman governor, for the first phase of his Roman trial	Pilate's judgment was, "I find no basis for a charge against him" (Jn 18:38)
"[Herod Antipas] plied him with many questions, but Jesus gave him no answer. The chief priests and the teachers of the law were standing there, vehemently accusing him"	Lk 23:9	NIV§160 NASB§234	The Death of Christ	early Friday morning of Passion Week, spring, A.D. 30	Pilate referred the case to Herod Antipas, whose jurisdiction included Galilee where Jesus had conducted so much of his ministry. This was the second phase of his Roman trial	Herod and his soldiers ridiculed and mocked Jesus, dressed him in an elegant robe, and sent him back to Pilate
"But with loud shouts [the chief priests, the rulers, and the people] insistently demanded that he be crucified, and their shouts prevailed"	Lk 23:23; cf. Mt 27:24-25; Jn 19:15	NIV§161 NASB§235	The Death of Christ	early Friday morning of Passion Week, spring, A.D. 30	In the third phase of the Roman trial, Pilate knew Jesus was an innocent man, so he offered to release him, but the people persuaded him to release Barabbas, an insurrectionist, instead	Pilate "released Barabbas to them. But he had Jesus flogged, and handed him over to be crucified" (Mt 27:26)
"[The governor's soldiers] stripped him and put a scarlet robe on him, and then twisted together a crown of thorns and set it on his head. They put a staff in his right hand and knelt in front of him and mocked him. 'Hail, king of the Jews,' they said. They spit on him, and took the staff and struck him on the head again and again"	Mt 27:28-30; cf. Mk 15:17-18	NIV§162 NASB§236	The Death of Christ	early Friday morning of Passion Week, spring, A.D. 30	After receiving custody of Jesus, the Roman soldiers did all they could to inflict physical and mental torture on Jesus	After the mocking, the soldiers led Jesus away to Golgotha, forcing Simon of Cyrene to carry the cross for him
"Here they crucified him, and with him two others—one on each side and Jesus in the middle"	Jn 19:18	NIV§164 NASB§238	The Death of Christ	9:00 A.M. to 3:00 P.M., Friday of Passion Week, spring, A.D. 30	The soldiers cast lots for his clothes as they kept watch over him at Golgotha	At the end of six hours of agony, Jesus "bowed his head and gave up his spirit" (Jn 19:30)

#40—Six Phases of Jesus' Trial

	Time	Location	Harmony Section Numbers	Scripture	Conveners	Person(s) in Charge
1	Friday before dawn	home of Annas	NIV§154 NASB§228	Jn 18:13-24	Jewish authorities	Annas, the former high priest
2	Friday before dawn	home of Caiaphas	NIV§155 NASB§229	Mt 26:57-68; Mk 14:53-65; Lk 22:54	Jewish authorities	Caiaphas, the high priest
3	Friday after dawn	the Sanhedrin council chamber	NIV§157 NASB§231	Mt 27:1; Mk 15:1a; Lk 22:66-71	Jewish authorities	Council of the elders
4	later Friday morning	the palace	NIV§159 NASB§233	Mt 27:2, 11-14; Mk 15:1b-5; Lk 23:1-5; Jn 18:28-38	Roman authorities	Pilate the governor
5	still later Friday morning	Herod's Jerusalem headquarters	NIV§160 NASB§234	Lk 23:6-12	Roman authorities	Herod Antipas, tetrarch of Galilee
6	still later Friday morning	the palace	NIV§161 NASB§235	Mt 27:15-26; Mk 15:6-15; Lk 23:13-25; Jn 18:39–19:16	Roman authorities	Pilate the governor

Subject of Interogation	Jesus' Defense	Court's Response	Other Features	Outcome
Jesus' disciples and his teaching	openness of his teaching	Jesus struck by one of the officers	Peter and another disciple present	Annas sent Jesus to Caiaphas
destruction and rebuilding of the temple	silence, then claim to be the coming Messiah	blasphemy, condemned to death, spit in his face, beaten	Peter present	kept in custody awaiting Phase #3
claim to be the Messiah	agreed that he is the Son of God	Jesus' admission accepted as guilt	Council formalized earlier verdict	to Roman authorities for Phase #4
forbidding to pay taxes and claiming to be king	admitted he was King of the Jews, then silence	not guilty	Jesus' kingdom not of earthly origin	referred to Herod Antipas for Phase #5
miracle-working abil-ity	silence	ridicule, mockery, robe for Jesus	accusations from chief priests and scribes	referred back to Pilate for Phase #6
place of origin	silence	not guilty, but scourging and crown of thorns	Pilate yielded to the Jewish leaders and mob	Jesus delivered to be crucified

#41—Seven Last Words of Christ on the Cross

Name	Scripture	Harmony Section Numbers	Period of Crucifixion	Circumstances
The Prayer for Forgiveness	Lk 23:34: "Father, forgive them, for they do not know what they are doing."	NIV§164 NASB§238	first three hours	one criminal on his right and one on his left; soldiers cast lots for his clothes
The Promise to the Repentant Criminal	Lk 23:43: "I tell you the truth, today you will be with me in paradise."	NIV§164 NASB§238	first three hours	Circumstances: in response to one criminal's request to be remembered by Jesus
The Provision for Jesus' Mother	Jn 19:26-27: "He said to his mother, 'Dear woman, here is your son,' and to the disciple, 'Here is your mother.'"	NIV§164 NASB§238	first three hours	Jesus saw his mother standing near John the disciple
The Cry of Separation from the Father	Mk 15:34: "*Eloi, Eloi, lama sabachthani?*"—which means, "My God, my God, why have you forsaken me?" Cf. Mt 27:46	NIV§165 NASB§239	last three hours	the land in darkness from 12:00 noon to about 3:00 P.M. when Jesus uttered this cry
The Acknowledgment of Thirst	Jn 19:28: "I am thirsty."	NIV§165 NASB§239	last three hours	Jesus realized Scripture had to be fulfilled (Ps 22:15) and asked for a drink
The Cry of Accomplishment	Jn 19:30: "It is finished."	NIV§165 NASB§239	last three hours	Jesus recognized the fulfillment of his scripturally appointed task
The Cry of Resignation	Lk 23:46: "Father, into your hands I commit my spirit."	NIV§165 NASB§239	last three hours	Jesus breathed his last breath until after his resurrection

Selected Bibliography

Bruce, A. B. *The Training of the Twelve*. 4th edition. New York: Hodder & Stoughton, 1906.

Bruce, F. F. *New Testament History*. Garden City, N. Y.: Doubleday, 1972.

Ferguson, Everett. *Backgrounds of Early Christianity*. 2nd Edition. Grand Rapids: Eerdmans, 1993.

Geisler, Norman L., and William E. Nix. Revised edition. *A General Introduction to the Bible*. Chicago: Moody, 1986.

Hoehner, Harold W. *Herod Antipas*. Cambridge: University Press, 1972.

Morgan, G. Campbell. *The Crises of Christ*. Old Tappan, N. J.: Fleming H. Revell, 1936.

Pentecost, J. Dwight. *The Words and Works of Jesus Christ: A Study of the Life of Christ*. Grand Rapids: Zondervan, 1981.

Scroggie, W. Graham. *A Guide to the Gospels*. London: Pickering & Inglis, 1948.

Tenney, Merrill C. *New Testament Survey* (Grand Rapids: Eerdmans, 1961).

Idem. *New Testament Times* (Grand Rapids: Eerdmans, 1965).

Thomas, Robert L., and F. David Farnell. *The Jesus Crisis: The Inroads of Historical Criticism into Evangelical Scholarship*. Grand Rapids: Kregel, 1998.

Thomas, Robert L., and Stanley N. Gundry. *A Harmony of the Gospels with Explanations and Essays (NASB)*. San Francisco: Harper-Collins, 1978.

Idem. *The NIV Harmony of the Gospels with Explanations and Essays*. San Francisco: Harper-Collins, 1988.

van Bruggen, Jakob. Translated by Nancy Forest-Flier. *Christ on Earth: The Gospel Narratives As History*. Grand Rapids: Baker, 1998.

We want to hear from you. Please send your comments about this book to us in care of the address below. Thank you.

GRAND RAPIDS, MICHIGAN 49530 USA

WWW.ZONDERVAN.COM

Printed in the USA
CPSIA information can be obtained
at www.ICGtesting.com
JSHW062057270124
55795JS00001B/1